Oxford School Spelling Dictionary

Robert Allen

Education Consultant Michele Chapman

OXFORD
UNIVERSITY PRESS

OXFORD
UNIVERSITY PRESS

Great Clarendon Street, Oxford OX2 6DP

Oxford University Press is a department of the University of Oxford.
It furthers the University's objective of excellence in research,
scholarship, and education by publishing worldwide in

Oxford New York

Auckland Bangkok Buenos Aires Cape Town Chennai
Dar es Salaam Delhi Hong Kong Istanbul Karachi Kolkata
Kuala Lumpur Madrid Melbourne Mexico City Mumbai Nairobi
São Paulo Taipei Tokyo Toronto

Oxford is a registered trade mark of Oxford University Press
in the UK and in certain other countries

British Library cataloguing in Publication Data available

Part of a 6-part set. Not to be sold separately.

ISBN 0-19-911201-0 (complete set)

ISBN 0-19-911263-0 *Oxford School Spelling Dictionary* (when part of this set)

10 9 8 7 6 5 4 3 2 1

Printed in the UK by Cox and Wyman

Introduction

The *Oxford School Spelling Dictionary* is a special dictionary designed to help students with their spelling. Generally speaking there are three main areas of spelling difficulty for users of English whatever their age.

- Some words are difficult because they have unusual or unpredictable features. **Eighth**, **guard**, and **niece** are often spelt wrongly because they have awkward letter sequences. **Disappear** and **embarrass** are confusing because some letters are doubled while others are not. Words such as **desperate** and **separate** seem inconsistent because one has an **e** in the middle where the other has an **a** for no apparent reason.

- Then there are words that are easily confused. **Vain**, **vein**, and **vane** sound the same but have very different meanings. Some words change their spelling according to how they are used. For example, **dependant** as a *noun* is spelt with an **a**, but as an *adjective*, it is spelt with an **e**.

- The third type of difficulty arises when suffixes and endings are added to words. It is not easy to remember to keep an **e** in **changeable**, to replace **y** with **i** in **happily**, and not to double the **p** in **galloping**.

With increased interest in spelling, reading, and writing in schools today we hope that the *Oxford School Spelling Dictionary* will provide a valuable tool offering useful strategies for dealing with spelling difficulties. We also hope that it will support teachers and parents whose task is to enable young writers to become confident, accurate spellers and to express themselves with a voice of their own.

How to use this book

Entries

Words are listed alphabetically in **bold** and the part of speech or word class (e.g. *noun*, *verb*, *adjective*) follows in italic. If the word has endings (called inflections), these are also listed below the headword.

Decide on the first sound of the word you are looking for. Some first sounds can be confusing. If you cannot find the word you are looking for, use the **Try also** tips which will guide you to other possible spellings.

Footnotes

Some words have footnotes attached to them. These identify words that you need to check that you have the right meaning. For example, at **bite** you will find a footnote to tell you that there is another word that sounds like it but is spelt a different way, **!byte**. Words that sound the same but are spelt differently are called homophones. Some footnotes also give extra information on usage and grammar.

Panels

There are about 250 panels which highlight particular problems. For example, you may want to know which words are spelt **-able** like **bendable**, and which ones are spelt **-ible** like **accessible**. Or you may want to know how you form plurals of nouns ending in **-f** such as **calf** or **roof**. Use these information panels to build your knowledge of spelling rules and practices.

It may be useful to keep a spelling jotter for new words. When using a new word, say it aloud several times before you write it down. When you go on to use it in your writing, try not to copy it but to write the word from memory.

Try also

Entry word

Panel

Inflections

Word class (part of speech)

selfishness
selfless *adjective*
  selflessly
self-service
★ sell *verb*
  sells
  selling
  sold
semaphore
semen

semi-
  semi- makes words
  meaning 'half', e.g.
  semi-automatic,
  semi-skimmed.
  A few words are spelt
  joined up, e.g.
  semicircle,
  semicolon, but most
  of them have hyphens.

semibreve *noun*
  semibreves
semicircle *noun*
  semicircles
semicircular
semicolon *noun*
  semicolons
semi-detached
semi-final *noun*
  semi-finals
semi-finalist *noun*
  semi-finalists
semitone *noun*
  semitones
semolina
senate
senator *noun*
  senators

send *verb*
  sends
  sending
  sent
senior *adjective* and
  noun
  seniors
seniority
sensation *noun*
  sensations
sensational *adjective*
  sensationally
sense *noun*
  senses
sense *verb*
  senses
  sensing
  sensed
senseless *adjective*
  senselessly
sensible *adjective*
  sensibly
sensitive *adjective*
  sensitively
sensitivity *noun*
  sensitivities
sensitize *verb*
  sensitizes
  sensitizing
  sensitized
sensor *noun*
  sensors
☆ sent see send
sentence *noun*
  sentences
sentence *verb*
  sentences
  sentencing
  sentenced
sentiment *noun*
  sentiments

sentimental
  adjective
  sentimentally
sentimentality
sentinel *noun*
  sentinels
sentry *noun*
  sentries
separable
separate *adjective*
  separately
separate *verb*
  separates
  separating
  separated
separation *noun*
  separations
September *noun*
  Septembers
septic
sequel *noun*
  sequels
sequence *noun*
  sequences
sequin *noun*
  sequins
serene *adjective*
  serenely
serenity
sergeant *noun*
  sergeants
sergeant major
  noun
  sergeant majors
○ serial *noun*
  serials
series *noun*
  series
serious *adjective*
  seriously

★ To sell something means 'to exchange it for money'. ! cell
☆ You use sent in e.g. *he was sent home*. ! cent, scent
○ A serial is a story or programme in separate parts. ! cereal

Footnote

Do not confuse with

Aa

-**a**
Most nouns ending in
-*a*, e.g. amoeba, gala,
have plurals ending in
-*as*, e.g. amoebas,
galas. A few technical
words have plurals
ending in -*ae*, e.g.
antennae.

aback

abacus *noun*
abacuses

abandon *verb*
abandons
abandoning
abandoned

abbey *noun*
abbeys

abbot *noun*
abbots

abbreviate *verb*
abbreviates
abbreviating
abbreviated

abbreviation *noun*
abbreviations

abdomen *noun*
abdomens

abdominal

abduct *verb*
abducts
abducting
abducted

abide *verb*
abides
abiding
abided

ability *noun*
abilities

ablaze

able *adjective*
abler
ablest

-**able and -ible**
You add -*able* to a
verb to make an
adjective that means
'able to be done', e.g.
bendable means 'able
to be bent'. Some
adjectives that have
this meaning end in
-*ible*, e.g. accessible,
convertible and
incredible. You
cannot use -*ible* to
make new words as
you can with -*able*.

ably

abnormal
abnormally

abnormality *noun*
abnormalities

aboard

abode *noun*
abodes

abolish *verb*
abolishes
abolishing
abolished

abolition

abominable

aboriginal

Aborigines

abort *verb*
aborts
aborting
aborted

abortion *noun*
abortions

abound *verb*
abounds
abounding
abounded

about

above

abrasive

abreast

abroad

abrupt

abscess *noun*
abscesses

abseil *verb*
abseils
abseiling
abseiled

absence *noun*
absences

absent

absentee *noun*
absentees

absent-minded
absent-mindedly

absolute
absolutely

absorb *verb*
absorbs
absorbing
absorbed

absorbent

absorption

abstract *adjective*
and *noun*
abstracts

abstract *verb*
abstracts
abstracting
abstracted

absurd
absurdly

absurdity *noun*
absurdities

abundance

abundant

abuse *verb*
abuses
abusing
abused

abuse *noun*
abuses

abusive
abusively

abysmal

abyss *noun*
abysses

academic

academy *noun*
academies

accelerate *verb*
accelerates
accelerating
accelerated

acceleration

accelerator *noun*
accelerators

accent *noun*
accents

accent *verb*
accents
accenting
accented

★ **accept** *verb*
accepts
accepting
accepted

acceptable

acceptance

access *noun*
accesses

access *verb*
accesses
accessing
accessed

accessibility

accessible

accession *noun*
accessions

accessory *noun*
accessories

accident *noun*
accidents

accidental
accidentally

acclaim *verb*
acclaims
acclaiming
acclaimed

accommodate *verb*
accommodates
accommodating
accommodated

accommodation

accompaniment
noun
accompaniments

accompanist *noun*
accompanists

accompany *verb*
accompanies
accompanying
accompanied

accomplish *verb*
accomplishes
accomplishing
accomplished

accomplished

accomplishment
noun
accomplishments

accord *noun*
accords

according
accordingly

accordion *noun*
accordions

account *noun*
accounts

account *verb*
accounts
accounting
accounted

accountancy

accountant *noun*
accountants

accumulate *verb*
accumulates
accumulating
accumulated

accumulation

accuracy

accurate
accurately

accusation *noun*
accusations

accuse *verb*
accuses
accusing
accused

accustomed

ace *noun*
aces

ache *noun*
aches

ache *verb*
aches
aching
ached

achieve *verb*
achieves
achieving
achieved

. . . .

★ To accept something is to take it. ! except.

achievement
achievements

acid noun
acids

acidic

acidity noun

acknowledge verb
acknowledges
acknowledging
acknowledged

acknowledgement
noun
acknowledgements

acne

acorn noun
acorns

acoustic

acoustics

acquaint verb
acquaints
acquainting
acquainted

acquaintance noun
acquaintances

acquire verb
acquires
acquiring
acquired

acquisition noun
acquisitions

acquit verb
acquits
acquitting
acquitted

acquittal noun
acquittals

acre noun
acres

acrobat noun
acrobats

acrobatic adjective
acrobatically

acrobatics

acronym noun
acronyms

across adverb and
preposition

act noun
acts

act verb
acts
acting
acted

action noun
actions

activate verb
activates
activating
activated

active

activity noun
activities

actor noun
actors

actress noun
actresses

actual
actually

acupuncture

acute

Adam's apple noun
Adam's apples

adapt verb
adapts
adapting
adapted

adaptable

adaptation

adaptor noun
adaptors

add verb
adds
adding
added

adder noun
adders

addict noun
addicts

addicted

addiction noun
addictions

addictive

addition noun
additions

additional

additive noun
additives

address noun
addresses

address verb
addresses
addressing
addressed

adenoids

adequate

adhere verb
adheres
adhering
adhered

adhesive noun
adhesives

adhesion

adhesive

Adi Granth

adjacent

adjective noun
adjectives

adjourn verb
adjourns
adjourning
adjourned
adjournment
adjudicate verb
adjudicates
adjudicating
adjudicated
adjudication
adjudicator
adjust verb
adjusts
adjusting
adjusted
adjustment noun
adjustments
administer verb
administers
administering
administered
administration noun
administrations
administrative
administrator
admirable
admirably
admiral noun
admirals
admiration
admire verb
admires
admiring
admired
admirer noun
admirers
admission noun
admissions
admit verb
admits

admitting
admitted
admittance
admittedly
ado
adolescence
adolescent noun
adolescents
adopt verb
adopts
adopting
adopted
adoption
adoptive
adorable
adorably
adoration
adore verb
adores
adoring
adored
adorn verb
adorns
adorning
adorned
adornment
adrenalin
adrift
adult noun
adults
adulterer
adultery
advance noun
advances
advance verb
advances
advancing
advanced
advanced
advantage noun

advantages
advantageous
★ **Advent**
adventure noun
adventures
adventurous
adjective
adventurously
adverb noun
adverbs
adversary noun
adversaries
adverse
adversity noun
adversities
advertise verb
advertises
advertising
advertised
advertisement
noun
advertisements
advice
advisable
advise verb
advises
advising
advised
adviser noun
advisers
advisory
advocate noun
advocates
advocate verb
advocates
advocating
advocated
aerial adjective and
noun
aerials

· ·

★ Use a capital A when you mean the period before Christmas.

aero-
You use *aero-* to make words to do with the air or aircraft, e.g. **aerobatics**. If the word is a long one you spell it with a hyphen, e.g. **aero-engineering**.

aerobatic

aerobatics

aerobics

aeronautical

aeronautics

aeroplane *noun*
aeroplanes

aerosol *noun*
aerosols

aesthetic
aesthetically

affair *noun*
affairs

★ **affect** *verb*
affects
affecting
affected

affection *noun*
affections

affectionate
affectionately

afflict *verb*
afflicts
afflicting
afflicted

affliction
afflictions

affluence

affluent

afford *verb*
affords

affording
afforded

afforestation

afloat *adjective* and *adverb*

afraid

afresh

African *adjective* and *noun*
Africans

aft

after

afternoon *noun*
afternoons

afterwards

again

against

age *noun*
ages

age *verb*
ages
ageing
aged

aged

agency *noun*
agencies

agenda *noun*
agendas

agent *noun*
agents

aggravate *verb*
aggravates
aggravating
aggravated

aggravation

aggression

aggressive
aggressively

aggressor
aggressors

agile

agility

agitate *verb*
agitates
agitating
agitated

agitation

agitator *noun*
agitators

agnostic *noun*
agnostics

ago

agonizing

agony *noun*
agonies

agree *verb*
agrees
agreeing
agreed

agreeable

agreement *noun*
agreements

agriculture

agricultural

aground

ahead

ahoy

aid *noun*
aids

aid *verb*
aids
aiding
aided

☆ **Aids**

ailing

ailment *noun*
ailments

aim *verb*
aims
aiming
aimed

. . . .

★ **Affect** means 'to make something change'. ! **effect**.
☆ Use a capital A when you mean the disease.

aim *noun*
aims

aimless
aimlessly

★ **air** *noun*
airs

air *verb*
airs
airing
aired

airborne

air-conditioned

air-conditioning

aircraft *noun*
aircraft

Airedale *noun*
Airedales

airfield *noun*
airfields

air force *noun*
air forces

airgun *noun*
airguns

airline *noun*
airlines

airlock *noun*
airlocks

airmail

airman *noun*
airmen

airport *noun*
airports

airship *noun*
airships

airstream *noun*
airstreams

airtight

airy *adjective*
airier
airiest
airily

☆ **aisle** *noun*
aisles

ajar

○ **akela** *noun*
akelas

alarm *verb*
alarms
alarming
alarmed

alarm *noun*
alarms

alas

albatross *noun*
albatrosses

album *noun*
albums

alcohol

alcoholic *adjective*
and *noun*
alcoholics

alcoholism

alcove *noun*
alcoves

✳ **ale** *noun*
ales

alert *verb*
alerts
alerting
alerted

alert *adjective* and
noun
alerts

algebra

algebraic

alias *noun*
aliases

alibi *noun*
alibis

alien *adjective* and
noun
aliens

alienate *verb*
alienates
alienating
alienated

alienation

alight

alike

alive

alkali *noun*
alkalis

alkaline

alkalinity

Allah

allegation *noun*
allegations

allege *verb*
alleges
alleging
alleged

allegedly

allegiance *noun*
allegiances

allegorical

allegory *noun*
allegories

allergic

allergy *noun*
allergies

alley *noun*
alleys

alliance *noun*
alliances

allied

alligator *noun*
alligators

- -

★ You can use a plural in the phrase *to put on airs*.
☆ An aisle is a passage in a church or cinema. **!** isle.
○ Akela is a Scout leader.
✳ You can use a plural when you mean 'different types of ale'.

allot verb
  allots
  allotting
  allotted
allotment noun
  allotments
allow verb
  allows
  allowing
  allowed
allowance noun
  allowances
alloy noun
  alloys
all right
all-round
all-rounder
ally noun
  allies
ally verb
  allies
  allying
  allied
almighty
almond noun
  almonds
almost
aloft
alone
along
alongside
★ **aloud**
alphabet noun
  alphabets
alphabetical
  alphabetically
alpine
already
Alsatian noun
  Alsatians

also
☆ **altar** noun
  altars
✪ **alter** verb
  alters
  altering
  altered
alteration
alternate
alternate verb
  alternates
  alternating
  alternated
alternately
alternation
**alternating
current**
alternative noun
  alternatives
alternative
alternator noun
  alternators
although conjunction
altitude noun
  altitudes
altogether
aluminium
always
amalgamate verb
  amalgamates
  amalgamating
  amalgamated
amalgamation
amateur adjective
  and noun
  amateurs
amateurish
amaze verb
  amazes
  amazing
  amazed

amazement
ambassador noun
  ambassadors
amber
ambiguity
  ambiguities
ambiguous
  ambiguously
ambition noun
  ambitions
ambitious
  ambitiously
amble verb
  ambles
  ambling
  ambled
ambulance noun
  ambulances
ambush noun
  ambushes
ambush verb
  ambushes
  ambushing
  ambushed
amen
amend verb
  amends
  amending
  amended
amendment
amenity noun
  amenities
American adjective
  and noun
  Americans
amiable
  amiably
amicable
  amicably
✳ **amid**

. . . .

★ **Aloud** means 'in a voice that can be heard'. ! allowed.
☆ An **altar** is a raised surface in religious ceremonies. ! alter.
✪ **Alter** means to change something. ! altar.
✳ You can also spell this word *amidst*.

amidships

ammonia

ammunition

amnesty noun
  amnesties

amoeba noun
  amoebas

★ among

amount noun
  amounts

amount verb
  amounts
  amounting
  amounted

amphibian adjective
  and noun
  amphibians

amphibious

ample adjective
  ampler
  amplest
  amply

amplification

amplifier noun
  amplifiers

amplify verb
  amplifies
  amplifying
  amplified

amputate verb
  amputates
  amputating
  amputated

amputation

amuse verb
  amuses
  amusing
  amused

amusement noun
  amusements

amusing

☆ an

anaemia

anaemic

anaesthetic noun
  anaesthetics

anaesthetist

anaesthetize verb
  anaesthetizes
  anaesthetizing
  anaesthetized

anagram noun
  anagrams

analogous

◐ analogue

analogy noun
  analogies

analyse verb
  analyses
  analysing
  analysed

analysis noun
  analyses

analytical

anarchism

anarchist noun
  anarchists

anarchy

anatomical

anatomy

-ance and -ence
Most nouns ending in
-ance come from
verbs, e.g.
disturbance,
endurance. Some
nouns end in -ence,
e.g. dependence,
obedience, and you
need to be careful not
to misspell these.

ancestor noun
  ancestors

ancestral

ancestry noun
  ancestries

anchor noun
  anchors

anchorage noun
  anchorages

ancient

anemone noun
  anemones

angel noun
  angels

angelic

anger

angle noun
  angles

angle verb
  angles
  angling
  angled

angler noun
  anglers

Anglican adjective
  and noun
  Anglicans

Anglo-Saxon
  adjective and noun
  Anglo-Saxons

angry adjective
  angrier
  angriest
  angrily

anguish

angular

animal noun
  animals

animated

animation

★ You can also spell this word *amongst*.

☆ You use *an* instead of *a* before a word beginning with a vowel, e.g. *an apple*, or before an abbreviation that sounds as though it begins with a vowel, e.g. *an MP*.

◐ You will sometimes see the spelling *analog*, especially when it is about computers.

animosity noun
animosities
aniseed
ankle noun
ankles
annex verb
annexes
annexing
annexed
annexation
annexe noun
annexes
annihilate verb
annihilates
annihilating
annihilated
annihilation
anniversary noun
anniversaries
announce verb
announces
announcing
announced
announcer
announcement noun
announcements
annoy verb
annoys
annoying
annoyed
annoyance noun
annoyances
annual adjective
annually
annual noun
annuals
★ **anonymity**
anonymous
anonymously
anorak noun
anoraks

anorexia
anorexic
another
answer noun
answers
answer verb
answers
answering
answered

-ant and -ent
Many adjectives end
in -ant, e.g. abundant,
important. Some
adjectives end in -ent,
e.g. dependent
(dependant is a
noun), permanent,
and you need to be
careful not to misspell
these.

antagonism
antagonistic
antagonize verb
antagonizes
antagonizing
antagonized
Antarctic adjective
and noun
anteater noun
anteaters
☆ **antelope** noun
antelope or
antelopes
antenna noun
antelopes
anthem noun
anthems
anthill noun
anthills
anthology noun
anthologies

anthracite
anthropologist
anthropology

anti-
anti- at the beginning
of a word makes a
word meaning
'against something'
or 'stopping
something', e.g.
antifreeze means 'a
liquid that stops
water from freezing'.
If the word you are
adding anti- to begins
with a vowel, you use
a hyphen, e.g.
anti-aircraft.

antibiotic noun
antibiotics
anticipate verb
anticipates
anticipating
anticipated
anticipation
anticlimax noun
anticlimaxes
anticlockwise
adverb and adjective
anticyclone noun
anticyclones
antidote noun
antidotes
antifreeze
⊙ **antipodes**
antiquated
antique adjective and
noun
antiques
antiseptic noun
antiseptics

★ The noun from **anonymous**.
☆ You use **antelope** when you mean a lot of animals and **antelopes** when you
    mean several you are thinking about separately.
⊙ A word Europeans use for Australia and New Zealand.

antler noun
  antlers
anus noun
  anuses
anvil noun
  anvils
anxiety noun
  anxieties
anxious
  anxiously
anybody
anyhow
anyone
anything
anyway
anywhere
apart
apartment noun
  apartments
apathetic
apathy
ape noun
  apes
aphid noun
  aphids
apiece
apologetic
  apologetically
apologize verb
  apologizes
  apologizing
  apologized
apology noun
  apologies
apostle noun
  apostles
apostrophe noun
  apostrophes
appal verb
  appals

  appalling
  appalled
appalling
apparatus noun
  apparatuses
apparent
  apparently
appeal verb
  appeals
  appealing
  appealed
appeal noun
  appeals
appear verb
  appears
  appearing
  appeared
appearance noun
  appearances
appease verb
  appeases
  appeasing
  appeased
appeasement
appendicitis
★ **appendix**
  appendixes or
  appendices
appetite noun
  appetites
appetizing
applaud verb
  applauds
  applauding
  applauded
applause
apple noun
  apples
appliance noun
  appliances

applicable
applicant noun
  applicants
application noun
  applications
applied
apply verb
  applies
  applying
  applied
appoint verb
  appoints
  appointing
  appointed
appointment noun
  appointments
appraisal
  appraisals
appraise verb
  appraises
  appraising
  appraised
appreciate verb
  appreciates
  appreciating
  appreciated
appreciation
appreciative
apprehension noun
apprehensive
apprentice noun
  apprentices
apprenticeship
approach verb
  approaches
  approaching
  approached
approach noun
  approaches
approachable
appropriate

. . . .

★ You use **appendixes** when you mean organs of the body and **appendices** when you mean parts of a book.

approval
approve *verb*
  approves
  approving
  approved
approximate
  approximately
apricot *noun*
  apricots
April
apron *noun*
  aprons
aptitude *noun*
  aptitudes
aquarium *noun*
  aquariums
aquatic
aqueduct *noun*
  aqueducts
★ **Arab** *noun*
  Arabs
★ **Arabian** *adjective*
☆ **Arabic**
☆ **arabic**
arable
arbitrary
arbitrate *verb*
  arbitrates
  arbitrating
  arbitrated
arbitration
arbitrator
○ **arc** *noun*
  arcs
arcade *noun*
  arcades
arch *noun*
  arches
arch *verb*
  arches

  arching
  arched
archaeology
archaeological
archaeologist
archbishop *noun*
  archbishops
archer *noun*
  archers
archery
architect *noun*
  architects
architecture

-archy
-archy at the end of a
word means 'rule or
government', e.g.
anarchy (= a lack of
rule) and monarchy
(= rule by a king or
queen). The plural
forms is -archies, e.g.
monarchies.

Arctic
are
area *noun*
  areas
arena *noun*
  arenas
aren't *abbreviation*
argue *verb*
  argues
  arguing
  argued
argument *noun*
  arguments
arid
aridity
arise *verb*
  arises

  arising
  arose
  arisen
aristocracy *noun*
  aristocracies
aristocrat *noun*
  aristocrats
aristocratic
arithmetic
arithmetical
✷ **ark** *noun*
  arks
arm *noun*
  arms
arm *verb*
  arms
  arming
  armed
armada *noun*
  armadas
armadillo *noun*
  armadillos
armaments
armchair *noun*
  armchairs
armful *noun*
  armfuls
armistice *noun*
  armistices
armour
armoured
armpit *noun*
  armpits
army *noun*
  armies
aroma *noun*
  aromas
aromatic
arose see **arise**
around

★ You use **Arab** when you mean a person or the people, and **Arabian** when you
  mean the place, e.g. *the Arabian desert.*
☆ You use **Arabic** when you mean the language, and **arabic** when you mean
  numbers, e.g. *arabic numerals.*
○ **Arc** means a curve. ! **ark**.
✷ **Ark** means a boat. ! **arc**.

ar - as

arouse *verb*
  arouses
  arousing
  aroused
arrange *verb*
  arranges
  arranging
  arranged
arrangement
array *noun*
  arrays
arrears
arrest *verb*
  arrests
  arresting
  arrested
arrest *noun*
  arrests
arrival
arrive *verb*
  arrives
  arriving
  arrived
arrogance
arrogant
arrow *noun*
  arrows
arsenal *noun*
  arsenals
arsenic
arson
artefact *noun*
  artefacts
artery *noun*
  arteries
artful
  artfully
arthritic
arthritis
article *noun*
  articles

articulate *adjective*
articulate *verb*
  articulates
  articulating
  articulated
artificial
  artificially
artillery *noun*
  artilleries
artist *noun*
  artists
artiste *noun*
  artistes
artistic
artistry
asbestos
ascend *verb*
  ascends
  ascending
  ascended
ascent *noun*
  ascents
★ **ash** *noun*
  ashes
ashamed
ashen
ashore
ashtray *noun*
  ashtrays
Asian *adjective* and
  noun
  Asians
aside
ask *verb*
  asks
  asking
  asked
asleep
aspect *noun*
  aspects

☆ **asphalt**
aspirin *noun*
  aspirins
ass *noun*
  asses
assassin *noun*
  assassins
assassinate *verb*
  assassinates
  assassinating
  assassinated
assassination *noun*
  assassinations
assault *verb*
  assaults
  assaulting
  assaulted
assault *noun*
  assaults
assemble *verb*
  assembles
  assembling
  assembled
assembly *noun*
  assemblies
assent
assert *verb*
  asserts
  asserting
  asserted
assertion
assertive
assess *verb*
  assesses
  assessing
  assessed
assessment
assessor

★ The tree and the burnt powder.
☆ Note that this word is not spelt *ash-*.

asset noun
assets

assign verb
assigns
assigning
assigned

assignment noun
assignments

assist verb
assists
assisting
assisted

assistance

assistant noun
assistants

associate verb
associates
associating
associated

associate noun
associates

association noun
associations

assorted

assortment

assume verb
assumes
assuming
assumed

assumption noun
assumptions

assurance noun
assurances

assure verb
assures
assuring
assured

asterisk noun
asterisks

asteroid noun
asteroids

asthma

asthmatic adjective
and noun
asthmatics

astonish verb
astonishes
astonishing
astonished

astonishment

astound verb
astounds
astounding
astounded

astride

astrologer

astrological

astrology

astronaut noun
astronauts

astronomer

astronomical

astronomy

-asy
Not many words end
in -asy. The most
important are
ecstasy, fantasy,
idiosyncrasy. There
are a lot of words
ending in -acy,
however, e.g.
accuracy.

★ **ate** see eat
atheist noun
atheists

atheism

athlete noun
athletes

athletic

athletics

atlas noun
atlases

atmosphere noun
atmospheres

atmospheric

atoll noun
atolls

atom noun
atoms

atomic

atrocious
atrociously

atrocity noun
atrocities

attach verb
attaches
attaching
attached

attached

attachment noun
attachments

attack verb
attacks
attacking
attacked

attack noun
attacks

attain verb
attains
attaining
attained

attainment

attempt verb
attempts
attempting
attempted

attempt noun
attempts

★ **Ate** is the past tense of eat e.g. *I ate an apple*. ! **eight**.

at - av

attend verb
attends
attending
attended

attendance noun
attendances

attendant noun
attendants

attention

attentive

attic noun
attics

attitude noun
attitudes

attract verb
attracts
attracting
attracted

attraction noun
attractions

attractive

auburn

auction noun
auctions

auctioneer

audibility

audible

audience noun
audiences

audio-
audio- makes words
with 'sound' or
'hearing' in their
meaning. Some of
them have hyphens,
e.g. **audio-visual** (= to
do with hearing and
seeing).

audiovisual

audition noun
auditions

auditorium noun
auditoriums

August

aunt noun
aunts

★ **auntie** noun
aunties

☆ **au pair** noun
au pairs

◉ **aural**

austere

austerity

Australian adjective
and noun
Australians

authentic
authentically

authenticity

author noun
authors

authority noun
authorities

authorize verb
authorizes
authorizing
authorized

autistic

auto-
auto- at the beginning
of a word means
'self', e.g.
autobiography (= a
biography of
yourself), **automatic**
(= done by itself). But
some words beginning
with auto- are to do
with cars, e.g.
autocross (= car
racing across
country).

autobiography
noun
autobiographies

autograph noun
autographs

automate verb
automates
automating
automated

automatic
automatically

automation

automobile noun
automobiles

autumn noun
autumns

autumnal

auxiliary adjective
and noun
auxiliaries

availability

available

avalanche noun
avalanches

avenue noun
avenues

average adjective
and noun
averages

average verb
averages
averaging
averaged

avert verb
averts
averting
averted

aviary noun
aviaries

aviation

avid

. . . .

★ You can also spell this word aunty.
☆ **Au pair** means a young person from another country who works in your house.
◉ **Aural** means 'to do with hearing'. ! oral.

avoid verb
 avoids
 avoiding
 avoided
avoidance
await verb
 awaits
 awaiting
 awaited
awake adjective
awake verb
 awakes
 awaking
 awoke
 awoken
awaken verb
 awakens
 awakening
 awakened
award noun
 awards
award verb
 awards
 awarding
 awarded
aware
awareness
awash
away
awe
awed
awful
 awfully
★ **awhile**
awkward
awoke see awake
awoken see awake
axe noun
 axes

axe verb
 axes
 axing
 axed
axis noun
 axes
axle noun
 axles
Aztec noun
 Aztecs
azure adjective

Bb

babble verb
 babbles
 babbling
 babbled
baboon noun
 baboons
baby noun
 babies
babyish
babysit verb
 babysits
 babysitting
 babysat
babysitter noun
 babysitters
bachelor noun
 bachelors
back noun
 backs
back verb
 backs
 backing
 backed

backache noun
 backaches
backbone noun
 backbones
background noun
 backgrounds
backing
backlash noun
 backlashes
backlog noun
 backlogs
backside noun
 backsides
backstroke
backward adjective
 and adverb
backwards adverb
backwater noun
 backwaters
backyard noun
 backyards
bacon
bacteria
bacterial
bad adjective
 worse
 worst
 badly
baddy noun
 baddies
badge noun
 badges
badger noun
 badgers
badger verb
 badgers
 badgering
 badgered
badminton

. . . .

★ **Awhile** means 'for a short time', e.g. *Wait here awhile*. You spell it as two words
  in e.g. *a short while*.

baffle *verb*
baffles
baffling
baffled

bag *noun*
bags

bag *verb*
bags
bagging
bagged

bagel *noun*
bagels

baggage

baggy *adjective*
baggier
baggiest

bagpipes

★ **bail** *noun*
bails

☆ **bail** *verb*
bails
bailing
bailed

Bairam *noun*
Bairams

Baisakhi

bait *noun*

bait *verb*
baits
baiting
baited

bake *verb*
bakes
baking
baked

baker *noun*
bakers

bakery *noun*
bakeries

baking powder

balance *noun*
balances

balance *verb*
balances
balancing
balanced

balcony *noun*
balconies

bald *adjective*
balder
baldest

◎ **bale** *noun*
bales

✳ **bale** *verb*
bales
baling
baled

ballad *noun*
ballads

ballerina *noun*
ballerinas

ballet *noun*
ballets

ballistic *adjective*

balloon *noun*
balloons

ballot *noun*
ballots

ballpoint *noun*
ballpoints

ballroom *noun*
ballrooms

balsa

bamboo *noun*
bamboos

ban *verb*
bans
banning
banned

banana *noun*
bananas

band *noun*
bands

band *verb*
bands
banding
banded

bandage *noun*
bandages

bandit *noun*
bandits

bandstand *noun*
bandstands

bandwagon *noun*
bandwagons

bandy *adjective*
bandier
bandiest

bang *noun*
bangs

bang *verb*
bangs
banging
banged

banger *noun*
bangers

banish *verb*
banishes
banishing
banished

banishment

banisters

banjo *noun*
banjos

bank *noun*
banks

bank *verb*
banks
banking
banked

banknote *noun*
banknotes

- -

★ **Bail** means 'money paid to let a prisoner out of prison' and 'a piece of wood put on the stumps in cricket'. ! **bale**.

☆ **Bail** means 'to pay money to let a prisoner out of prison' and 'to scoop water out of a boat'. ! **bale**.

◎ **Bale** means 'a large bundle'. ! **bail**.

✳ **Bale** means 'to jump out of an aircraft'. ! **bail**.

bankrupt
bankruptcy
banner *noun*
  banners
banquet *noun*
  banquets
baptism *noun*
  baptisms
★ **Baptist** *noun*
  Baptists
baptize *verb*
  baptizes
  baptizing
  baptized
bar *noun*
  bars
bar *verb*
  bars
  barring
  barred
barb *noun*
  barbs
barbarian *noun*
  barbarians
barbaric
barbarism
barbarity *noun*
  barbarities
barbarous *adjective*
barbecue *noun*
  barbecues
barber *noun*
  barbers
bar code *noun*
  bar codes
bard *noun*
  bards
☆ **bare** *adjective*
  barer
  barest
bareback

barely
bargain *noun*
  bargains
bargain *verb*
  bargains
  bargaining
  bargained
barge *noun*
  barges
barge *verb*
  barges
  barging
  barged
baritone *noun*
  baritones
bark *noun*
  barks
bark *verb*
  barks
  barking
  barked
barley
barman *noun*
  barmen
bar mitzvah *noun*
  bar mitzvahs
barnacle *noun*
  barnacles
barnyard *noun*
  barnyards
barometer *noun*
  barometers
barometric
baron *noun*
  barons
baroness *noun*
  baronesses
baronial
barrack *verb*
  barracks
  barracking

barracked
◉ **barracks** *plural noun*
barrage *noun*
  barrages
barrel *noun*
  barrels
barren
barricade *noun*
  barricades
barricade *verb*
  barricades
  barricading
  barricaded
barrier *noun*
  barriers
barrister *noun*
  barristers
barrow *noun*
  barrows
barter *verb*
  barters
  bartering
  bartered
✱ **base** *noun*
  bases
base *verb*
  bases
  basing
  based
baseball *noun*
  baseballs
basement *noun*
  basements
bash *verb*
  bashes
  bashing
  bashed
bash *noun*
  bashes
bashful
  bashfully

★ You use a capital B when you mean a member of the Christian Church.
☆ Bare means 'naked' or 'not covered'. ! bear.
◉ Barracks is plural but sometimes has a singular verb, e.g. *The Barracks is over there.*
✱ Base means 'a place where things are controlled'. ! **bass**.

basic
basically

basin noun
basins

basis noun
bases

bask verb
basks
basking
basked

basket noun
baskets

basketball noun
basketballs

basketful noun
basketfuls

★ **bass** noun
basses

bassoon noun
bassoons

bastard noun
bastards

bat noun
bats

bat verb
bats
batting
batted

batch noun
batches

bath noun
baths

bath verb
baths
bathing
bathed

bathe verb
bathes
bathing
bathed

bathroom noun
bathrooms

☆ **baton** noun
batons

batsman noun
batsmen

battalion noun
battalions

◎ **batten** noun
battens

batter verb
batters
battering
battered

batter noun

battery noun
batteries

battle noun
battles

battlefield noun
battlefields

battlements

battleship noun
battleships

bawl verb
bawls
bawling
bawled

bay noun
bays

bayonet noun
bayonets

bazaar noun
bazaars

✳ **beach** noun
beaches

beacon noun
beacons

bead noun
beads

beady adjective
beadier
beadiest

beagle noun
beagles

beak noun
beaks

beaker noun
beakers

beam noun
beams

beam verb
beams
beaming
beamed

✱ **bean** noun
beans

✳ **bear** verb
bears
bearing
bore
borne

✳ **bear** noun
bears

bearable

beard noun
beards

bearded

bearing noun
bearings

beast noun
beasts

beastly

beat verb
beats
beating
beat
beaten

beat noun
beats

beautiful
beautifully

. . . .

★ **Bass** means 'a singer with a low voice'. ! **base.**
☆ A **baton** is a stick used by a conductor in an orchestra. ! **batten.**
◎ A **batten** is a flat strip of wood. ! **baton.**
✳ **Beach** means 'sandy part of the seashore'. ! **beech.**
✱ A **bean** is a vegetable. ! **been.**
✳ To **bear** something is to carry it and a **bear** is an animal. ! **bare.**

beautify verb
beautifies
beautifying
beautified

beauty noun
beauties

beaver noun
beavers

becalmed

became see become

because

beckon verb
beckons
beckoning
beckoned

become verb
becomes
becoming
became
become

bedclothes

bedding

bedlam

bedraggled

bedridden

bedroom noun
bedrooms

bedside

bedspread noun
bedspreads

bedstead noun
bedsteads

bedtime

bee noun
bees

★ **beech** noun
beeches

beef

beefburger noun
beefburgers

beefeater noun
beefeaters

beefy adjective
beefier
beefiest

beehive noun
beehives

beeline

☆ **been** see be

beer noun
beers

beet noun
beet or beets

beetle noun
beetles

beetroot noun
beetroot

before

beforehand

beg verb
begs
begging
begged

began see begin

beggar noun
beggars

begin verb
begins
beginning
began
begun

beginner noun
beginners

beginning noun
beginnings

begrudge verb
begrudges
begrudging
begrudged

begun see begin

behalf

behave verb
behaves
behaving
behaved

behaviour

behead verb
beheads
beheading
beheaded

behind adverb and
preposition

behind noun
behinds

beige noun

being noun
beings

belch verb
belches
belching
belched

belch noun
belches

belfry noun
belfries

belief noun
beliefs

believe verb
believes
believing
believed

believable

believer

bellow verb
bellows
bellowing
bellowed

bellows

belly noun
bellies

• •

★ **Beech** means 'a tree'. ! **beach**.
☆ You use **been** in e.g. *I've been to the zoo*. ! **bean**.

be - bi

belong verb
belongs
belonging
belonged

belongings

beloved

below

belt noun
belts

belt verb
belts
belting
belted

bench noun
benches

bend verb
bends
bending
bent

bend noun
bends

beneath

benefaction

benefactor noun
benefactors

benefit noun
benefits

beneficial
beneficially

benevolence

benevolent

bent see bend

bequeath verb
bequeaths
bequeathing
bequeathed

bequest

★ **bereaved**

bereavement

☆ **bereft**

beret noun
berets

berry noun
berries

berserk

berth noun
berths

beside

besides

besiege verb
besieges
besieging
besieged

bestseller noun
bestsellers

bet noun
bets

bet verb
bets
betting
bet
betted

betray verb
betrays
betraying
betrayed

betrayal

better adjective and adverb

better verb
betters
bettering
bettered

between

⊙ **beware** verb

bewilder verb
bewilders
bewildering
bewildered

bewilderment

bewitch verb
bewitches

bewitching
bewitched

beyond

bi-
bi- at the beginning of a word means 'two', e.g. bicycle (= a machine with two wheels), bilateral (= having two sides).

bias noun
biases

biased

bib noun
bibs

Bible noun
Bibles

biblical

bicycle noun
bicycles

bid noun
bids

bid verb
bids
bidding
bid

bide verb
bides
biding
bided

big adjective
bigger
biggest

bigamist

bigamous

bigamy

bike noun
bikes

bikini noun
bikinis

. . . .

★ You use **bereaved** when you mean a person with a close relative who has died.
　! bereft.

☆ You use **bereft** when you mean 'deprived of something', e.g. *bereft of hope*.
　! bereaved.

⊙ **Beware** has no other forms.

bile

bilge *noun*
bilges

bilingual

billiards

billion *noun*
billions

billionth

billow *noun*
billows

billow *verb*
billows
billowing
billowed

billy goat *noun*
billy goats

binary

bind *verb*
binds
binding
bound

bingo

binoculars

bio-
bio- at the beginning
of a word means 'life',
e.g. biography (= a
story of a person's
life), biology (= the
study of living things).

biodegradable

biographer

biographical

biography *noun*
biographies

biological

biologist

biology

bionic

biosphere

birch *noun*
birches

bird *noun*
birds

birdseed

Biro *noun*
Biros

birth *noun*
births

birth control

birthday *noun*
birthdays

birthmark *noun*
birthmarks

birthplace *noun*
birthplaces

biscuit *noun*
biscuits

bisect *verb*
bisects
bisecting
bisected

bishop *noun*
bishops

bison *noun*
bison

bit *noun*
bits

bit see **bite**

bitch *noun*
bitches

bitchy *adjective*
bitchier
bitchiest

bite *verb*
bites
biting
bit
bitten

★ **bite** *noun*
bites

bitter

black *adjective*
blacker
blackest

black *noun*
blacks

blackberry *noun*
blackberries

blackbird *noun*
blackbirds

blackboard *noun*
blackboards

blacken *verb*
blackens
blackening
blackened

blackmail *verb*
blackmails
blackmailing
blackmailed

blackout *noun*
blackouts

blacksmith *noun*
blacksmiths

bladder *noun*
bladders

blade *noun*
blades

blame *verb*
blames
blaming
blamed

blame *noun*

blancmange *noun*
blancmanges

blank *adjective* and
noun
blanks

blanket *noun*
blankets

· ·

★ A bite is an act of biting. ! byte.

blare *verb*
blares
blaring
blared

blaspheme *verb*
blasphemes
blaspheming
blasphemed

blasphemous

blasphemy

blast *noun*
blasts

blast *verb*
blasts
blasting
blasted

blast-off

blaze *noun*
blazes

blaze *verb*
blazes
blazing
blazed

blazer *noun*
blazers

bleach *noun*
bleaches

bleach *verb*
bleaches
bleaching
bleached

bleak *adjective*
bleaker
bleakest

bleary *adjective*
blearier
bleariest
blearily

bleat *noun*
bleats

bleat *verb*
bleats
bleating
bleated

bleed *verb*
bleeds
bleeding
bled

bleep *noun*
bleeps

blemish *noun*
blemishes

blend *verb*
blends
blending
blended

blend *noun*
blends

bless *verb*
blesses
blessing
blessed

blessing *noun*
blessings

★ **blew** see **blow**

blight *noun*
blights

blind *adjective*
blinder
blindest

blind *verb*
blinds
blinding
blinded

blind *noun*
blinds

blindfold *noun*
blindfolds

blindfold *verb*
blindfolds
blindfolding
blindfolded

blindfold

blink *verb*
blinks
blinking
blinked

bliss

blissful
blissfully

blister *noun*
blisters

blitz *noun*
blitzes

blizzard *noun*
blizzards

bloated

block *noun*
blocks

block *verb*
blocks
blocking
blocked

blockade *noun*
blockades

blockage *noun*
blockages

blond *adjective*
blonder
blondest

☆ **blonde** *noun*
blondes

blood

bloodhound *noun*
bloodhounds

bloodshed

bloodshot

bloodstream

bloodthirsty
adjective
bloodthirstier
bloodthirstiest

. . . .

★ You use **blew** in e.g. *the wind blew hard*. ! **blue**.

☆ You use **blonde** when you are talking about a girl or woman.

bloody *adjective*
  bloodier
  bloodiest
bloom *verb*
  blooms
  blooming
  bloomed
bloom *noun*
  blooms
blossom *noun*
  blossoms
blossom *verb*
  blossoms
  blossoming
  blossomed
blot *noun*
  blots
blot *verb*
  blots
  blotting
  blotted
blotch *noun*
  blotches
blotchy *adjective*
  blotchier
  blotchiest
blouse *noun*
  blouses
blow *noun*
  blows
blow *verb*
  blows
  blowing
  blew
  blown
blowlamp *noun*
  blowlamps
blowtorch *noun*
  blowtorches
blue *adjective*
  bluer
  bluest

★ **blue** *noun*
  blues
bluebell *noun*
  bluebells
bluebottle *noun*
  bluebottles
blueprint *noun*
  blueprints
bluff *verb*
  bluffs
  bluffing
  bluffed
bluff *noun*
  bluffs
blunder *verb*
  blunders
  blundering
  blundered
blunder *noun*
  blunders
blunt *adjective*
  blunter
  bluntest
blur *verb*
  blurs
  blurring
  blurred
blur *noun*
  blurs
blush *verb*
  blushes
  blushing
  blushed
bluster *verb*
  blusters
  blustering
  blustered
blustery
boa constrictor *noun*
  boa constrictors

☆ **boar** *noun*
  boars
✪ **board** *noun*
  boards
board *verb*
  boards
  boarding
  boarded
boarder *noun*
  boarders
board game *noun*
  board games
boast *verb*
  boasts
  boasting
  boasted
boastful
  boastfully
boat *noun*
  boats
boating
bob *verb*
  bobs
  bobbing
  bobbed
bobble *noun*
  bobbles
bobsled *noun*
  bobsleds
bobsleigh *noun*
  bobsleighs
bodice *noun*
  bodices
bodily
body *noun*
  bodies
bodyguard *noun*
  bodyguards

. . . .

★ **Blue** is the colour. **! blew.**
☆ A **boar** is a wild pig. **! bore.**
✪ A **board** is a piece of wood. **! bored.**

boggy *adjective*
boggier
boggiest

bogus

boil *verb*
boils
boiling
boiled

boil *noun*
boils

boiler *noun*
boilers

boisterous
boisterously

bold *adjective*
bolder
boldest

bollard *noun*
bollards

bolster *verb*
bolsters
bolstering
bolstered

bolster *noun*
bolsters

bolt *noun*
bolts

bolt *verb*
bolts
bolting
bolted

bomb *noun*
bombs

bomb *verb*
bombs
bombing
bombed

bombard *verb*
bombards
bombarding
bombarded

bombardment

bomber *noun*
bombers

bond *noun*
bonds

bondage

bone *noun*
bones

bonfire *noun*
bonfires

bonnet *noun*
bonnets

bonus *noun*
bonuses

bony *adjective*
bonier
boniest

boo *verb*
boos
booing
booed

booby *noun*
boobies

book *noun*
books

book *verb*
books
booking
booked

bookcase *noun*
bookcases

booklet *noun*
booklets

bookmaker *noun*
bookmakers

bookmark *noun*
bookmarks

boom *noun*
booms

boom *verb*
booms
booming
boomed

boomerang *noun*
boomerangs

boost *verb*
boosts
boosting
boosted

booster *noun*
boosters

boot *noun*
boots

boot *verb*
boots
booting
booted

booth *noun*
booths

border *noun*
borders

borderline

bore *verb*
bores
boring
bored

★ bore *noun*
bores

boredom

boring

☆ born

✿ borne see bear

borough *noun*
boroughs

borrow *verb*
borrows
borrowing
borrowed

bosom *noun*
bosoms

- -

★ **Bore** means 'something boring'. ! **boar**.
☆ You use **born** in e.g. *He was born in June*. ! **borne**.
✿ You use **borne** in e.g. *She has borne three children* and *The cost is borne by the government*. ! **born**.

boss noun
bosses

boss verb
bosses
bossing
bossed

bossy adjective
bossier
bossiest

botanical

botanist

botany

both

bother verb
bothers
bothering
bothered

bother noun

bottle noun
bottles

bottle verb
bottles
bottling
bottled

bottleneck noun
bottlenecks

bottom noun
bottoms

bottomless

★ **bough** noun
boughs

bought

boulder noun
boulders

bounce verb
bounces
bouncing
bounced

bounce noun
bounces

bouncing

bouncy adjective
bouncier
bounciest

bound verb
bounds
bounding
bounded

bound adjective and noun
bounds

bound see **bind**

boundary noun
boundaries

bounds

bouquet noun
bouquets

bout noun
bouts

boutique noun
boutiques

☆ **bow** noun
bows

❂ **bow** verb
bows
bowing
bowed

bowels

bowl noun
bowls

bowl verb
bowls
bowling
bowled

bow-legged

bowler noun
bowlers

bowling

bowls

bow tie noun
bow ties

box noun
boxes

box verb
boxes
boxing
boxed

boxer noun
boxers

Boxing Day noun

boy noun
boys

boycott verb
boycotts
boycotting
boycotted

boyfriend noun
boyfriends

boyhood

boyish

bra noun
bras

brace noun
braces

bracelet noun
bracelets

braces

bracken

bracket noun
brackets

bracket verb
brackets
bracketing
bracketed

brag verb
brags
bragging
bragged

- -

★ A **bough** is a part of a tree. ! bow.
☆ A **bow** is a knot with loops and rhymes with 'go'. A **bow** is also the front of a
    ship or a bending of the body and rhymes with 'cow'.
❂ To **bow** is to bend the body and rhymes with 'cow'.

br

braid noun
braids

braille

brain noun
brains

brainy adjective
brainier
brainiest

★ **brake** noun
brakes

bramble noun
brambles

branch noun
branches

branch verb
branches
branching
branched

brand noun
brands

brand verb
brands
branding
branded

brandish verb
brandishes
brandishing
brandished

brand-new

brandy noun
brandies

brass

brassière noun
brassières

brassy adjective
brassier
brassiest

brave adjective
braver
bravest

brave noun
braves

bravery

brawl noun
brawls

brawn

brawny adjective
brawnier
brawniest

bray verb
brays
braying
brayed

brazen

brazier noun
braziers

☆ **breach** noun
breaches

bread

breadth noun
breadths

breadwinner noun
breadwinners

◐ **break** verb
breaks
breaking
broke
broken

break noun
breaks

breakable

breakage noun
breakages

breakdown noun
breakdowns

breaker noun
breakers

breakfast noun
breakfasts

breakneck

breakthrough noun
breakthroughs

breakwater noun
breakwaters

breast noun
breasts

breaststroke

breath noun
breaths

breathalyse
breathalyses
breathalysing
breathalysed

breathalyser noun
breathalysers

breathe verb
breathes
breathing
breathed

breather noun
breathers

breathless

breathtaking

bred see breed

✳ **breech** noun
breeches

breeches

breed verb
breeds
breeding
bred

breed noun
breeds

breeder noun
breeders

breeze noun
breezes

breezy adjective
breezier
breeziest

brethren

- -

★ A brake is what makes a car stop. ! break.
☆ A breach is a gap or a breaking of a rule. ! breech.
◐ To break something is to make it go into pieces. ! brake.
✳ A breech is a part of a gun. ! breach.

brevity

brew verb
brews
brewing
brewed

brewer noun
brewers

brewery noun
breweries

★ **briar** noun
briars

bribe noun
bribes

bribe verb
bribes
bribing
bribed

bribery

brick noun
bricks

bricklayer noun
bricklayers

bride noun
brides

☆ **bridal**

bridegroom noun
bridegrooms

bridesmaid noun
bridesmaids

bridge noun
bridges

⊙ **bridle** noun
bridles

brief adjective
briefer
briefest

brief noun
briefs

brief verb
briefs
briefing
briefed

briefcase noun
briefcases

brigade noun
brigades

brigadier noun
brigadiers

brigand noun
brigands

bright adjective
brighter
brightest

brighten verb
brightens
brightening
brightened

brilliance

brilliant

brim noun
brims

brimming

brine

bring verb
brings
bringing
brought

brink

brisk adjective
brisker
briskest

bristle noun
bristles

bristly
bristlier
bristliest

British

Briton noun
Britons

brittle adjective
brittler
brittlest

✱ **broach** verb
broaches
broaching
broached

broad adjective
broader
broadest
broadly

broadcast noun
broadcasts

broadcast verb
broadcasts
broadcasting
broadcast

broadcaster

broaden verb
broadens
broadening
broadened

broad-minded

broadside noun
broadsides

brochure noun
brochures

brogue noun
brogues

broke see break
broken see break
bronchitis

bronze

✶ **brooch** noun
brooches

brood noun
broods

brood verb
broods
brooding
brooded

. . . .

★ **Briar** means 'a prickly bush' and 'a pipe'. You will sometimes see it spelt *brier*.
☆ **Bridal** means 'to do with a **bride**'. ! **bridle**.
⊙ A **bridle** is part of a horse's harness. ! **bridal**.
✱ **Broach** means 'to mention something'. ! **brooch**.
✶ A **brooch** is an ornament you wear. ! **broach**.

broody *adjective*
broodier
broodiest

brook *noun*
brooks

broom *noun*
brooms

broomstick *noun*
broomsticks

broth *noun*
broths

brother *noun*
brothers

brotherly

brother-in-law *noun*
brothers-in-law

brought see bring

brow *noun*
brows

brown *adjective*
browner
brownest

★ **brownie** *noun*
brownies

☆ **Brownie** *noun*
Brownies

browse *verb*
browses
browsing
browsed

bruise *noun*
bruises

bruise *verb*
bruises
bruising
bruised

brunette *noun*
brunettes

brush *noun*
brushes

brush *verb*
brushes
brushing
brushed

Brussels sprout *noun*
Brussels sprouts

brutal
brutally

brutality
brutalities

brute *noun*
brutes

bubble *noun*
bubbles

bubble *verb*
bubbles
bubbling
bubbled

bubble gum

bubbly *adjective*
bubblier
bubbliest

buccaneer *noun*
buccaneers

buck *noun*
bucks

buck *verb*
bucks
bucking
bucked

bucket *noun*
buckets

bucketful *noun*
bucketfuls

buckle *noun*
buckles

buckle *verb*
buckles
buckling
buckled

bud *noun*
buds

Buddhism

Buddhist

budding

budge *verb*
budges
budging
budged

budgerigar *noun*
budgerigars

budget *noun*
budgets

budget *verb*
budgets
budgeting
budgeted

budgie *noun*
budgies

buff

buffalo *noun*
buffalo or
buffaloes

buffer *noun*
buffers

buffet *noun*
buffets

bug *noun*
bugs

bug *verb*
bugs
bugging
bugged

bugle *noun*
bugles

bugler

build *verb*
builds
building
built

. . . .

★ A brownie is a chocolate cake.
☆ A Brownie is a junior Guide.

builder noun
builders
building noun
buildings
built-in
built-up
bulb noun
bulbs
bulge noun
bulges
bulge verb
bulges
bulging
bulged
bulk
bulky adjective
bulkier
bulkiest
bull noun
bulls
bulldog noun
bulldogs
bulldoze verb
bulldozes
bulldozing
bulldozed
bulldozer noun
bulldozers
bullet noun
bullets
bulletin noun
bulletins
bulletproof
bullfight noun
bullfights
bullfighter
bullion
bullock noun
bullocks
bull's-eye noun
bull's-eyes

bully verb
bullies
bullying
bullied
bully noun
bullies
bulrush noun
bulrushes
★ **bulwark** noun
bulwarks
☆ **bulwarks** plural noun
bum noun
bums
bumble-bee noun
bumble-bees
bump verb
bumps
bumping
bumped
bump noun
bumps
bumper adjective
and noun
bumpers
bumpy adjective
bumpier
bumpiest
bunch noun
bunches
bundle noun
bundles
bundle verb
bundles
bundling
bundled
bung verb
bungs
bunging
bunged

bung noun
bungs
bungalow noun
bungalows
bungle verb
bungles
bungling
bungled
bungler
bunk noun
bunks
bunk bed noun
bunk beds
bunker noun
bunkers
bunny noun
bunnies
bunsen burner noun
bunsen burners
buoy noun
buoys
buoyancy
buoyant
burden noun
burdens
burdensome
❂ **bureau** noun
bureaux
burglar noun
burglars
burglary noun
burglaries
burgle verb
burgles
burgling
burgled
burial noun
burials
burly adjective
burlier
burliest

. . . .

★ A bulwark is a strong wall.
☆ Bulwarks are the sides of a ship.
❂ Bureau is a French word used in English. It means 'a writing desk' or 'an office'.

★ **burn** verb
  burns
  burning
  burnt or burned

burn noun
  burns

burner noun
  burners

burning

burp noun
  burps

burp verb
  burps
  burping
  burped

burr noun
  burrs

burrow noun
  burrows

burrow verb
  burrows
  burrowing
  burrowed

burst verb
  bursts
  bursting
  burst

burst noun
  bursts

bury verb
  buries
  burying
  buried

bus noun
  buses

bus stop noun
  bus stops

bush noun
  bushes

bushy adjective
  bushier
  bushiest

busily

business noun
  businesses

businesslike

busker noun
  buskers

bust verb
  busts
  busting
  bust

bust noun
  busts

bust adjective

bustle verb
  bustles
  bustling
  bustled

busy adjective
  busier
  busiest

busybody noun
  busybodies

☆ **but**

butcher noun
  butchers

butchery

butler noun
  butlers

✿ **butt** noun
  butts

✳ **butt** verb
  butts
  butting
  butted

butter

buttercup noun
  buttercups

butterfingers noun
  butterfingers

butterfly noun
  butterflies

butterscotch noun
  butterscotches

buttocks

button noun
  buttons

button verb
  buttons
  buttoning
  buttoned

buttonhole noun
  buttonholes

buttress noun
  buttresses

buy verb
  buys
  buying
  bought

buy noun
  buys

buyer

buzz noun
  buzzes

buzz verb
  buzzes
  buzzing
  buzzed

buzzard noun
  buzzards

buzzer noun
  buzzers

✴ **by** preposition

✳ **bye** noun
  byes

bye-bye

by-election noun
  by-elections

by-law noun
  by-laws

. . . .

★ You use **burned** in e.g. *I burned the cakes.* You use **burnt** in e.g. *I can smell burnt cakes.* You use **burned** or **burnt** in e.g. *I have burned/burnt the cakes.*

☆ You use **but** in e.g. *I like fish but I'm not hungry.* **! butt.**

✿ A **butt** is a barrel or part of a gun. **! but.**

✳ **Butt** means 'to hit with your head'. **! but.**

✴ You use **by** in e.g. *a book by J. K. Rowling.* **! bye.**

✳ You use **bye** in e.g. *bye for now.* **! by.**

bypass noun
bypasses
by-product noun
by-products
bystander noun
bystanders
★ **byte** noun

Cc

CAB abbreviation
cab noun
cabs
cabaret noun
cabarets
cabbage noun
cabbages
cabin noun
cabins
cabinet noun
cabinets
cable noun
cables
cackle verb
cackles
cackling
cackled
cackle noun
cackles
cactus noun
cacti
☆ **caddie** noun
caddies
○ **caddy** noun
caddies
cadet noun
cadets

cadge verb
cadges
cadging
cadged
cafe noun
cafes
cafeteria noun
cafeterias
caffeine
caftan noun
caftans use **kaftan**
cage noun
cages
cagey adjective
cagier
cagiest
cagoule noun
cagoules
cake noun
cakes
caked
calamine
calamitous
calamity noun
calamities
calcium
calculate verb
calculates
calculating
calculated
calculation
calculator noun
calculators
calendar noun
calendars
✳ **calf** noun
calves
calico
call noun
calls

call verb
calls
calling
called
calling noun
callings
callipers
callous
calm adjective
calmer
calmest
calmly
calmness
calorie noun
calories
✽ **calves** see **calf**
calypso noun
calypsos
camcorder noun
camcorders
came see **come**
camel noun
camels
camera noun
cameras
cameraman
camouflage
camp noun
camps
camp verb
camps
camping
camped
campaign noun
campaigns
camper noun
campers

• •

★ A **byte** is a unit in computing. ! bite.
☆ A **caddie** is a person who helps a golfer. ! caddy.
○ A **caddy** is a container for tea. ! caddie.
✳ **Calf** means 'a young cow' and 'a part of your leg'.
✽ **Calves** is the plural of calf. ! carves.

campaign verb
campaigns
campaigning
campaigned

campsite noun
campsites

campus noun
campuses

can verb
could

★ **can** verb
cans
canning
canned

can noun
cans

canal noun
canals

canary noun
canaries

cancel verb
cancels
cancelling
cancelled

cancellation noun
cancellations

cancer noun
cancers

candidate noun
candidates

candle noun
candles

candlelight

candlestick noun
candlesticks

candy noun
candies

candyfloss

cane noun
canes

cane verb
canes
caning
caned

canine

cannabis

canned music

cannibal noun
cannibals

cannibalism

☆ **cannon** noun
cannon or cannons

cannonball noun
cannonballs

cannot

canoe noun
canoes

canoe verb
canoes
canoeing
canoed

canoeist

✪ **canon** noun
canons

canopy noun
canopies

can't verb

canteen noun
canteens

canter verb
canters
cantering
cantered

canton noun
cantons

✳ **canvas** noun
canvases

● **canvass** verb
canvasses
canvassing
canvassed

canyon noun
canyons

cap verb
caps
capping
capped

cap noun
caps

capable
capably

capability

capacity noun
capacities

cape noun
capes

caper verb
capers
capering
capered

caper noun
capers

capital noun
capitals

capitalism

capitalist

capsize verb
capsizes
capsizing
capsized

capsule noun
capsules

captain noun
captains

caption noun
captions

captivating

captive adjective and
noun
captives

★ This verb **can** means 'to put food in a can', and it has normal forms.
☆ A **cannon** is a gun. ! canon. You use **cannons** in e.g. *There are ten cannons on the walls* and **cannon** in e.g. *They use all their cannon.*
✪ A **canon** is a member of the clergy. ! cannon.
✳ **Canvas** means 'a strong cloth'. ! canvass.
● **Canvass** means 'to ask people for their support'. ! canvas.

captivity

captor noun
  captors

capture verb
  captures
  capturing
  captured

capture noun

car noun
  cars

caramel noun
  caramels

carat noun
  carats

caravan noun
  caravans

carbohydrate noun
  carbohydrates

carbon

car-boot sale noun
  car-boot sales

carburettor noun
  carburettors

carcass noun
  carcasses

card noun
  cards

cardboard

cardigan noun
  cardigans

cardinal noun
  cardinals

cardphone noun
  cardphones

care noun
  cares

care verb
  cares
  caring
  cared

career noun
  careers

career verb
  careers
  careering
  careered

carefree

careful adjective
  carefully

careless adjective
  carelessly
  carelessness

caress verb
  caresses
  caressing
  caressed

caress noun
  caresses

caretaker noun
  caretakers

cargo noun
  cargoes

Caribbean

caricature noun
  caricatures

carnation noun
  carnations

carnival noun
  carnivals

carnivore noun
  carnivores

carnivorous

carol noun
  carols

caroller

carolling

carp noun
  carp

carpenter noun
  carpenters

carpentry

carpet noun
  carpets

carriage noun
  carriages

carriageway noun
  carriageways

carrier noun
  carriers

carrot noun
  carrots

carry verb
  carries
  carrying
  carried

cart noun
  carts

cart verb
  carts
  carting
  carted

carthorse noun
  carthorses

cartilage

carton noun
  cartons

cartoon noun
  cartoons

cartoonist

cartridge noun
  cartridges

cartwheel noun
  cartwheels

★ **carve** verb
  carves
  carving
  carved

cascade noun
  cascades

case noun
  cases

. . . .

★ You use **carves** in e.g. *He carves the meat with a knife.* ! **calves.**

cash verb
 cashes
 cashing
 cashed
cash noun
cashier noun
 cashiers
cash register noun
 cash registers
cask noun
 casks
casket noun
 caskets
casserole noun
 casseroles
cassette noun
 cassettes
cast verb
 casts
 casting
 cast
cast noun
 casts
castanets plural
 noun
castaway noun
 castaways
castle noun
 castles
castor noun
 castors
castor sugar
casual adjective
 casually
casualty noun
 casualties
cat noun
 cats
catalogue noun
 catalogues

catalyst noun
 catalysts
catamaran noun
 catamarans
catapult noun
 catapults
catastrophe noun
 catastrophes
catastrophic
catch verb
 catches
 catching
 caught
catch noun
 catches
catching
catchphrase noun
 catchphrases
catchy adjective
 catchier
 catchiest
category noun
 categories
cater verb
 caters
 catering
 catered
caterer noun
 caterers
caterpillar noun
 caterpillars
cathedral noun
 cathedrals
Catherine wheel
 noun
 Catherine wheels
cathode noun
 cathodes
Catholic adjective
 and noun
 Catholics

catkin noun
 catkins
Cat's-eye noun
 Cat's-eyes
cattle
caught see **catch**
cauldron noun
 cauldrons
cauliflower noun
 cauliflowers
cause verb
 causes
 causing
 caused
cause noun
 causes
caution noun
 cautions
cautious adjective
 cautiously
cavalier noun
 cavaliers
cavalry noun
 cavalries
cave noun
 caves
cave verb
 caves
 caving
 caved
caveman noun
 cavemen
cavern noun
 caverns
cavity noun
 cavities
CD
CD-ROM noun

cease verb
ceases
ceasing
ceased

ceasefire noun
ceasefires

ceaseless adjective
ceaselessly

cedar noun
cedars

ceiling noun
ceilings

celebrate verb
celebrates
celebrating
celebrated

celebration noun
celebrations

celebrity noun
celebrities

celery

★ **cell** noun
cells

cellar noun
cellars

cello noun
cellos

cellular

celluloid

cellulose

Celsius

Celt noun
Celts

Celtic

cement

cemetery noun
cemeteries

censor verb
censors
censoring
censored

☆ **censor** noun
censors

censorship

censure verb
censures
censured
censuring

○ **censure** noun

census noun
censuses

✳ **cent** noun
cents

centenary noun
centenaries

centigrade

centimetre noun
centimetres

centipede noun
centipedes

central adjective
centrally

centre noun
centres

centrifugal force

centurion noun
centurions

century noun
centuries

ceramic adjective

ceramics plural noun

✱ **cereal** noun
cereals

ceremony noun
ceremonies

ceremonial adjective
ceremonially

certain

certainly

certainty noun
certainties

certificate noun
certificates

certify verb
certifies
certifying
certified

chaffinch noun
chaffinches

chain noun
chains

chair noun
chairs

chairlift noun
chairlifts

chairman noun
chairmen

chairperson noun
chairpersons

chalet noun
chalets

chalk noun
chalks

chalky adjective
chalkier
chalkiest

challenge verb
challenges
challenging
challenged

challenge noun
challenges

challenger noun
challengers

chamber noun
chambers

champagne

champion noun
champions

championship noun
championships

. . . .

★ A **cell** is a small room or a part of an organism. ! **sell**.
☆ A **censor** is someone who makes sure books and films are suitable for people to see. ! **censure**.
○ **Censure** means 'harsh criticism'. ! **censor**.
✳ A **cent** is a coin used in America. ! **scent, sent**.
✱ A **cereal** is something you eat. ! **serial**.

chance noun
chances

chancel noun
chancels

chancellor noun
chancellors

Chancellor of the Exchequer

chandelier noun
chandeliers

change verb
changes
changing
changed

change noun
changes

changeable

channel noun
channels

chant noun
chants

chant verb
chants
chanting
chanted

chaos

chaotic adjective
chaotically

chap noun
chaps

chapatti noun
chapattis

chapel noun
chapels

chapped

chapter noun
chapters

char verb
chars
charring
charred

character noun
characters

characteristic adjective
characteristically

characteristic noun
characteristics

characterize verb
characterizes
characterizing
characterized

charades plural noun

charcoal

charge verb
charges
charging
charged

charge noun
charges

chariot noun
chariots

charioteer noun
charioteers

charitable adjective
charitably

charity noun
charities

charm verb
charms
charming
charmed

charm noun
charms

charming

chart noun
charts

charter noun
charters

charter verb
charters
chartering
chartered

charwoman noun
charwomen

chase verb
chases
chasing
chased

chase noun
chases

chasm noun
chasms

chassis noun
chassis

chat verb
chats
chatting
chatted

chat noun
chats

chatty adjective
chattier
chattiest

★ **château** noun
châteaux

chatter verb
chatters
chattering
chattered

chauffeur noun
chauffeurs

chauvinism

chauvinist

☆ **cheap** adjective
cheaper
cheapest

cheat verb
cheats
cheating
cheated

cheat noun
cheats

· ·

★ **Château** is a French word used in English. It means 'a castle or large house'.

☆ **Cheap** means 'not costing much'. ! **cheep**.

check verb
  checks
  checking
  checked
check noun
  checks
checkmate noun
  checkmates
checkout noun
  checkouts
check-up noun
  check-ups
cheek noun
  cheeks
cheek verb
  cheeks
  cheeking
  cheeked
cheeky adjective
  cheekier
  cheekiest
  cheekily
★ **cheep** verb
  cheeps
  cheeping
  cheeped
cheer verb
  cheers
  cheering
  cheered
cheer noun
  cheers
cheerful adjective
  cheerfully
cheerio
cheese noun
  cheeses
cheesy adjective
  cheesier
  cheesiest
cheetah noun
  cheetahs

chef noun
  chefs
chemical adjective
  chemically
chemical noun
  chemicals
chemist noun
  chemists
chemistry
cheque noun
  cheques
chequebook noun
  chequebooks
chequered
cherish verb
  cherishes
  cherishing
  cherished
cherry noun
  cherries
chess
chest noun
  chests
chestnut noun
  chestnuts
chest of drawers
  noun
  chests of drawers
chew verb
  chews
  chewing
  chewed
chewy adjective
  chewier
  chewiest
☆ **chic**
chick noun
  chicks
chicken noun
  chickens

chicken verb
  chickens
  chickening
  chickened
chickenpox
chief adjective
  chiefly
chief noun
  chiefs
chieftain noun
  chieftains
chilblain noun
  chilblains
child noun
  children
childhood noun
  childhoods
childish
childminder noun
  childminders
childproof
chill noun
  chills
chill verb
  chills
  chilling
  chilled
❍ **chilli** noun
  chillies
✳ **chilly** adjective
  chillier
  chilliest
chime noun
  chimes
chime verb
  chimes
  chiming
  chimed
chimney noun
  chimneys

• •

★ **Cheep** is the noise a bird makes. ! **cheap**.
☆ **Chic** is a French word and means 'smart or elegant'. There is no word *chicly*.
❍ A **chilli** is a type of hot pepper, added to meat or vegetable dishes. ! **chilly**.
✳ You use **chilly** to describe cold, bleak weather or atmosphere. ! **chilli**.

ch

chimpanzee *noun*
chimpanzees

chin *noun*
chins

china

chink *noun*
chinks

chip *noun*
chips

chip *verb*
chips
chipping
chipped

chirp *verb*
chirps
chirping
chirped

chirpy *adjective*
chirpier
chirpiest

chisel *noun*
chisels

chisel *verb*
chisels
chiselling
chiselled

chivalrous *adjective*
chivalrously

chivalry

chlorine

chlorophyll

choc ice *noun*
choc ices

chock-a-block

chock-full

chocolate *noun*
chocolates

choice *noun*
choices

choir *noun*
choirs

choirboy *noun*
choirboys

choirgirl *noun*
choirgirls

choke *verb*
chokes
choking
choked

choke *noun*
chokes

cholera

cholesterol

choose *verb*
chooses
choosing
chose
chosen

choosy *adjective*
choosier
choosiest

chop *verb*
chops
chopping
chopped

chop *noun*
chops

chopper *noun*
choppers

choppy *adjective*
choppier
choppiest

chopsticks

choral

★ **chord** *noun*
chords

chore *noun*
chores

chorister *noun*
choristers

chorus *noun*
choruses

chose see **choose**

chosen see **choose**

christen *verb*
christens
christening
christened

christening

Christian *adjective*
and *noun*
Christians

Christianity

Christmas *noun*
Christmases

chrome

chromium

chromosome *noun*
chromosomes

chronic *adjective*
chronically

chronicle *noun*
chronicles

chronological
adjective
chronologically

chronology

chrysalis *noun*
chrysalises

chrysanthemum
noun
chrysanthemums

chubby *adjective*
chubbier
chubbiest

chuck *verb*
chucks
chucking
chucked

chuckle *verb*
chuckles
chuckling
chuckled

★ A **chord** is a number of musical notes played together. ! **cord**.

chuckle noun
　chuckles
chug verb
　chugs
　chugging
　chugged
chum noun
　chums
chummy adjective
　chummier
　chummiest
chunk noun
　chunks
chunky adjective
　chunkier
　chunkiest
church noun
　churches
churchyard noun
　churchyards
churn noun
　churns
churn verb
　churns
　churning
　churned
★ **chute** noun
　chutes
chutney noun
　chutneys
cider noun
　ciders
cigar noun
　cigars
cigarette noun
　cigarettes
cinder noun
　cinders
cine camera noun
　cine cameras
cinema noun
　cinemas

cinnamon
circle noun
　circles
circle verb
　circles
　circling
　circled
circuit noun
　circuits
circular adjective and noun
　circulars
circulate verb
　circulates
　circulating
　circulated
circulation noun
　circulations
circumference noun
　circumferences
circumstance noun
　circumstances
circus noun
　circuses
cistern noun
　cisterns
citizen noun
　citizens
citizenship
citric acid
citrus
city noun
　cities
civic
civil
civilian noun
　civilians
civilization noun
　civilizations

civilize verb
　civilizes
　civilizing
　civilized
clad
claim verb
　claims
　claiming
　claimed
claim noun
　claims
claimant noun
　claimants
clam noun
　clams
clamber verb
　clambers
　clambering
　clambered
clammy adjective
　clammier
　clammiest
clamp noun
　clamps
clamp verb
　clamps
　clamping
　clamped
clan noun
　clans
clang verb
　clangs
　clanging
　clanged
clanger noun
　clangers
clank verb
　clanks
　clanking
　clanked

. . . .

★ A **chute** is a funnel for sending things down. ! **shoot**.

clap verb
 claps
 clapping
 clapped

clap noun
 claps

clapper noun
 clappers

clarification

clarify verb
 clarifies
 clarifying
 clarified

clarinet noun
 clarinets

clarinettist

clarity

clash verb
 clashes
 clashing
 clashed

clash noun
 clashes

clasp verb
 clasps
 clasping
 clasped

clasp noun
 clasps

class noun
 classes

class verb
 classes
 classing
 classed

classic noun
 classics

classic

classical adjective
 classically

classification

classified

classify verb
 classifies
 classifying
 classified

classmate noun
 classmates

classroom noun
 classrooms

clatter noun

clatter verb
 clatters
 clattering
 clattered

★ **clause** noun
 clauses

☆ **claw** noun
 claws

✪ **claw** verb
 claws
 clawing
 clawed

clay

clayey

clean adjective
 cleaner
 cleanest
 cleanly

clean verb
 cleans
 cleaning
 cleaned

cleaner noun
 cleaners

cleanliness

cleanse verb
 cleanses
 cleansing
 cleansed

cleanser

clear adjective
 clearer
 clearest
 clearly

clear verb
 clears
 clearing
 cleared

clearance noun
 clearances

clearing noun
 clearings

clef noun
 clefs

clench verb
 clenches
 clenching
 clenched

clergy

clergyman noun
 clergymen

clergywoman noun
 clergywomen

clerical

clerk noun
 clerks

clever adjective
 cleverer
 cleverest

cliché noun
 clichés

click noun
 clicks

client noun
 clients

cliff noun
 cliffs

cliffhanger noun
 cliffhangers

climate noun
 climates

. . . .

★ A **clause** is a part of a sentence or contract. ! **claws**.
☆ **Claws** are the hard sharp nails that some animals have on their feet. ! **clause**.
✪ To **claw** is to scratch, maul, or pull a person or thing.

climatic

climax *noun*
climaxes

climb *verb*
climbs
climbing
climbed

climb *noun*
climbs

climber *noun*
climbers

cling *verb*
clings
clinging
clung

clingfilm

clinic *noun*
clinics

clink *verb*
clinks
clinking
clinked

clip *verb*
clips
clipping
clipped

clip *noun*
clips

clipboard *noun*
clipboards

clipper *noun*
clippers

clippers *plural noun*

clipping *noun*
clippings

cloak *noun*
cloaks

cloakroom *noun*
cloakrooms

clobber *verb*
clobbers
clobbering
clobbered

clock *noun*
clocks

clockwise

clockwork

clog *verb*
clogs
clogging
clogged

clog *noun*
clogs

cloister *noun*
cloisters

clone *noun*
clones

clone *verb*
clones
cloning
cloned

close *verb*
closes
closing
closed

close *adjective* and
noun
closer
closest
closely

close *noun*
closes

close-up *noun*
close-ups

closure *noun*
closures

clot *noun*
clots

clot *verb*
clots
clotting
clotted

cloth *noun*
cloths

clothe *verb*
clothes
clothing
clothed

clothes

clothing

cloud *noun*
clouds

cloud *verb*
clouds
clouding
clouded

cloudless

cloudy *adjective*
cloudier
cloudiest

clout *verb*
clouts
clouting
clouted

clove *noun*
cloves

clover

clown *noun*
clowns

clown *verb*
clowns
clowning
clowned

club *noun*
clubs

club *verb*
clubs
clubbing
clubbed

cluck *verb*
clucks
clucking
clucked

clue noun
clues
clueless
clump noun
clumps
clumsiness
clumsy adjective
clumsier
clumsiest
clumsily
clung see cling
cluster noun
clusters
clutch verb
clutches
clutching
clutched
clutch noun
clutches
clutter verb
clutters
cluttering
cluttered
clutter noun

co-
co- makes words
meaning 'together',
e.g. a **co-pilot** is
another pilot who sits
together with the
chief pilot. You often
need a hyphen, e.g.
co-author, co-driver,
but some words are
spelt joined up, e.g.
cooperate,
coordinate.

coach verb
coaches
coaching
coached

coach noun
coaches
coal
★ **coarse** adjective
coarser
coarsest
coarsely
coast noun
coasts
coast verb
coasts
coasting
coasted
coastal
coastguard noun
coastguards
coastline
coat noun
coats
coat verb
coats
coating
coated
coating noun
coatings
coax verb
coaxes
coaxing
coaxed
cobalt
cobbled
cobbler noun
cobblers
cobbles plural noun
cobblestone noun
cobblestones
cobra noun
cobras
cobweb noun
cobwebs

cock noun
cocks
cock verb
cocks
cocking
cocked
cockerel noun
cockerels
cocker spaniel noun
cocker spaniels
cockle noun
cockles
cockney noun
cockneys
cockpit noun
cockpits
cockroach noun
cockroaches
cocky adjective
cockier
cockiest
cocoa noun
cocoas
coconut noun
coconuts
cocoon noun
cocoons
☆ **cod** noun
cod
code noun
codes
code verb
codes
coding
coded
coeducation
coeducational
coffee noun
coffees
coffin noun
coffins

★ **Coarse** means 'rough' or 'crude'. ! **course**.
☆ You use **cod** for the plural: *The sea is full of cod.*

cog noun
cogs

cohort noun
cohorts

coil verb
coils
coiling
coiled

coil noun
coils

coin noun
coins

coin verb
coins
coining
coined

coinage noun
coinages

coincide verb
coincides
coinciding
coincided

coincidence noun
coincidences

coincidentally

coke

cola noun
colas

colander noun
colanders

cold adjective
colder
coldest
coldly

cold noun
colds

cold-blooded

coldness

coleslaw

collaborate verb
collaborates
collaborating
collaborated

collaboration

collaborator

collage noun
collages

collapse verb
collapses
collapsing
collapsed

collapse noun
collapses

collapsible

collar noun
collars

collate verb
collates
collating
collated

colleague noun
colleagues

collect verb
collects
collecting
collected

collection noun
collections

collective

collector

college noun
colleges

collide verb
collides
colliding
collided

collie noun
collies

collision noun
collisions

colloquial adjective
colloquially

colon noun
colons

★ **colonel** noun
colonels

colonial

colonist noun
colonists

colony noun
colonies

colossal adjective
colossally

colour noun
colours

colour verb
colours
colouring
coloured

colour-blind

coloured

colourful adjective
colourfully

colouring

colourless

colt noun
colts

column noun
columns

coma noun
comas

comb noun
combs

comb verb
combs
combing
combed

combat noun
combats

combat verb
combats
combating
combated

★ A **colonel** is an army officer. ! **kernel**.

combatant noun
combatants

combination noun
combinations

combine verb
combines
combining
combined

combine noun
combines

combustion

come verb
comes
coming
came

comeback noun
comebacks

comedian noun
comedians

comedy noun
comedies

comet noun
comets

comfort verb
comforts
comforting
comforted

comfort noun
comforts

comfortable
adjective
comfortably

comic adjective and
noun
comics

comical adjective
comically

comma noun
commas

command verb
commands
commanding
commanded

command noun
commands

commander noun
commanders

commandment
noun
commandments

commando noun
commandos

commemorate verb
commemorates
commemorating
commemorated

commemoration

commence verb
commences
commencing
commenced

commencement

commend verb
commends
commending
commended

commendable

commendation

comment verb
comments
commenting
commented

comment noun
comments

commentary noun
commentaries

commentate

commentator noun
commentators

commerce

commercial
adjective
commercially

commercial noun
commercials

commercialized

commit verb
commits
committing
committed

commitment noun
commitments

committee noun
committees

commodity noun
commodities

common adjective
commoner
commonest

common noun
commons

commonplace

commonwealth
noun
commonwealths

commotion noun
commotions

communal adjective
communally

commune noun
communes

communicate verb
communicates
communicating
communicated

communication
noun
communications

communicative

communion noun
communions

communism

communist *noun*
communists

community *noun*
communities

commute

commuter *noun*
commuters

compact *adjective*
compactly

compact *noun*
compacts

compact disc *noun*
compact discs

companion *noun*
companions

companionship

company *noun*
companies

comparable
adjective
comparably

comparative
adjective
comparatively

comparative *noun*
comparatives

compare *verb*
compares
comparing
compared

comparison *noun*
comparisons

compartment *noun*
compartments

compass *noun*
compasses

compassion

compassionate
adjective
compassionately

compatible *adjective*
compatibly

compel *verb*
compels
compelling
compelled

compensate *verb*
compensates
compensating
compensated

compensation *noun*
compensations

compère *noun*
compères

compete *verb*
competes
competing
competed

competence

competent *adjective*
competently

competition *noun*
competitions

competitive
adjective
competitively

competitor *noun*
competitors

compilation *noun*
compilations

compile *verb*
compiles
compiling
compiled

compiler *noun*
compilers

complacent
adjective
complacently

complain *verb*
complains
complaining
complained

complaint *noun*
complaints

★ **complement** *noun*
complements

☆ **complementary**

complete *adjective*
completely

complete *verb*
completes
completing
completed

completion

complex *adjective*
and *noun*
complexes

complexion *noun*
complexions

complexity *noun*
complexities

complicated

complication *noun*
complications

✪ **compliment** *noun*
compliments

✳ **complimentary**

component *noun*
components

compose *verb*
composes
composing
composed

composer *noun*
composers

composition *noun*
compositions

compost

compound *noun*
compounds

. . . .

★ A **complement** is a thing that completes something. ! **compliment**.
☆ Something **complementary** completes something. ! **complimentary**.
✪ A **compliment** is something good you say about someone. ! **complement**.
✳ Something **complimentary** praises someone. ! **complementary**.

comprehend verb
comprehends
comprehending
comprehended
comprehension
noun
comprehensions
comprehensive
adjective
comprehensively
comprehensive
noun
comprehensives
compress verb
compresses
compressing
compressed
compression
comprise verb
comprises
comprising
comprised
compromise noun
compromises
compromise verb
compromises
compromising
compromised
compulsory
computation
compute verb
computes
computing
computed
computer noun
computers
comrade noun
comrades
comradeship
con verb
cons
conning
conned

concave
conceal verb
conceals
concealing
concealed
concealment
conceit
conceited
conceive verb
conceives
conceiving
conceived
concentrate verb
concentrates
concentrating
concentrated
concentrated
concentration noun
concentrations
concentric
concept noun
concepts
conception noun
conceptions
concern verb
concerns
concerning
concerned
concern noun
concerns
concerning
concert noun
concerts
concertina noun
concertinas
concerto noun
concertos
concession noun
concessions

concise adjective
concisely
conclude verb
concludes
concluding
concluded
conclusion noun
conclusions
concrete adjective
and noun
concussion
condemn verb
condemns
condemning
condemned
condemnation
condensation
condense verb
condenses
condensing
condensed
condition noun
conditions
condom noun
condoms
conduct verb
conducts
conducting
conducted
conduct noun
conduction
conductor noun
conductors
cone noun
cones
confectioner noun
confectioners
confectionery

confer verb
confers
conferring
conferred

conference noun
conferences

confess verb
confesses
confessing
confessed

confession noun
confessions

confetti

confide verb
confides
confiding
confided

confidence noun
confidences

confident adjective
confidently

confidential adjective
confidentially

confine verb
confines
confining
confined

confinement

confirm verb
confirms
confirming
confirmed

confirmation

confiscate verb
confiscates
confiscating
confiscated

confiscation noun
confiscations

conflict verb
conflicts
conflicting
conflicted

conflict noun
conflicts

conform verb
conforms
conforming
conformed

conformity

confront verb
confronts
confronting
confronted

confrontation noun
confrontations

confuse verb
confuses
confusing
confused

confusion noun
confusions

congested

congestion

congratulate verb
congratulates
congratulating
congratulated

congratulations plural noun

congregation noun
congregations

congress noun
congresses

congruence

congruent

conical

conifer noun
conifers

coniferous

conjunction noun
conjunctions

conjure verb
conjures
conjuring
conjured

conjuror noun
conjurors

★ **conker** noun
conkers

connect verb
connects
connecting
connected

connection noun
connections

conning tower noun
conning towers

☆ **conquer** verb
conquers
conquering
conquered

conqueror noun
conquerors

conquest noun
conquests

conscience

conscientious adjective
conscientiously

conscious adjective
consciously

consciousness

conscription

consecutive adjective
consecutively

consensus

consent verb
consents
consenting
consented

....

★ A **conker** is the fruit of a horse chestnut tree. ! conquer.
☆ To **conquer** means 'to invade or take over'. ! conker.

consent noun
consequence noun
  consequences
consequently
conservation
conservationist
conservative
★ **Conservative** noun
  Conservatives
conservatory noun
  conservatories
conserve verb
  conserves
  conserving
  conserved
consider verb
  considers
  considering
  considered
considerable
  adjective
  considerably
considerate
  adjective
  considerately
consideration noun
  considerations
consist verb
  consists
  consisting
  consisted
consistency noun
  consistencies
consistent adjective
  consistently
consolation noun
  consolations
console verb
  consoles
  consoling
  consoled

consonant noun
  consonants
conspicuous
  adjective
  conspicuously
conspiracy noun
  conspiracies
conspirator
conspire verb
  conspires
  conspiring
  conspired
constable noun
  constables
constancy
constant adjective
  constantly
constant noun
  constants
constellation noun
  constellations
constipated
constipation
constituency noun
  constituencies
constituent noun
  constituents
constitute verb
  constitutes
  constituting
  constituted
constitution noun
  constitutions
constitutional
construct verb
  constructs
  constructing
  constructed
construction noun
  constructions

constructive
consul noun
  consuls
consult verb
  consults
  consulting
  consulted
consultant noun
  consultants
consultation noun
  consultations
consume verb
  consumes
  consuming
  consumed
consumer noun
  consumers
consumption
contact noun
  contacts
contact verb
  contacts
  contacting
  contacted
contagious
contain verb
  contains
  containing
  contained
container noun
  containers
contaminate verb
  contaminates
  contaminating
  contaminated
contamination
contemplate verb
  contemplates
  contemplating
  contemplated
contemplation

★ Use a capital C when you mean a member of the political party.

contemporary
adjective and noun
contemporaries

contempt

contemptible
adjective
contemptibly

contemptuous
adjective
contemptuously

contend verb
contends
contending
contended

contender noun
contenders

content adjective and
noun

contented adjective
contentedly

contentment

contents plural noun

contest verb
contests
contesting
contested

contest noun
contests

contestant noun
contestants

context noun
contexts

continent noun
continents

continental

continual adjective
continually

continuation

continue verb
continues
continuing
continued

continuous adjective
continuously

continuity

contour noun
contours

contraception

contraceptive noun
contraceptives

contract verb
contracts
contracting
contracted

contract noun
contracts

contraction noun
contractions

contractor noun
contractors

contradict verb
contradicts
contradicting
contradicted

contradiction noun
contradictions

contradictory

contraflow noun
contraflows

contraption noun
contraptions

contrary adjective
and noun

contrast verb
contrasts
contrasting
contrasted

contrast noun
contrasts

contribute verb
contributes
contributing
contributed

contribution noun
contributions

contributor noun
contributors

contrivance noun
contrivances

contrive verb
contrives
contriving
contrived

control verb
controls
controlling
controlled

control noun
controls

controller noun
controllers

controversial
adjective
controversially

controversy noun
controversies

conundrum noun
conundrums

convalescence

convalescent

convection

convector noun
convectors

convenience noun
conveniences

convenient adjective
conveniently

convent noun
convents

convention noun
conventions

conventional adjective
conventionally

converge verb
converges
converging
converged

conversation noun
conversations

conversational adjective
conversationally

converse verb
converses
conversing
conversed

converse noun

conversion noun
conversions

convert verb
converts
converting
converted

convert noun
converts

convertible

convex

convey verb
conveys
conveying
conveyed

conveyor belt noun
conveyor belts

convict verb
convicts
convicting
convicted

convict noun
convicts

conviction noun
convictions

convince verb
convinces
convincing
convinced

convoy noun
convoys

cook verb
cooks
cooking
cooked

cook noun
cooks

cooker noun
cookers

cookery

cool adjective
cooler
coolest
coolly

cool verb
cools
cooling
cooled

cooler

coolness

coop noun
coops

cooperate verb
cooperates
cooperating
cooperated

cooperation

cooperative

coordinate verb
coordinates
coordinating
coordinated

coordinate noun
coordinates

coordination

coordinator noun
coordinators

coot noun
coots

cop verb
cops
copping
copped

cop noun
cops

cope verb
copes
coping
coped

copier noun
copiers

copper noun
coppers

copper sulphate

copy verb
copies
copying
copied

copy noun
copies

coral

★ **cord** noun
cords

cordial adjective
cordially

cordial noun
cordials

cordiality

corduroy

core noun
cores

corgi noun
corgis

cork noun
corks

corkscrew noun
corkscrews

. . . .

★ A **cord** is a piece of thin rope. ! chord.

cormorant noun
  cormorants

corn noun
  corns

corned beef

corner noun
  corners

corner verb
  corners
  cornering
  cornered

cornet noun
  cornets

cornfield noun
  cornfields

cornflakes

cornflour

cornflower noun
  cornflowers

Cornish

Cornish pasty noun
  Cornish pasties

corny adjective
  cornier
  corniest

coronation noun
  coronations

coroner noun
  coroners

corporal noun
  corporals

corporal adjective

corporation noun
  corporations

★ **corps** noun
  corps

☆ **corpse** noun
  corpses

corpuscle noun
  corpuscles

corral noun
  corrals

correct adjective
  correctly

correct verb
  corrects
  correcting
  corrected

correction noun
  corrections

correctness

correspond verb
  corresponds
  corresponding
  corresponded

correspondence

correspondent noun
  correspondents

corridor noun
  corridors

corrode verb
  corrodes
  corroding
  corroded

corrosion

corrosive

corrugated

corrupt

corruption

corset noun
  corsets

cosmetics plural noun

cosmic

cosmonaut noun
  cosmonauts

cost verb
  costs
  costing
  cost

cost noun
  costs

costly adjective
  costlier
  costliest

costume noun
  costumes

cosy adjective
  cosier
  cosiest

cosy noun
  cosies

cot noun
  cots

cottage noun
  cottages

cotton

couch noun
  couches

cough verb
  coughs
  coughing
  coughed

cough noun
  coughs

could see can
couldn't

⊙ **council** noun
  councils

✳ **councillor** noun
  councillors

✱ **counsel** noun
  counsels

counsel verb
  counsels
  counselling
  counselled

✼ **counsellor** noun
  counsellors

. . . .

★ A **corps** is a unit of soldiers. ! **corpse**.
☆ A **corpse** is a dead body. ! **corps**.
⊙ A **council** is a group of people who run the affairs of a town. ! **counsel**.
✳ A **councillor** is a member of a council. ! **counsellor**.
✱ **Counsel** means 'advice'. ! **council**.
✼ A **counsellor** is someone who gives advice. ! **councillor**.

count verb
counts
counting
counted

count noun
counts

countdown noun
countdowns

countenance noun
countenances

counter-
counter- makes words
meaning 'opposite',
e.g. a **counter-claim**
is a claim someone
makes in response to
a claim from someone
else. You often need a
hyphen, but some
words are spelt joined
up, e.g. **counteract**,
counterbalance.

counter noun
counters

counterfeit

countess noun
countesses

countless

country noun
countries

countryman noun
countrymen

countryside

countrywoman
noun
countrywomen

county noun
counties

couple noun
couples

couple verb
couples
coupling
coupled

coupling noun
couplings

coupon noun
coupons

courage

courageous
adjective
courageously

courgette noun
courgettes

courier noun
couriers

★ **course** noun
courses

court noun
courts

court verb
courts
courting
courted

courteous adjective
courteously

courtesy noun
courtesies

court martial noun
courts martial

courtship

courtyard noun
courtyards

cousin noun
cousins

cove noun
coves

cover verb
covers
covering
covered

cover noun
covers

coverage

cover-up noun
cover-ups

cow noun
cows

coward noun
cowards

cowardice

cowardly

cowboy noun
cowboys

cowslip noun
cowslips

cox noun
coxes

coxswain noun
coxswains

coy adjective
coyly

coyness

crab noun
crabs

crack verb
cracks
cracking
cracked

crack noun
cracks

cracker noun
crackers

crackle verb
crackles
crackling
crackled

crackling

cradle noun
cradles

craft noun
crafts

- -

★ You use **course** in e.g. a French course. ! **coarse**.

craftsman noun
craftsmen

craftsmanship

crafty adjective
craftier
craftiest
craftily

craftiness

crag noun
crags

craggy adjective
craggier
craggiest

cram verb
crams
cramming
crammed

cramp verb
cramps
cramping
cramped

cramp noun
cramps

crane noun
cranes

crane verb
cranes
craning
craned

crane-fly noun
crane-flies

crank verb
cranks
cranking
cranked

crank noun
cranks

cranky adjective
crankier
crankiest

cranny noun
crannies

crash verb
crashes
crashing
crashed

crash noun
crashes

crate noun
crates

crater noun
craters

crave verb
craves
craving
craved

crawl verb
crawls
crawling
crawled

crawl noun
crawls

crayon noun
crayons

craze noun
crazes

craziness

crazy adjective
crazier
craziest
crazily

creak verb
creaks
creaking
creaked

creak noun
creaks

creaky adjective
creakier
creakiest

cream noun
creams

creamy adjective
creamier
creamiest

crease verb
creases
creasing
creased

crease noun
creases

create verb
creates
creating
created

creation noun
creations

creative adjective
creatively

creativity

creator noun
creators

creature noun
creatures

crèche noun
crèches

credibility

credible adjective
credibly

credit verb
credits
crediting
credited

credit noun

creditable adjective
creditably

creditor noun
creditors

creed noun
creeds

creek noun
creeks

creep verb
creeps
creeping
crept

creep noun
creeps

creeper noun
creepers

creepy adjective
creepier
creepiest

cremate verb
cremates
cremating
cremated

cremation noun
cremations

crematorium noun
crematoria

creosote

crêpe noun
crêpes

crept see **creep**

crescendo noun
crescendos

crescent noun
crescents

cress

crest noun
crests

crevice noun
crevices

crew noun
crews

crib verb
cribs
cribbing
cribbed

crib noun
cribs

★ **cricket** noun
crickets

cricketer noun
cricketers

cried see **cry**

crime noun
crimes

criminal adjective
and noun
criminals

crimson

crinkle verb
crinkles
crinkling
crinkled

crinkly adjective
crinklier
crinkliest

cripple verb
cripples
crippling
crippled

cripple noun
cripples

crisis noun
crises

crisp adjective
crisper
crispest

crisp noun
crisps

criss-cross adjective

critic noun
critics

critical adjective
critically

criticism noun
criticisms

criticize verb
criticizes
criticizing
criticized

croak verb
croaks
croaking
croaked

croak noun
croaks

☆ **crochet**

crock noun
crocks

crockery

crocodile noun
crocodiles

crocus noun
crocuses

croft noun
crofts

crofter

croissant noun
croissants

crook noun
crooks

crook verb
crooks
crooking
crooked

crooked

croon verb
croons
crooning
crooned

crop noun
crops

crop verb
crops
cropping
cropped

★ Cricket means 'a game' and 'an insect like a grasshopper'.
☆ Crochet is a kind of needlework. ! crotchet.

cross-
cross- makes words meaning 'across', e.g. a *cross-channel ferry* is one that goes across the English Channel. You usually need a hyphen, but some words are spelt joined up, e.g. **crossroads** and **crosswind**.

cross *adjective*
crossly

cross *verb*
crosses
crossing
crossed

cross *noun*
crosses

crossbar *noun*
crossbars

crossbow *noun*
crossbows

cross-country

cross-examine *verb*
cross-examines
cross-examining
cross-examined

cross-examination *noun*
cross-examinations

cross-eyed

crossing *noun*
crossings

cross-legged

crossness

crossroads *noun*
crossroads

cross-section *noun*
cross-sections

crosswise

crossword *noun*
crosswords

★ **crotchet** *noun*
crotchets

crouch *verb*
crouches
crouching
crouched

crow *noun*
crows

crow *verb*
crows
crowing
crowed

crowbar *noun*
crowbars

crowd *noun*
crowds

crowd *verb*
crowds
crowding
crowded

crown *noun*
crowns

crown *verb*
crowns
crowning
crowned

crow's-nest *noun*
crow's-nests

crucial *adjective*
crucially

crucifix *noun*
crucifixes

☆ **crucifixion** *noun*
crucifixions

crucify *verb*
crucifies
crucifying
crucified

crude *adjective*
cruder
crudest

cruel *adjective*
crueller
cruellest
cruelly

cruelty *noun*
cruelties

cruise *verb*
cruises
cruising
cruised

cruise *noun*
cruises

cruiser *noun*
cruisers

crumb *noun*
crumbs

crumble *verb*
crumbles
crumbling
crumbled

crumbly *adjective*
crumblier
crumbliest

crumpet *noun*
crumpets

crumple *verb*
crumples
crumpling
crumpled

crunch *noun*
crunches

crunch *verb*
crunches
crunching
crunched

crunchy *adjective*
crunchier
crunchiest

. . . . ★ . . .

★ A **crotchet** is a note in music. ! **crochet**.
☆ Use a capital C when you are talking about Christ.

crusade noun
crusades

crusader noun
crusaders

crush verb
crushes
crushing
crushed

crush noun
crushes

crust noun
crusts

crustacean noun
crustaceans

crutch noun
crutches

cry verb
cries
crying
cried

cry noun
cries

crypt noun
crypts

crystal noun
crystals

crystalline

crystallize verb
crystallizes
crystallizing
crystallized

cub noun
cubs

cubbyhole noun
cubbyholes

cube noun
cubes

cube verb
cubes
cubing
cubed

cubic

cubicle noun
cubicles

cuboid noun
cuboids

cuckoo noun
cuckoos

cucumber noun
cucumbers

cud

cuddle verb
cuddles
cuddling
cuddled

cuddly

★ **cue** noun
cues

cuff verb
cuffs
cuffing
cuffed

cuff noun
cuffs

cul-de-sac noun
cul-de-sacs or
culs-de-sac

culminate verb
culminates
culminating
culminated

culmination

culprit noun
culprits

cult noun
cults

cultivate verb
cultivates
cultivating
cultivated

cultivation

cultivated

culture noun
cultures

cultural adjective
culturally

cultured

cunning

cup noun
cups

cup verb
cups
cupping
cupped

cupboard noun
cupboards

cupful noun
cupfuls

curate noun
curates

curator noun
curators

☆ **curb** verb
curbs
curbing
curbed

curd noun
curds

curdle verb
curdles
curdling
curdled

cure verb
cures
curing
cured

cure noun
cures

curfew noun
curfews

★ A **cue** is a signal for action or a stick used in snooker. ! **queue**.
☆ To **curb** a feeling is to restrain it. ! **kerb**.

curiosity noun
curiosities
curious adjective
curiously
curl verb
curls
curling
curled
curl noun
curls
curly adjective
curlier
curliest
★ **currant** noun
currants
currency noun
currencies
☆ **current** noun
currents
current adjective
currently
curriculum noun
curriculums or
curricula
curry verb
curries
currying
curried
curry noun
curries
curse verb
curses
cursing
cursed
curse noun
curses
cursor noun
cursors
curtain noun
curtains

curtsy verb
curtsies
curtsying
curtsied
curtsy noun
curtsies
curvature noun
curvatures
curve verb
curves
curving
curved
curve noun
curves
cushion noun
cushions
cushion verb
cushions
cushioning
cushioned
custard
custom noun
customs
customary adjective
customarily
customer noun
customers
customize noun
customizes
customizing
customized
cut verb
cuts
cutting
cut
cut noun
cuts
cute adjective
cuter
cutest

cutlass noun
cutlasses
cutlery
cutlet noun
cutlets
cut-out noun
cut-outs
cut-price
cutter noun
cutters
cutting noun
cuttings
cycle noun
cycles
cycle verb
cycles
cycling
cycled
cyclist noun
cyclists
cyclone noun
cyclones
cyclonic
○ **cygnet** noun
cygnets
cylinder noun
cylinders
cylindrical
cymbal noun
cymbals
cynic noun
cynics
cynical adjective
cynically
cynicism
cypress noun
cypresses

· ·

★ A **currant** is a small dried grape. ! current.
☆ A **current** is a flow of water, air, or electricity. ! currant.
○ A **cygnet** is a young swan. ! signet.

Dd

dab verb
dabs
dabbing
dabbed

dab noun
dabs

dabble verb
dabbles
dabbling
dabbled

dachshund noun
dachshunds

dad noun
dads

daddy noun
daddies

daddy-long-legs
noun
daddy-long-legs

daffodil noun
daffodils

daft adjective
dafter
daftest

dagger noun
daggers

dahlia noun
dahlias

daily adjective and
adverb

daintiness

dainty adjective
daintier
daintiest
daintily

dairy noun
dairies

daisy noun
daisies

dale noun
dales

Dalmatian noun
Dalmatians

dam noun
dams

★ **dam** verb
dams
damming
dammed

damage verb
damages
damaging
damaged

damage noun
damages plural noun

☆ **Dame** noun
Dames

◐ **dame** noun
dames

✳ **damn** verb
damns
damning
damned

damned

damp adjective and
noun
damper
dampest

dampen verb
dampens
dampening
dampened

damson noun
damsons

dance verb
dances
dancing
danced

dance noun
dances

dancer noun
dancers

dandelion noun
dandelions

dandruff

danger noun
dangers

dangerous adjective
dangerously

dangle verb
dangles
dangling
dangled

dappled

dare verb
dares
daring
dared

dare noun
dares

daredevil noun
daredevils

daring

dark adjective and
noun
darker
darkest

darken verb
darkens
darkening
darkened

darkness

darkroom noun
darkrooms

darling noun
darlings

darn verb
darns
darning
darned

★ **Dam** means 'to build a dam across water'. ! **damn**.
☆ Use a capital D when it is a title, e.g. *Dame Jane Smith*.
◐ Use a small d when you mean a pantomime woman played by a man.
✳ **Damn** means 'to say that something is very bad'. ! **dam**.

dart noun
darts
dartboard noun
dartboards
dash verb
dashes
dashing
dashed
dash noun
dashes
dashboard noun
dashboards
★ **data** plural noun
database noun
databases
date noun
dates
date verb
dates
dating
dated
daughter noun
daughters
dawdle verb
dawdles
dawdling
dawdled
dawn noun
dawns
dawn verb
dawns
dawning
dawned
day noun
days
daybreak
daydream verb
daydreams
daydreaming
daydreamed
daylight

day-to-day
daze verb
dazes
dazing
dazed
daze noun
dazzle verb
dazzles
dazzling
dazzled

de-
de- makes verbs with an opposite meaning, e.g. deactivate means 'to stop something working'. You need a hyphen when the word begins with an e or i, e.g. de-escalate, **de-ice**.

dead
deaden verb
deadens
deadening
deadened
dead end noun
dead ends
deadline noun
deadlines
deadlock
deadly adjective
deadlier
deadliest
deaf adjective
deafer
deafest
deafness
deafen verb
deafens
deafening
deafened

deal verb
deals
dealing
dealt
deal noun
deals
dealer noun
dealers
dean noun
deans
☆ **dear** adjective
dearer
dearest
death noun
deaths
deathly
debatable
debate noun
debates
debate verb
debates
debating
debated
debris
debt noun
debts
debtor noun
debtors
debug verb
debugs
debugging
debugged
début noun
débuts
decade noun
decades
decay verb
decays
decaying
decayed

★ **Data** is strictly a plural noun, but is often used as a singular noun: *Here is the data.*

☆ **Dear** means 'loved' or 'expensive'. ! deer.

decay noun
deceased
deceit
deceitful adjective
  deceitfully
deceive verb
  deceives
  deceiving
  deceived
December
decency
decent adjective
  decently
deception noun
  deceptions
deceptive
decibel noun
  decibels
decide verb
  decides
  deciding
  decided
deciduous
decimal noun
  decimals
decimalization
decimalize verb
  decimalizes
  decimalizing
  decimalized
decipher verb
  deciphers
  deciphering
  deciphered
decision noun
  decisions
decisive adjective
  decisively
deck noun
  decks

deckchair noun
  deckchairs
declaration noun
  declarations
declare verb
  declares
  declaring
  declared
decline verb
  declines
  declining
  declined
decode verb
  decodes
  decoding
  decoded
decompose verb
  decomposes
  decomposing
  decomposed
decorate verb
  decorates
  decorating
  decorated
decoration noun
  decorations
decorative
decorator noun
  decorators
decoy noun
  decoys
decrease verb
  decreases
  decreasing
  decreased
decrease noun
  decreases
decree noun
  decrees

decree verb
  decrees
  decreeing
  decreed
decrepit
dedicate verb
  dedicates
  dedicating
  dedicated
dedication
deduce verb
  deduces
  deducing
  deduced
deduct verb
  deducts
  deducting
  deducted
deductible
deduction noun
  deductions
deed noun
  deeds
deep adjective
  deeper
  deepest
  deeply
deepen verb
  deepens
  deepening
  deepened
deep-freeze noun
  deep-freezes
★ **deer** noun
  deer
deface verb
  defaces
  defacing
  defaced
default noun
  defaults

★ A **deer** is an animal. ! **dear.**

defeat verb
  defeats
  defeating
  defeated

defeat noun
  defeats

defect noun
  defects

defect verb
  defects
  defecting
  defected

defective adjective
  defectively

defence noun
  defences

defenceless

defend verb
  defends
  defending
  defended

defendant noun
  defendants

defender noun
  defenders

defensible

defensive adjective
  defensively

defer verb
  defers
  deferring
  deferred

deferment

defiance

defiant adjective
  defiantly

deficiency noun
  deficiencies

deficient

deficit noun
  deficits

defile verb
  defiles
  defiling
  defiled

define verb
  defines
  defining
  defined

definite adjective
  definitely

definition noun
  definitions

deflate verb
  deflates
  deflating
  deflated

deflect verb
  deflects
  deflecting
  deflected

deflection

deforestation

deformed

deformity noun
  deformities

defrost verb
  defrosts
  defrosting
  defrosted

deft adjective
  defter
  deftest
  deftly

defuse verb
  defuses
  defusing
  defused

defy verb
  defies
  defying
  defied

degenerate verb
  degenerates
  degenerating
  degenerated

degeneration

degradation

degrade verb
  degrades
  degrading
  degraded

degree noun
  degrees

dehydrated

dehydration

de-ice verb
  de-ices
  de-icing
  de-iced

de-icer

deity noun
  deities

dejected

dejection

delay verb
  delays
  delaying
  delayed

delay noun
  delays

delegate noun
  delegates

delegate verb
  delegates
  delegating
  delegated

delegation

delete verb
  deletes
  deleting
  deleted

deletion

deliberate *adjective*
deliberately

deliberate *verb*
deliberates
deliberating
deliberated

deliberation

delicacy *noun*
delicacies

delicate *adjective*
delicately

delicatessen *noun*
delicatessens

delicious *adjective*
deliciously

delight *verb*
delights
delighting
delighted

delight *noun*
delights

delightful *adjective*
delightfully

delinquency

delinquent *noun*
delinquents

delirious *adjective*
deliriously

delirium *noun*

deliver *verb*
delivers
delivering
delivered

delivery *noun*
deliveries

delta *noun*
deltas

delude *verb*
deludes
deluding
deluded

deluge *noun*
deluges

deluge *verb*
deluges
deluging
deluged

delusion *noun*
delusions

de luxe

demand *verb*
demands
demanding
demanded

demand *noun*
demands

demanding

demerara

demist *verb*
demists
demisting
demisted

demo *noun*
demos

democracy *noun*
democracies

democrat *noun*
democrats

democratic *adjective*
democratically

demolish *verb*
demolishes
demolishing
demolished

demolition

demon *noun*
demons

demonstrate *verb*
demonstrates
demonstrating
demonstrated

demonstration
noun
demonstrations

demonstrator *noun*
demonstrators

demoralize *verb*
demoralizes
demoralizing
demoralized

demote *verb*
demotes
demoting
demoted

den *noun*
dens

denial *noun*
denials

denim

denominator *noun*
denominators

denote *verb*
denotes
denoting
denoted

denounce *verb*
denounces
denouncing
denounced

denunciation

dense *adjective*
denser
densest
densely

density *noun*

dent *noun*
dents

dental

dentist *noun*
dentists

dentistry

denture *noun*
dentures

deny *verb*
denies
denying
denied

deodorant *noun*
deodorants

depart *verb*
departs
departing
departed

department *noun*
departments

departure *noun*
departures

depend *verb*
depends
depending
depended

dependable

★ **dependant** *noun*
dependants

dependence

☆ **dependent** *adjective*

depict *verb*
depicts
depicting
depicted

deplorable *adjective*
deplorably

deplore *verb*
deplores
deploring
deplored

deport *verb*
deports
deporting
deported

deposit *verb*
deposits
depositing
deposited

deposit *noun*
deposits

depot *noun*
depots

depress *verb*
depresses
depressing
depressed

depression *noun*
depressions

deprivation

deprive *verb*
deprives
depriving
deprived

depth *noun*
depths

deputize *verb*
deputizes
deputizing
deputized

deputy *noun*
deputies

derail *verb*
derails
derailing
derailed

derby *noun*
derbies

derelict

deride *verb*
derides
deriding
derided

derision

derive *verb*
derives
deriving
derived

derrick *noun*
derricks

derv

○ **descant** *noun*
descants

descend *verb*
descends
descending
descended

descendant *noun*
descendants

✳ **descent**

describe *verb*
describes
describing
described

description *noun*
descriptions

descriptive *adjective*
descriptively

✱ **desert** *noun*
deserts

desert *verb*
deserts
deserting
deserted

deserter *noun*
deserters

desertion

deserve *verb*
deserves
deserving
deserved

design *verb*
designs
designing
designed

design *noun*
designs

designate *verb*
designates
designating
designated

★ **Dependant** is a noun: *She has three dependants.* ! **dependent**.
☆ **Dependent** is an adjective: *She has three dependent children.* ! **dependant**.
○ **Descant** is a term in music. ! **descent**.
✳ **Descent** is a way down. ! **descant**.
✱ A **desert** is a very dry area of land. ! **dessert**.

designer noun
  designers
desirable
desire verb
  desires
  desiring
  desired
desire noun
  desires
desk noun
  desks
desktop
desolate
desolation
despair verb
  despairs
  despairing
  despaired
despair noun
despatch verb
  use dispatch
desperate adjective
  desperately
desperation
despicable adjective
  despicably
despise verb
  despises
  despising
  despised
despite
★ **dessert** noun
  desserts
dessertspoon noun
  dessertspoons
destination noun
  destinations
destined
destiny noun
  destinies

destroy verb
  destroys
  destroying
  destroyed
destroyer noun
  destroyers
destruction
destructive
detach verb
  detaches
  detaching
  detached
detachable
detached
detachment noun
  detachments
detail noun
  details
detain verb
  detains
  detaining
  detained
detect verb
  detects
  detecting
  detected
detection
detector
detective noun
  detectives
detention noun
  detentions
deter verb
  deters
  deterring
  deterred
detergent noun
  detergents
deteriorate verb
  deteriorates
  deteriorating
  deteriorated

deterioration
determination
determine verb
  determines
  determining
  determined
determined
deterrence
deterrent noun
  deterrents
detest verb
  detests
  detesting
  detested
detestable
detonate verb
  detonates
  detonating
  detonated
detonation
detonator
detour noun
  detours
☆ **deuce**
devastate verb
  devastates
  devastating
  devastated
devastation
develop verb
  develops
  developing
  developed
development noun
  developments
device noun
  devices
devil noun
  devils

★ A **dessert** is a sweet pudding. ! desert.
☆ **Deuce** is a score in tennis. ! juice.

devilish

devilment

devious *adjective*
deviously

devise *verb*
devises
devising
devised

devolution

devote *verb*
devotes
devoting
devoted

devotee

devotion

devour *verb*
devours
devouring
devoured

devout

★ **dew**

dewy

☆ **dhoti** *noun*
dhotis

diabetes

diabetic

diabolical *adjective*
diabolically

diagnose *verb*
diagnoses
diagnosing
diagnosed

diagnosis *noun*
diagnoses

diagonal *adjective*
diagonally

diagonal *noun*
diagonals

diagram *noun*
diagrams

dial *noun*
dials

dial *verb*
dials
dialling
dialled

dialect *noun*
dialects

dialogue *noun*
dialogues

diameter *noun*
diameters

diamond *noun*
diamonds

diaphragm *noun*
diaphragms

diarrhoea

diary *noun*
diaries

dice *noun*
dice

dictate *verb*
dictates
dictating
dictated

dictation

dictator *noun*
dictators

dictatorial *adjective*
dictatorially

dictionary *noun*
dictionaries

did see do

diddle *verb*
diddles
diddling
diddled

didn't *verb*

die *verb*
dies
dying
died

diesel *noun*
diesels

diet *noun*
diets

diet *verb*
diets
dieting
dieted

differ *verb*
differs
differing
differed

difference *noun*
differences

different *adjective*
differently

difficult

difficulty *noun*
difficulties

dig *verb*
digs
digging
dug

dig *noun*
digs

digest *verb*
digests
digesting
digested

digestible

digestion

digestive

digger

digit *noun*
digits

digital *adjective*
digitally

. . . .

★ **Dew** is moisture on grass and plants. ! due.
☆ A **dhoti** is a piece of clothing worn by Hindus.

dignified

dignity

dike *noun*
use **dyke**

dilemma *noun*
dilemmas

dilute *verb*
dilutes
diluting
diluted

dilution

dim *adjective*
dimmer
dimmest
dimly

dimension *noun*
dimensions

diminish *verb*
diminishes
diminishing
diminished

dimple *noun*
dimples

din *noun*
dins

dine *verb*
dines
dining
dined

★ **diner** *noun*
diners

☆ **dinghy** *noun*
dinghies

○ **dingy** *adjective*
dingier
dingiest

✳ **dinner** *noun*
dinners

dinosaur *noun*
dinosaurs

dioxide *noun*
dioxides

dip *verb*
dips
dipping
dipped

dip *noun*
dips

diphtheria

diploma *noun*
diplomas

diplomacy

diplomat

diplomatic *adjective*
diplomatically

dire *adjective*
direr
direst

direct *adjective*
directly

direct *verb*
directs
directing
directed

direction *noun*
directions

director *noun*
directors

directory *noun*
directories

dirt

dirtiness

dirty *adjective*
dirtier
dirtiest
dirtily

dis-
dis- makes a word with an opposite meaning, e.g. **disobey** means 'to refuse to obey' and **disloyal** means 'not loyal'. These words are spelt joined up.

disability *noun*
disabilities

disabled

disadvantage *noun*
disadvantages

disagree *verb*
disagrees
disagreeing
disagreed

disagreeable *adjective*
disagreeably

disagreement *noun*
disagreements

disappear *verb*
disappears
disappearing
disappeared

disappearance *noun*
disappearances

disappoint *verb*
disappoints
disappointing
disappointed

disappointing

disappointment *noun*
disappointments

disapproval

- -

★ A **diner** is someone who eats dinner. ! **dinner**.
☆ A **dinghy** is a small sailing boat. ! **dingy**.
○ **Dingy** means 'dirty-looking, drab, dull-coloured'. ! **dinghy**.
✳ **Dinner** is a meal. ! **diner**.

disapprove verb
disapproves
disapproving
disapproved
disarm verb
disarms
disarming
disarmed
disarmament
disaster noun
disasters
disastrous adjective
disastrously
★ **disc** noun
discs
discard verb
discards
discarding
discarded
discharge verb
discharges
discharging
discharged
disciple noun
disciples
discipline
disc jockey noun
disc jockeys
disclose verb
discloses
disclosing
disclosed
disclosure
disco noun
discos
discomfort
disconnect verb
disconnects
disconnecting
disconnected
disconnection

discontent
discontented
discotheque noun
discotheques
discount noun
discounts
discourage verb
discourages
discouraging
discouraged
discouragement
discover verb
discovers
discovering
discovered
discovery noun
discoveries
discreet adjective
discreetly
discriminate verb
discriminates
discriminating
discriminated
discrimination
discus noun
discuses
discuss verb
discusses
discussing
discussed
discussion noun
discussions
disease noun
diseases
diseased
disgrace verb
disgraces
disgracing
disgraced
disgrace noun
disgraceful adjective
disgracefully

disguise verb
disguises
disguising
disguised
disguise noun
disguises
disgust verb
disgusts
disgusting
disgusted
disgust noun
disgusting
dish noun
dishes
dish verb
dishes
dishing
dished
dishcloth noun
dishcloths
dishevelled
dishonest adjective
dishonestly
dishonesty
dishwasher noun
dishwashers
disinfect verb
disinfects
disinfecting
disinfected
disinfectant noun
disinfectants
disintegrate verb
disintegrates
disintegrating
disintegrated
disintegration
disinterested
☆ **disk** noun
disks

★ A **disc** is a flat round object. ! **disk**.
☆ A **disk** is what you put in a computer. ! **disc**.

di

dislike verb
dislikes
disliking
disliked

dislike noun
dislikes

dislocate verb
dislocates
dislocating
dislocated

dislodge verb
dislodges
dislodging
dislodged

disloyal adjective
disloyally

disloyalty

dismal adjective
dismally

dismantle verb
dismantles
dismantling
dismantled

dismay

dismayed

dismiss verb
dismisses
dismissing
dismissed

dismissal

dismount verb
dismounts
dismounting
dismounted

disobedience

disobedient

disobey verb
disobeys
disobeying
disobeyed

disorder noun
disorders

disorderly

dispatch verb
dispatches
dispatching
dispatched

dispense verb
dispenses
dispensing
dispensed

dispenser noun
dispensers

dispersal

disperse verb
disperses
dispersing
dispersed

display verb
displays
displaying
displayed

display noun
displays

displease verb
displeases
displeasing
displeased

disposable

disposal

dispose verb
disposes
disposing
disposed

disprove verb
disproves
disproving
disproved

dispute noun
disputes

disqualification

disqualify verb
disqualifies
disqualifying
disqualified

disregard verb
disregards
disregarding
disregarded

disrespect

disrespectful
adjective
disrespectfully

disrupt verb
disrupts
disrupting
disrupted

disruption

disruptive

dissatisfaction

dissatisfied

dissect verb
dissects
dissecting
dissected

dissection

dissolve verb
dissolves
dissolving
dissolved

dissuade verb
dissuades
dissuading
dissuaded

distance noun
distances

distant adjective
distantly

distil verb
distils
distilling
distilled

distillery noun
distilleries

distinct adjective
distinctly

distinction noun
distinctions

distinctive

distinguish verb
distinguishes
distinguishing
distinguished

distinguished

distort verb
distorts
distorting
distorted

distortion noun
distortions

distract verb
distracts
distracting
distracted

distraction noun
distractions

distress verb
distresses
distressing
distressed

distress noun

distribute verb
distributes
distributing
distributed

distribution

distributor

district noun
districts

distrust

distrustful

disturb verb
disturbs
disturbing
disturbed

disturbance noun
disturbances

disused

ditch noun
ditches

dither verb
dithers
dithering
dithered

divan noun
divans

dive verb
dives
diving
dived

diver noun
divers

diverse

diversify verb
diversifies
diversifying
diversified

diversion noun
diversions

diversity

divert verb
diverts
diverting
diverted

divide verb
divides
dividing
divided

dividend noun
dividends

dividers plural noun

divine adjective
divinely

divine verb
divines
divining
divined

divinity

divisible

division noun
divisions

divorce verb
divorces
divorcing
divorced

divorce noun
divorces

★ **Diwali**

dizziness

dizzy adjective
dizzier
dizziest
dizzily

do verb
does
doing
did
done

docile adjective
docilely

dock noun
docks

dock verb
docks
docking
docked

dock noun
docks

docker noun
dockers

dockyard noun
dockyards

doctor noun
doctors

doctrine noun
doctrines

• •

★ **Diwali** is a Hindu festival.

document *noun*
documents

documentary *noun*
documentaries

doddery

dodge *verb*
dodges
dodging
dodged

dodge *noun*
dodges

dodgem *noun*
dodgems

dodgy *adjective*
dodgier
dodgiest

★ doe *noun*
does

doesn't *abbreviation*

dog *noun*
dogs

dog-eared

dogged *adjective*
doggedly

doldrums *plural noun*

dole *verb*
doles
doling
doled

dole *noun*

doll *noun*
dolls

dollar *noun*
dollars

dolly *noun*
dollies

dolphin *noun*
dolphins

-dom
-dom makes nouns,
e.g. **kingdom**. Other
noun suffixes are
-hood, -ment, -ness,
and **-ship.**

domain *noun*
domains

dome *noun*
domes

domestic *adjective*
domestically

domesticated

dominance

dominant *adjective*
dominantly

dominate *verb*
dominates
dominating
dominated

domination

dominion *noun*
dominions

domino *noun*
dominoes

donate *verb*
donates
donating
donated

donation *noun*
donations

done *see* do

donkey *noun*
donkeys

donor *noun*
donors

don't *abbreviation*

doodle *verb*
doodles
doodling
doodled

doodle *noun*
doodles

doom *verb*
dooms
dooming
doomed

doom *noun*

door *noun*
doors

doorstep *noun*
doorsteps

doorway *noun*
doorways

dope *noun*
dopes

dopey *adjective*
dopier
dopiest

dormitory *noun*
dormitories

dose *noun*
doses

dossier *noun*
dossiers

dot *verb*
dots
dotting
dotted

dot *noun*
dots

dottiness

dotty *adjective*
dottier
dottiest
dottily

double *adjective*
doubly

double *noun*
doubles

★ A doe is a female deer. ! **dough.**

double verb
doubles
doubling
doubled

double-cross verb
double-crosses
double-crossing
double-crossed

double-decker noun
double-deckers

doubt verb
doubts
doubting
doubted

doubt noun
doubts

doubtful adjective
doubtfully

doubtless

★ **dough**

doughnut noun
doughnuts

doughy adjective
doughier
doughiest

dove noun
doves

dowel noun
dowels

down

downcast

downfall noun
downfalls

downhill

downpour noun
downpours

downright adjective

downs plural noun

downstairs

downstream

downward adjective
and adverb

downwards adverb

downy adjective
downier
downiest

doze verb
dozes
dozing
dozed

dozen noun
dozens

dozy adjective
dozier
doziest

drab adjective
drabber
drabbest

draft verb
drafts
drafting
drafted

draft noun
drafts

drag verb
drags
dragging
dragged

drag noun

dragon noun
dragons

dragonfly noun
dragonflies

drain verb
drains
draining
drained

drain noun
drains

drainage

drake noun
drakes

drama noun
dramas

dramatic adjective
dramatically

dramatist noun
dramatists

dramatization

dramatize verb
dramatizes
dramatizing
dramatized

drank see **drink**

drape verb
drapes
draping
draped

drastic adjective
drastically

draught noun
draughts

draughty adjective
draughtier
draughtiest

draughts noun

draughtsman noun
draughtsmen

☆ **draw** verb
draws
drawing
drew
drawn

draw noun
draws

drawback noun
drawbacks

drawbridge noun
drawbridges

○ **drawer** noun
drawers

. . . .

★ **Dough** is a mixture of flour and water used for baking. ! **doe**.
☆ To **draw** is to make a picture with a pencil, pen, or crayon. ! **drawer**.
○ A **drawer** is part of a cupboard. ! **draw**.

drawing noun
  drawings
drawl verb
  drawls
  drawling
  drawled
dread verb
  dreads
  dreading
  dreaded
dread noun
dreadful adjective
  dreadfully
dreadlocks
dream noun
  dreams
dream verb
  dreams
  dreaming
  dreamt or dreamed
dreamy adjective
  dreamier
  dreamiest
dreariness
dreary adjective
  drearier
  dreariest
  drearily
dredge verb
  dredges
  dredging
  dredged
dredger
drench verb
  drenches
  drenching
  drenched
dress verb
  dresses
  dressing
  dressed

dress noun
  dresses
dresser noun
  dressers
dressing noun
  dressings
dressmaker noun
  dressmakers
drew see draw
dribble verb
  dribbles
  dribbling
  dribbled
dried see dry
drier noun
  driers
drift verb
  drifts
  drifting
  drifted
drift noun
  drifts
driftwood
drill verb
  drills
  drilling
  drilled
drill noun
  drills
drink verb
  drinks
  drinking
  drank
  drunk
drink noun
  drinks
drinker noun
  drinkers
drip noun
  drips

drip verb
  drips
  dripping
  dripped
dripping
drive verb
  drives
  driving
  drove
  driven
drive noun
  drives
driver noun
  drivers
drizzle verb
  drizzles
  drizzling
  drizzled
drizzle noun
drone verb
  drones
  droning
  droned
drone noun
  drones
drool verb
  drools
  drooling
  drooled
droop verb
  droops
  drooping
  drooped
drop verb
  drops
  dropping
  dropped
drop noun
  drops
droplet noun
  droplets

drought noun
 droughts
drove see **drive**
drown verb
 drowns
 drowning
 drowned
drowsiness
drowsy adjective
 drowsier
 drowsiest
 drowsily
drug noun
 drugs
drug verb
 drugs
 drugging
 drugged
Druid noun
 Druids
drum noun
 drums
drum verb
 drums
 drumming
 drummed
drummer noun
 drummers
drumstick noun
 drumsticks
drunk see **drink**
drunk adjective and
 noun
 drunks
drunkard noun
 drunkards
dry adjective
 drier
 driest
 drily

dry verb
 dries
 drying
 dried
dryness
★ **dual** adjective
 dually
dub verb
 dubs
 dubbing
 dubbed
duchess noun
 duchesses
duck noun
 ducks
duck verb
 ducks
 ducking
 ducked
duckling noun
 ducklings
duct noun
 ducts
dud noun
 duds
☆ **due**
◉ **duel** noun
 duels
duet noun
 duets
duff
duffel coat noun
 duffel coats
dug see **dig**
dugout noun
 dugouts
duke noun
 dukes

dull adjective
 duller
 dullest
 dully
dullness
duly
dumb adjective
 dumber
 dumbest
dumbfounded
dummy noun
 dummies
dump verb
 dumps
 dumping
 dumped
dump noun
 dumps
dumpling noun
 dumplings
dumpy adjective
 dumpier
 dumpiest
dune noun
 dunes
dung
dungarees
dungeon noun
 dungeons
duo noun
 duos
duplicate noun
 duplicates
duplicate verb
 duplicates
 duplicating
 duplicated
duplication
durability
durable
duration
during

. . . .

★ **Dual** means 'having two parts'. ! **duel**.
☆ **Due** means 'expected'. ! **dew**.
◉ A **duel** is a fight between two people. ! **dual**.

dusk

dust

dust verb
dusts
dusting
dusted

dustbin noun
dustbins

duster noun
dusters

dustman noun
dustmen

dustpan noun
dustpans

dusty adjective
dustier
dustiest

dutiful adjective
dutifully

duty noun
duties

duvet noun
duvets

dwarf noun
dwarfs or dwarves

dwarf verb
dwarfs
dwarfing
dwarfed

dwell verb
dwells
dwelling
dwelt

dwelling noun
dwellings

dwindle verb
dwindles
dwindling
dwindled

★ **dye** verb
dyes
dyeing
dyed

dye noun
dyes

dying see die

dyke noun
dykes

dynamic adjective
dynamically

dynamite

dynamo noun
dynamos

dynasty noun
dynasties

dyslexia

dyslexic

dystrophy noun

Ee

e-
e- stands for
'electronic' and
makes words about
computers and the
Internet, e.g. email
(spelt joined up),
e-commerce and
e-shopping (spelt with
hyphens).

each

eager adjective
eagerly

eagerness

eagle noun
eagles

ear noun
ears

earache

eardrum noun
eardrums

earl noun
earls

early adjective and
adverb
earlier
earliest

earmark verb
earmarks
earmarking
earmarked

earn verb
earns
earning
earned

earnest adjective
earnestly

earnings plural noun

earphones

earring noun
earrings

earth noun
earths

earthenware

earthly

earthquake noun
earthquakes

earthworm noun
earthworms

earthy adjective
earthier
earthiest

earwig noun
earwigs

ease verb
eases
easing
eased

ease noun

★ **Dye** means 'to change the colour of something'. ! die.

easel *noun*
easels

east *adjective* and
adverb

★ **east** *noun*

Easter

easterly *adjective*
and *noun*
easterlies

eastern

eastward *adjective*
and *adverb*

eastwards *adverb*

easy *adjective* and
adverb
easier
easiest
easily

eat *verb*
eats
eating
ate
eaten

eatable

eaves

ebb *verb*
ebbs
ebbing
ebbed

ebb

ebony

eccentric

eccentricity *noun*
eccentricities

echo *verb*
echoes
echoing
echoed

echo *noun*
echoes

éclair *noun*
éclairs

eclipse *noun*
eclipses

ecological

ecology

economic

economical *adjective*
economically

economics

economist *noun*
economists

economize *verb*
economizes
economizing
economized

economy *noun*
economies

ecstasy *noun*
ecstasies

ecstatic *adjective*
ecstatically

eczema

-ed and -t
Some verbs ending in
l, m, n, and p have
past forms and past
participles ending in
-ed and -t, e.g.
burned/burnt, leaped/
leapt. Both forms are
correct, and the -t
form is especially
common when it
comes before a noun,
e.g. burnt cakes.

edge *noun*
edges

edge *verb*
edges
edging
edged

edgeways

edgy *adjective*
edgier
edgiest

edible

edit *verb*
edits
editing
edited

edition *noun*
editions

editor *noun*
editors

editorial *noun*
editorials

educate *verb*
educates
educating
educated

education

educational

educator

eel *noun*
eels

eerie *adjective*
eerier
eeriest
eerily

eeriness

☆ **effect** *noun*
effects

effective *adjective*
effectively

effectiveness

effeminate

effervescence

effervescent

efficiency

efficient *adjective*
efficiently

- -

★ You use a capital E in **the East**, meaning China, Japan, etc.
☆ An **effect** is something that is caused by something else. ! **affect**.

effort *noun*
efforts

effortless *adjective*
effortlessly

egg *noun*
eggs

egg *verb*
eggs
egging
egged

-ei- and -ie-
The rule 'i before e
except after c' is true
when it is pronounced
-ee-, e.g. thief,
ceiling. There are a
few exceptions, of
which the most
important are **seize**
and **protein**.

★ **Eid**

eiderdown *noun*
eiderdowns

☆ **eight**

eighteen

eighteenth

✿ **eighth** *adjective* and
noun
eighthly

eightieth

eighty *noun*
eighties

either

eject *verb*
ejects
ejecting
ejected

ejection

elaborate *adjective*
elaborately

elaborate *verb*
elaborates
elaborating
elaborated

elaboration

elastic

elated

elation

elbow *noun*
elbows

elbow *verb*
elbows
elbowing
elbowed

elder *adjective* and
noun
elders

elderberry *noun*
elderberries

elderly

eldest

elect *verb*
elects
electing
elected

election *noun*
elections

electorate

electric

electrical *adjective*
electrically

electrician *noun*
electricians

electricity

electrification

electrify *verb*
electrifies
electrifying
electrified

electrocute *verb*
electrocutes

electrocuting
electrocuted

electrocution

electromagnet
noun
electromagnets

electron *noun*
electrons

electronic *adjective*
electronically

electronics

elegance

elegant *adjective*
elegantly

element *noun*
elements

elementary

elephant *noun*
elephants

elevate *verb*
elevates
elevating
elevated

elevation *noun*
elevations

eleven

eleventh

elf *noun*
elves

eligibility

eligible

eliminate *verb*
eliminates
eliminating
eliminated

elimination

élite *noun*
élites

elk *noun*
elk *or* elks

★ **Eid** is a Muslim festival.
☆ **Eight** is the number. ! **ate**.
✿ Note that there are two h's in **eighth**.

ellipse *noun*
  ellipses
elliptical *adjective*
  elliptically
elm *noun*
  elms
elocution
eloquence
eloquent
else
elsewhere
elude *verb*
  eludes
  eluding
  eluded
elusive *adjective*
  elusively
elves see **elf**
★ **email** *noun*
  emails
email *verb*
  emails
  emailing
  emailed
emancipate *verb*
  emancipates
  emancipating
  emancipated
emancipation
embankment *noun*
  embankments
embark *verb*
  embarks
  embarking
  embarked
embarkation
☆ **embarrass** *verb*
  embarrasses
  embarrassing
  embarrassed

embarrassment
embassy *noun*
  embassies
embedded
embers *plural noun*
emblem *noun*
  emblems
embrace *verb*
  embraces
  embracing
  embraced
embroider *verb*
  embroiders
  embroidering
  embroidered
embroidery *noun*
  embroideries
embryo *noun*
  embryos
emerald *noun*
  emeralds
emerge *verb*
  emerges
  emerging
  emerged
emergence
emergency *noun*
  emergencies
emery paper
emigrant *noun*
  emigrants
emigrate *verb*
  emigrates
  emigrating
  emigrated
emigration
eminence
eminent
○ **emission** *noun*
  emissions

emit *verb*
  emits
  emitting
  emitted
emotion *noun*
  emotions
emotional *adjective*
  emotionally
emperor *noun*
  emperors
emphasis *noun*
  emphases
emphasize *verb*
  emphasizes
  emphasizing
  emphasized
emphatic *adjective*
  emphatically
empire *noun*
  empires
employ *verb*
  employs
  employing
  employed
employee *noun*
  employees
employer *noun*
  employers
employment
empress *noun*
  empresses
empties *plural noun*
emptiness
empty *adjective*
  emptier
  emptiest
empty *verb*
  empties
  emptying
  emptied
emu *noun*
  emus

. . . .

★ **Email** is short for **electronic mail**.
☆ Note that there are two rs in **embarrass** and **embarrassment**.
○ An **emission** is something that escapes, like fumes. ! **omission**.

emulsion noun
emulsions

enable verb
enables
enabling
enabled

enamel noun
enamels

encampment noun
encampments

-ence
See the note at -ance.

enchant verb
enchants
enchanting
enchanted

enchantment

encircle verb
encircles
encircling
encircled

enclose verb
encloses
enclosing
enclosed

enclosure

encore noun
encores

encounter verb
encounters
encountering
encountered

encourage verb
encourages
encouraging
encouraged

encouragement

encyclopedia noun
encyclopedias

encyclopedic

end verb
ends
ending
ended

end noun
ends

endanger verb
endangers
endangering
endangered

endeavour verb
endeavours
endeavouring
endeavoured

ending noun
endings

endless adjective
endlessly

endurance

endure verb
endures
enduring
endured

enemy noun
enemies

energetic adjective
energetically

energy noun
energies

enforce verb
enforces
enforcing
enforced

enforceable

enforcement

engage verb
engages
engaging
engaged

engagement noun
engagements

engine noun
engines

engineer noun
engineers

engineering

engrave verb
engraves
engraving
engraved

engraver

engrossed

engulf verb
engulfs
engulfing
engulfed

enhance verb
enhances
enhancing
enhanced

enhancement

enjoy verb
enjoys
enjoying
enjoyed

enjoyable

enjoyment

enlarge verb
enlarges
enlarging
enlarged

enlargement noun
enlargements

enlist verb
enlists
enlisting
enlisted

enmity noun
enmities

★ **enormity** noun
enormities

★ An **enormity** is a wicked act. If you mean 'large size', use **enormousness**.

enormous adjective
enormously
enormousness
enough
enquire verb
enquires
enquiring
enquired
★ **enquiry** noun
enquiries
enrage verb
enrages
enraging
enraged
enrich verb
enriches
enriching
enriched
enrichment
enrol verb
enrols
enrolling
enrolled
enrolment
ensemble noun
ensembles
ensue verb
ensues
ensuing
ensued
ensure verb
ensures
ensuring
ensured

-ent
See the note at -ant.

entangle verb
entangles
entangling
entangled

entanglement
enter verb
enters
entering
entered
enterprise noun
enterprises
enterprising
entertain verb
entertains
entertaining
entertained
entertainer noun
entertainers
entertainment
noun
entertainments
enthusiasm noun
enthusiasms
enthusiast noun
enthusiasts
enthusiastic
adjective
enthusiastically
entire adjective
entirely
entirety
entitle verb
entitles
entitling
entitled
entrance noun
entrances
entrance verb
entrances
entrancing
entranced
entrant noun
entrants

entreat verb
entreats
entreating
entreated
entreaty noun
entreaties
entrust verb
entrusts
entrusting
entrusted
entry noun
entries
envelop verb
envelops
enveloping
enveloped
envelope noun
envelopes
envious adjective
enviously
environment noun
environments
environmental
environmentalist
noun
environmentalists
envy verb
envies
envying
envied
envy noun
enzyme noun
enzymes
epic noun
epics
epidemic noun
epidemics
epilepsy
epileptic adjective
and noun
epileptics
epilogue noun
epilogues

★ An **enquiry** is a question. ! **inquiry**.

episode noun
episodes

epistle noun
epistles

epitaph noun
epitaphs

epoch noun
epochs

equal adjective
equally

equal verb
equals
equalling
equalled

equal noun
equals

equality

equalize verb
equalizes
equalizing
equalized

equalizer noun
equalizers

equation noun
equations

equator

equatorial

equestrian

equilateral

equilibrium noun
equilibria

equinox noun
equinoxes

equip verb
equips
equipping
equipped

equipment

equivalence

equivalent

-er and -est

-er and -est make adjectives and adverbs meaning 'more' or 'most', e.g. **faster, slowest**. You can do this when the word has one syllable, and when a consonant comes at the end of the word after a single vowel you double it, e.g. **fatter, bigger**. You can use -er and -est with some two-syllable adjectives, e.g. **commoner, pleasantest**, and words ending in y, which change to -ier and -iest, e.g. **angrier, happiest**.

-er and -or

-er makes nouns meaning 'a person or thing that does something', e.g. a **helper** is a person who helps and an **opener** is a tool that opens things. You can make new words this way, e.g. **complainer, repairer**. Some words end in -or, e.g. **actor, visitor**, but you can't use -or to make new words.

---

era noun
eras

erase verb
erases
erasing
erased

eraser

erect adjective

erect verb
erects
erecting
erected

erection noun
erections

ermine noun
ermine

erode verb
erodes
eroding
eroded

erosion

errand noun
errands

erratic adjective
erratically

erroneous adjective
erroneously

error noun
errors

erupt verb
erupts
erupting
erupted

eruption

escalate verb
escalates
escalating
escalated

escalation

escalator noun
escalators

escape verb
escapes
escaping
escaped

escape noun
escapes

escort verb
escorts
escorting
escorted

escort noun
escorts

Eskimo noun
Eskimos or Eskimo

especially

espionage

esplanade noun
esplanades

-ess
makes nouns for
female people and
animals, e.g.
manageress, lioness.

essay noun
essays

essence noun
essences

essential adjective
essentially

essential noun
essentials

establish verb
establishes
establishing
established

establishment noun
establishments

estate noun
estates

esteem verb
esteems
esteeming
esteemed

estimate noun
estimates

estimate verb
estimates
estimating
estimated

estuary noun
estuaries

etch verb
etches
etching
etched

etching noun
etchings

eternal adjective
eternally

eternity

ether

ethnic

etymology noun
etymologies

eucalyptus noun
eucalyptuses

euphemism noun
euphemisms

euphemistic
adjective
euphemistically

Eurasian

European adjective
and noun
Europeans

euthanasia

evacuate verb
evacuates
evacuating
evacuated

evacuation

evacuee

evade verb
evades
evading
evaded

evaluate verb
evaluates
evaluating
evaluated

evaluation

evangelical

evangelism

evangelist noun
evangelists

evaporate verb
evaporates
evaporating
evaporated

evaporation

evasion noun
evasions

evasive

eve noun
eves

even adjective
evenly

even adverb

even verb
evens
evening
evened

evening noun
evenings

evenness

event noun
events

eventful adjective
eventfully

eventual adjective
eventually

ever

evergreen adjective
and noun
evergreens

everlasting

every
everybody
everyday
everyone
everything
everywhere

evict verb
  evicts
  evicting
  evicted

eviction

evidence

evident adjective
  evidently

evil adjective
  evilly

evil noun
  evils

evolution

evolutionary

evolve verb
  evolves
  evolving
  evolved

★ **ewe** noun
  ewes

ex-
ex- makes nouns with
the meaning 'former'
or 'who used to be',
e.g. ex-president,
ex-wife. You use a
hyphen to make these
words.

exact adjective
  exactly

exactness

exaggerate verb
  exaggerates
  exaggerating
  exaggerated

exaggeration

exalt verb
  exalts
  exalting
  exalted

exam noun
  exams

examination noun
  examinations

examine verb
  examines
  examining
  examined

examiner noun
  examiners

example noun
  examples

exasperate verb
  exasperates
  exasperating
  exasperated

exasperation

excavate verb
  excavates
  excavating
  excavated

excavation noun
  excavations

excavator noun
  excavators

exceed verb
  exceeds
  exceeding
  exceeded

exceedingly

excel verb
  excels
  excelling
  excelled

excellence

excellent adjective
  excellently

☆ **except**

exception noun
  exceptions

exceptional
  adjective
  exceptionally

excerpt noun
  excerpts

excess noun
  excesses

excessive adjective
  excessively

exchange verb
  exchanges
  exchanging
  exchanged

exchange noun
  exchanges

excitable adjective
  excitably

excite verb
  excites
  exciting
  excited

excitedly

excitement noun
  excitements

exclaim verb
  exclaims
  exclaiming
  exclaimed

exclamation noun
  exclamations

* *

★ A ewe is a female sheep. ! yew, you.
☆ You use except in e.g. everyone except me. ! accept.

exclude verb
excludes
excluding
excluded

exclusion

exclusive adjective
exclusively

excrement

excrete verb
excretes
excreting
excreted

excretion

excursion noun
excursions

excusable

excuse verb
excuses
excusing
excused

excuse noun
excuses

execute verb
executes
executing
executed

execution noun
executions

executioner noun
executioners

executive noun
executives

exempt adjective

exemption noun

exercise noun
exercises

★ **exercise** verb
exercises
exercising
exercised

exert verb
exerts
exerting
exerted

exertion noun
exertions

exhale verb
exhales
exhaling
exhaled

exhalation

exhaust verb
exhausts
exhausting
exhausted

exhaust noun
exhausts

exhaustion

exhibit verb
exhibits
exhibiting
exhibited

exhibit noun
exhibits

exhibition noun
exhibitions

exhibitor noun
exhibitors

exile verb
exiles
exiling
exiled

exile noun
exiles

exist verb
exists
existing
existed

existence noun
existences

exit verb
exits

exiting
exited

exit noun
exits

exorcism

exorcist

☆ **exorcize** verb
exorcizes
exorcizing
exorcized

exotic adjective
exotically

expand verb
expands
expanding
expanded

expanse noun
expanses

expansion

expect verb
expects
expecting
expected

expectant adjective
expectantly

expectation noun
expectations

expedition noun
expeditions

expel verb
expels
expelling
expelled

expenditure

expense noun
expenses

expensive

experience verb
experiences
experiencing
experienced

· ·

★ To **exercise** is to keep your body fit. ! **exorcise**.
☆ To **exorcise** is to get rid of evil spirits. ! **exercise**.

experience noun
experiences

experienced

experiment verb
experiments
experimenting
experimented

experiment noun
experiments

experimental
adjective
experimentally

experimentation

expert adjective and
noun
experts

expertise

expire verb
expires
expiring
expired

expiry

explain verb
explains
explaining
explained

explanation noun
explanations

explanatory

explode verb
explodes
exploding
exploded

exploit noun
exploits

exploit verb
exploits
exploiting
exploited

exploitation

exploration noun
explorations

exploratory

explore verb
explores
exploring
explored

explorer noun
explorers

explosion noun
explosions

explosive adjective
and noun
explosives

export verb
exports
exporting
exported

export noun
exports

exporter noun
exporters

expose verb
exposes
exposing
exposed

exposure noun
exposures

express adjective and
noun
expresses

express verb
expresses
expressing
expressed

expression noun
expressions

expressive adjective
expressively

expulsion noun
expulsions

exquisite adjective
exquisitely

extend verb
extends
extending
extended

extension noun
extensions

extensive adjective
extensively

extent noun
extents

exterior noun
exteriors

exterminate verb
exterminates
exterminating
exterminated

extermination

external adjective
externally

extinct

extinction

extinguish verb
extinguishes
extinguishing
extinguished

extinguisher noun
extinguishers

extra adjective and
noun
extras

extract verb
extracts
extracting
extracted

extract noun
extracts

extraction noun
extractions

extraordinary
adjective
extraordinarily

extrasensory

extraterrestrial
adjective and *noun*
extraterrestrials

extravagance

extravagant
adjective
extravagantly

extreme *adjective*
extremely

extreme *noun*
extremes

extremity *noun*
extremities

exuberance

exuberant *adjective*
exuberantly

exult *verb*
exults
exulting
exulted

exultant

exultation

eye *noun*
eyes

eye *verb*
eyes
eyeing
eyed

eyeball *noun*
eyeballs

eyebrow *noun*
eyebrows

eyelash *noun*
eyelashes

eyelid *noun*
eyelids

eyepiece *noun*
eyepieces

eyesight

eyesore *noun*
eyesores

eyewitness *noun*
eyewitnesses

Ff

-f
Most nouns ending in
-f have plurals ending
in -ves, e.g. **shelf -
shelves**, but some
have plurals ending in
-fs, e.g. **chiefs**. Nouns
ending in -ff have
plurals ending in -ffs,
e.g. **cuffs**.

fable *noun*
fables

fabric *noun*
fabrics

fabricate *verb*
fabricates
fabricating
fabricated

fabulous *adjective*
fabulously

face *noun*
faces

face *verb*
faces
facing
faced

facet *noun*
facets

facetious *adjective*
facetiously

facial *adjective*
facially

facilitate *verb*
facilitates
facilitating
facilitated

facility *noun*
facilities

fact *noun*
facts

factor *noun*
factors

factory *noun*
factories

factual *adjective*
factually

fad *noun*
fads

fade *verb*
fades
fading
faded

faeces

fag *noun*
fags

fagged

faggot *noun*
faggots

Fahrenheit

fail *verb*
fails
failing
failed

fail *noun*
fails

failing *noun*
failings

failure *noun*
failures

faint *adjective*
fainter
faintest
faintly

faint *verb*
faints
fainting
fainted

faint-hearted

faintness

fair *adjective*
fairer
fairest

★ **fair** *noun*
fairs

fairground *noun*
fairgrounds

fairly

fairness

fairy *noun*
fairies

fairyland

faith *noun*
faiths

faithful *adjective*
faithfully

faithfulness

fake *noun*
fakes

fake *verb*
fakes
faking
faked

faker

falcon *noun*
falcons

falconry

fall *verb*
falls
falling
fell
fallen

fall *noun*
falls

fallacious *adjective*
fallaciously

fallacy *noun*
fallacies

fallen see fall

fallout

fallow

falls *plural noun*

false *adjective*
falser
falsest
falsely

falsehood *noun*
falsehoods

falseness

falter *verb*
falters
faltering
faltered

fame

famed

familiar *adjective*
familiarly

familiarity

family *noun*
families

famine *noun*
famines

famished

famous *adjective*
famously

fan *verb*
fans
fanning
fanned

fan *noun*
fans

fanatic *noun*
fanatics

fanatical *adjective*
fanatically

fanciful *adjective*
fancifully

fancy *adjective*
fancier
fanciest

fancy *verb*
fancies
fancying
fancied

fancy *noun*
fancies

fanfare *noun*
fanfares

fang *noun*
fangs

fantastic *adjective*
fantastically

fantasy *noun*
fantasies

far *adjective* and
adverb
farther
farthest

far-away

farce *noun*
farces

farcical *adjective*
farcically

fare *verb*
fares
faring
fared

☆ **fare** *noun*
fares

farewell

far-fetched

. . . .

★ A **fair** is a group of outdoor entertainments or an exhibition. **! fare.**
☆ A **fare** is money you pay, for example on a bus. **! fair.**

farm noun
farms
farm verb
farms
farming
farmed
farmer noun
farmers
farmhouse noun
farmhouses
farmyard noun
farmyards
★ **farther**
☆ **farthest**
farthing noun
farthings
fascinate verb
fascinates
fascinating
fascinated
fascination
fascism
fascist noun
fascists
fashion noun
fashions
fashion verb
fashions
fashioning
fashioned
fashionable
fast adjective and
adverb
faster
fastest
fast verb
fasts
fasting
fasted

fasten verb
fastens
fastening
fastened
fastener
fastening
fat adjective
fatter
fattest
fat noun
fats
fatal adjective
fatally
fatality noun
fatalities
○ **fate** noun
fates
father noun
fathers
father-in-law noun
fathers-in-law
fathom noun
fathoms
fathom verb
fathoms
fathoming
fathomed
fatigue
fatigued
fatten verb
fattens
fattening
fattened
fattening
fatty adjective
fattier
fattiest
fault noun
faults
fault verb
faults

faulting
faulted
faultless adjective
faultlessly
faulty adjective
faultier
faultiest
fauna
favour noun
favours
favour verb
favours
favouring
favoured
favourable adjective
favourably
favourite adjective
and noun
favourites
favouritism
fawn noun
fawns
fax noun
faxes
fax verb
faxes
faxing
faxed

-fe
Most nouns ending
in -fe have plurals
ending in -ves,
e.g. life - lives.

fear noun
fears
fear verb
fears
fearing
feared
fearful adjective
fearfully

★ You can use **farther** or **further** in e.g. farther up the road. See **further**.
☆ You can use **farthest** or **furthest** in e.g. the place farthest from here. See
    furthest.
○ **Fate** is a power that is thought to make things happen. ! **fête**.

fearless *adjective*
fearlessly
fearsome
feasible
feast *noun*
feasts
feast *verb*
feasts
feasting
feasted
★ **feat** *noun*
feats
feather *noun*
feathers
feathery
feature *noun*
features
feature *verb*
features
featuring
featured
☆ **February** *noun*
Februaries
fed see **feed**
federal
federation
fee *noun*
fees
feeble *adjective*
feebler
feeblest
feebly
feed *verb*
feeds
feeding
fed
feed *noun*
feeds
feedback

feel *verb*
feels
feeling
felt
feel *noun*
feeler *noun*
feelers
feeling *noun*
feelings
○ **feet** see **foot**
feline
fell see **fall**
fell *verb*
fells
felling
felled
fell *noun*
fells
fellow *noun*
fellows
fellowship *noun*
fellowships
felt see **feel**
felt *noun*
felt-tip pen *or*
felt-tipped pen
noun
felt-tip pens *or*
felt-tipped pens
female *adjective* and
noun
females
feminine
femininity
feminism
feminist *noun*
feminists
fen *noun*
fens

fence *noun*
fences
fence *verb*
fences
fencing
fenced
fencer *adjective*
fencers
fencing
fend *verb*
fends
fending
fended
fender *noun*
fenders
ferment *verb*
ferments
fermenting
fermented
fermentation
ferment
fern *noun*
ferns
ferocious *adjective*
ferociously
ferocity
ferret *noun*
ferrets
ferret *verb*
ferrets
ferreting
ferreted
ferry *noun*
ferries
ferry *verb*
ferries
ferrying
ferried
fertile
fertility
fertilization

....

★ A feat is an achievement. ! feet.
☆ Note that **February** has two rs.
○ Feet is the plural of foot. ! feat.

fertilize verb
 fertilizes
 fertilizing
 fertilized

fertilizer noun
 fertilizers

fervent adjective
 fervently

fervour

festival noun
 festivals

festive

festivity

festoon verb
 festoons
 festooning
 festooned

fetal

fetch verb
 fetches
 fetching
 fetched

★ **fête** noun
 fêtes

fetlock noun
 fetlocks

fetters plural noun

☆ **fetus** noun
 fetuses

feud noun
 feuds

feudal

feudalism

fever noun
 fevers

fevered

feverish adjective
 feverishly

few adjective
 fewer
 fewest

fez noun
 fezzes

⊘ **fiancé** noun
 fiancés

✳ **fiancée** noun
 fiancées

fiasco noun
 fiascos

fib noun
 fibs

fibber noun
 fibbers

fibre noun
 fibres

fibreglass

fibrous

fickle

fiction noun
 fictions

fictional adjective
 fictionally

fictitious adjective
 fictitiously

fiddle verb
 fiddles
 fiddling
 fiddled

fiddle noun
 fiddles

fiddler noun
 fiddlers

fiddling

fiddly

fidelity

fidget verb
 fidgets
 fidgeting
 fidgeted

fidgety

field noun
 fields

field verb
 fields
 fielding
 fielded

fielder noun
 fielders

field Marshal noun
 field Marshals

fieldwork

fiend noun
 fiends

fiendish adjective
 fiendishly

fierce adjective
 fiercer
 fiercest
 fiercely

fierceness

fiery adjective
 fierier
 fieriest

fife noun
 fifes

fifteen

fifteenth

fifth

fifthly

fiftieth

fifty noun
 fifties

fig noun
 figs

fight verb
 fights
 fighting
 fought

fight noun
 fights

. . . .

★ A fête is an outdoor entertainment with stalls. ! fate.
☆ You will also see this word spelt foetus.
⊘ A woman's fiancé is the man who is going to marry her.
✳ A man's fiancée is the woman who is going to marry him.

fighter noun
fighters

figurative adjective
figuratively

figure noun
figures

figure verb
figures
figuring
figured

filament noun
filaments

file verb
files
filing
filed

file noun
files

filings plural noun

fill verb
fills
filling
filled

fill noun
fills

filler noun
fillers

fillet noun
fillets

filling noun
fillings

filly noun
fillies

film noun
films

film verb
films
filming
filmed

filter noun
filters

filter verb
filters
filtering
filtered

filth

filthy adjective
filthier
filthiest

fin noun
fins

final adjective
finally

final noun
finals

finale noun
finales

finalist noun
finalists

finality

finance

finance verb
finances
financing
financed

finances plural noun

financial adjective
financially

financier noun
financiers

finch noun
finches

find verb
finds
finding
found

finder noun
finders

findings plural noun

fine adjective
finer
finest
finely

fine noun
fines

fine verb
fines
fining
fined

finger noun
fingers

finger verb
fingers
fingering
fingered

fingernail noun
fingernails

fingerprint noun
fingerprints

finicky

finish verb
finishes
finishing
finished

finish noun
finishes

★ **fir** noun
firs

fire noun
fires

fire verb
fires
firing
fired

firearm noun
firearms

firefighter noun
firefighters

fireman noun
firemen

fireplace noun
fireplaces

fireproof

★ A fir is a tree. ! fur.

fireside noun
  firesides
firewood
firework noun
  fireworks
firm adjective
  firmer
  firmest
  firmly
firm noun
  firms
firmness
first adjective and
  adverb
  firstly
first-class
first floor noun
  first floors
first-hand adjective
first-rate
fish noun
  fish or fishes
fish verb
  fishes
  fishing
  fished
fisherman noun
  fishermen
fishmonger noun
  fishmongers
fishy adjective
  fishier
  fishiest
fission
fist noun
  fists
fit adjective
  fitter
  fittest

fit verb
  fits
  fitting
  fitted
fit noun
  fits
fitness
fitter noun
  fitters
fitting adjective
fitting noun
  fittings
five
fiver noun
  fivers
fix verb
  fixes
  fixing
  fixed
fix noun
  fixes
fixture noun
  fixtures
fizz verb
  fizzes
  fizzing
  fizzed
fizzy adjective
  fizzier
  fizziest
fizzle verb
  fizzles
  fizzling
  fizzled
fjord noun
  fjords
flabbergasted
flabby adjective
  flabbier
  flabbiest

flag noun
  flags
flag verb
  flags
  flagging
  flagged
flagpole noun
  flagpoles
flagship noun
  flagships
flagstaff noun
  flagstaffs
flagstone noun
  flagstones
★ **flair** noun
flake noun
  flakes
flake verb
  flakes
  flaking
  flaked
flaky adjective
  flakier
  flakiest
flame noun
  flames
flame verb
  flames
  flaming
  flamed
flamingo noun
  flamingos
flan noun
  flans
flank noun
  flanks
flannel noun
  flannels
flap noun
  flaps

★ **Flair** is a special talent. **!** flare.

flap verb
flaps
flapping
flapped

flapjack noun
flapjacks

★ **flare** noun
flares

flare verb
flares
flaring
flared

flash noun
flashes

flash verb
flashes
flashing
flashed

flashback noun
flashbacks

flashy adjective
flashier
flashiest

flask noun
flasks

flat adjective
flatter
flattest
flatly

flat noun
flats

flatness

flatten verb
flattens
flattening
flattened

flatter verb
flatters
flattering
flattered

flatterer noun
flatterers

flattery

flaunt verb
flaunts
flaunting
flaunted

flavour noun
flavours

flavour verb
flavours
flavouring
flavoured

flavouring

flaw noun
flaws

flawed

flawless adjective
flawlessly

flax

☆ **flea** noun
fleas

fleck noun
flecks

❍ **flee** verb
flees
fleeing
fled

fleece noun
fleeces

fleece verb
fleeces
fleecing
fleeced

fleecy adjective
fleecier
fleeciest

fleet noun
fleets

fleeting

flesh

fleshy adjective
fleshier
fleshiest

✴ **flew** see fly

flex noun
flexes

flex verb
flexes
flexing
flexed

flexibility

flexible adjective
flexibly

flick verb
flicks
flicking
flicked

flick noun
flicks

flicker verb
flickers
flickering
flickered

flight noun
flights

flimsy adjective
flimsier
flimsiest

flinch verb
flinches
flinching
flinched

fling verb
flings
flinging
flung

flint noun
flints

flinty adjective
flintier
flintiest

- -

★ A flare is a bright light. ! flair.
☆ A flea is an insect. ! flee.
❍ To flee is to run away. ! flea.
✴ Flew is the past of fly. ! flu, flue.

flip verb
  flips
  flipping
  flipped
flippancy
flippant adjective
  flippantly
flipper noun
  flippers
flirt verb
  flirts
  flirting
  flirted
flirtation
flit verb
  flits
  flitting
  flitted
float verb
  floats
  floating
  floated
float noun
  floats
flock verb
  flocks
  flocking
  flocked
flock noun
  flocks
flog verb
  flogs
  flogging
  flogged
flood verb
  floods
  flooding
  flooded
flood noun
  floods
floodlight noun
  floodlights

floodlit
floor noun
  floors
floor verb
  floors
  flooring
  floored
floorboard noun
  floorboards
flop verb
  flops
  flopping
  flopped
flop noun
  flops
floppy adjective
  floppier
  floppiest
floppy disk noun
  floppy disks
flora
floral
florist noun
  florists
floss
flounder verb
  flounders
  floundering
  floundered
★ **flour**
flourish verb
  flourishes
  flourishing
  flourished
floury adjective
  flourier
  flouriest
flow verb
  flows
  flowing
  flowed

flow noun
  flows
☆ **flower** noun
  flowers
flower verb
  flowers
  flowering
  flowered
flowerpot noun
  flowerpots
flowery
flown
○ **flu**
fluctuate verb
  fluctuates
  fluctuating
  fluctuated
fluctuation
✳ **flue** noun
  flues
fluency
fluent adjective
  fluently
fluff
fluffy adjective
  fluffier
  fluffiest
fluid noun
  fluids
fluke noun
  flukes
flung see **fling**
fluorescent
fluoridation
fluoride
flurry noun
  flurries
flush verb
  flushes
  flushing
  flushed

★ **Flour** is powder used in making bread. ! **flower**.
☆ A **flower** is a part of a plant. ! **flour**.
○ **Flu** is an illness. ! **flew, flue**.
✳ A **flue** is a pipe for smoke and fumes. ! **flew, flu**.

flush noun
flushes

flush adjective

flustered

flute noun
flutes

flutter verb
flutters
fluttering
fluttered

flutter noun
flutters

fly verb
flies
flying
flew
flown

fly noun
flies

flyleaf noun
flyleaves

flyover noun
flyovers

flywheel noun
flywheels

foal noun
foals

foam noun

foam verb
foams
foaming
foamed

foamy adjective
foamier
foamiest

focal

focus verb
focuses
focusing
focused

focus noun
focuses or foci

fodder

foe noun
foes

foetus noun use fetus

fog noun
fogs

★ **foggy** adjective
foggier
foggiest

foghorn noun
foghorns

☆ **fogy** noun
fogies

foil verb
foils
foiling
foiled

foil noun
foils

fold verb
folds
folding
folded

fold noun
folds

folder noun
folders

foliage

folk

folklore

follow verb
follows
following
followed

follower noun
followers

fond adjective
fonder
fondest
fondly

fondness

font noun
fonts

food noun
foods

fool noun
fools

fool verb
fools
fooling
fooled

foolhardiness

foolhardy
adjective
foolhardier
foolhardiest

foolish adjective
foolishly

foolishness

foolproof

✪ **foot** noun
feet

football noun
footballs

footballer noun
footballers

foothill noun
foothills

foothold noun
footholds

footing

footlights

footnote noun
footnotes

footpath noun
footpaths

footprint noun
footprints

footstep noun
footsteps

- -

★ **Foggy** means 'covered in fog'. ! fogy.
☆ A **fogy** is someone with old-fashioned ideas. ! foggy.
✪ The plural is **foot** in e.g. *a six-foot pole.*

★ **for** preposition and conjunction

forbid verb
forbids
forbidding
forbade
forbidden

force verb
forces
forcing
forced

force noun
forces

forceful adjective
forcefully

forceps plural noun

forcible adjective
forcibly

ford verb
fords
fording
forded

ford noun
fords

☆ **fore** adjective and noun

forecast verb
forecasts
forecasting
forecast
forecasted

forecast noun
forecasts

forecourt noun
forecourts

forefathers plural noun

forefinger noun
forefingers

○ **foregone** adjective

foreground noun
foregrounds

forehead noun
foreheads

foreign

foreigner noun
foreigners

foreman noun
foremen

foremost

forename noun
forenames

foresee verb
foresees
foreseeing
foresaw
foreseen

foreseeable

foresight

forest noun
forests

forester noun
foresters

forestry

foretell verb
foretells
foretelling
foretold

✱ **forever** adverb

forfeit verb
forfeits
forfeiting
forfeited

forfeit noun
forfeits

forgave see **forgive**

forge verb
forges
forging
forged

forge noun
forges

forgery noun
forgeries

forget verb
forgets
forgetting
forgot
forgotten

forgetful

forgetfulness

forget-me-not noun
forget-me-nots

forgive verb
forgives
forgiving
forgave
forgiven

forgiveness

fork noun
forks

fork verb
forks
forking
forked

fork-lift truck noun
fork-lift trucks

forlorn

form verb
forms
forming
formed

form noun
forms

formal adjective
formally

formality noun
formalities

format noun
formats

formation noun
formations

· ·

★ You use **for** in phrases like *a present for you*. ! **fore**.
☆ You use **fore** in phrases like *come to the fore*. ! **for**.
○ You can use **foregone** in *a foregone conclusion*.
✱ You use **forever** in e.g. *They are forever complaining*. You can also use **for ever** in e.g. *The rain seemed to go on for ever*.

former *adjective*
formerly

formidable *adjective*
formidably

formula *noun*
formulas *or*
formulae

formulate *verb*
formulates
formulating
formulated

forsake *verb*
forsakes
forsaking
forsook
forsaken

fort *noun*
forts

★ **forth**

fortieth

fortification *noun*
fortifications

fortify *verb*
fortifies
fortifying
fortified

fortnight *noun*
fortnights

fortnightly

fortress *noun*
fortresses

fortunate *adjective*
fortunately

fortune *noun*
fortunes

fortune-teller *noun*
fortune-tellers

forty *noun*
forties

forward *adjective*
and *adverb*

forward *noun*
forwards

forwards *adverb*

fossil *noun*
fossils

fossilized

foster *verb*
fosters
fostering
fostered

foster child *noun*
foster children

foster parent *noun*
foster parents

fought see fight

☆ **foul** *adjective*
fouler
foulest
foully

○ **foul** *verb*
fouls
fouling
fouled

✳ **foul** *noun*
fouls

foulness

found *verb*
founds
founding
founded

found see find

foundation *noun*
foundations

founder *noun*
founders

founder *verb*
founders
foundering
foundered

foundry *noun*
foundries

fountain *noun*
fountains

four *noun*
fours

fourteen *noun*
fourteens

fourteenth

✳ **fourth**

fourthly

✳ **fowl** *noun*
fowl or fowls

fox *noun*
foxes

fox *verb*
foxes
foxing
foxed

foxglove *noun*
foxgloves

foxy *adjective*
foxier
foxiest

foyer *noun*
foyers

fraction *noun*
fractions

fractionally

fracture *verb*
fractures
fracturing
fractured

fracture *noun*
fractures

fragile *adjective*
fragilely

fragility

fragment *noun*
fragments

fragmentary

fragmentation

- -

★ You use **forth** in e.g. *to go forth*. ! **fourth**.
☆ **Foul** means 'dirty' or 'disgusting'. ! **fowl**.
○ To **foul** is to break a rule in a game. ! **fowl**.
✳ A **foul** is breaking a rule in a game. ! **fowl**.
✳ You use **fourth** in e.g. *for the fourth time*. ! **forth**.
✳ A **fowl** is a kind of bird. ! **foul**.

fragrance noun
fragrances
fragrant
frail adjective
frailer
frailest
frailly
frailty noun
frailties
frame verb
frames
framing
framed
frame noun
frames
framework noun
frameworks
★ **franc** noun
francs
franchise noun
franchises
☆ **frank** adjective
franker
frankest
frankly
○ **frank** verb
franks
franking
franked
frankness
frantic adjective
frantically
fraud noun
frauds
fraudulent adjective
fraudulently
fraught
frayed
freak noun
freaks

freakish
freckle noun
freckles
freckled
free adjective
freer
freest
freely
free verb
frees
freeing
freed
freedom noun
freedoms
freehand adjective
freewheel verb
freewheels
freewheeling
freewheeled
✳ **freeze** verb
freezes
freezing
froze
frozen
freezer noun
freezers
freight
freighter noun
freighters
frenzied
frenzy noun
frenzies
frequency noun
frequencies
frequent adjective
frequently
frequent verb
frequents
frequenting
frequented

fresh adjective
fresher
freshest
freshly
freshness
freshen verb
freshens
freshening
freshened
freshwater
fret verb
frets
fretting
fretted
fretful adjective
fretfully
fretsaw noun
fretsaws
fretwork
friar noun
friars
friary noun
friaries
friction
Friday noun
Fridays
fridge noun
fridges
friend noun
friends
friendless
friendliness
friendly adjective
friendlier
friendliest
friendship noun
friendships
✴ **frieze** noun
friezes
frigate noun
frigates

★ A **franc** is a French unit of money. ! **frank**.
☆ **Frank** means 'speaking honestly'. ! **franc**.
○ To **frank** is to mark a letter with a postmark. ! **franc**.
✳ To **freeze** is to be very cold. ! **frieze**.
✴ A **frieze** is a strip of designs along a wall. ! **freeze**.

fright noun
frights

frighten verb
frightens
frightening
frightened

frightful adjective
frightfully

frill noun
frills

frilled

frilly adjective
frillier
frilliest

fringe noun
fringes

fringed

frisk verb
frisks
frisking
frisked

friskiness

frisky adjective
friskier
friskiest
friskily

fritter verb
fritters
frittering
frittered

fritter noun
fritters

frivolous adjective
frivolously

frivolity noun
frivolities

frizzy adjective
frizzier
frizziest

★ **fro**

frock noun
frocks

frog noun
frogs

frogman noun
frogmen

frolic noun
frolics

frolicsome

frolic verb
frolics
frolicking
frolicked

front noun
fronts

frontier noun
frontiers

frost
noun
frosts

frost verb
frosts
frosting
frosted

frostbite

frostbitten

frosty adjective
frostier
frostiest

froth noun

froth verb
froths
frothing
frothed

frothy adjective
frothier
frothiest

froth verb
froths
frothing
frothed

frown verb
frowns
frowning
frowned

frown noun
frowns

froze see **freeze**
frozen see **freeze**
frugal adjective
frugally

frugality

fruit noun
fruit or fruits

fruitful adjective
fruitfully

fruitless adjective
fruitlessly

fruity adjective
fruitier
fruitiest

frustrate verb
frustrates
frustrating
frustrated

frustration noun
frustrations

fry verb
fries
frying
fried

fudge

fuel noun
fuels

fuel verb
fuels
fuelling
fuelled

fug noun
fugs

fuggy adjective
fuggier
fuggiest

★ You use **fro** in to and fro.

fugitive noun
fugitives

-ful
-ful makes nouns for amounts, e.g. **handful**, **spoonful**. The plural of these words ends in -fuls, e.g. **handfuls**. -ful also makes adjectives, e.g. **graceful**, and when the adjective ends in -y following a consonant, you change the y to i, e.g. **beauty - beautiful**.

fulcrum noun
fulcra or fulcrums

fulfil verb
fulfils
fulfilling
fulfilled

fulfilment

full adjective
fully

fullness

fumble verb
fumbles
fumbling
fumbled

fume verb
fumes
fuming
fumed

fumes plural noun

fun

function verb
functions
functioning
functioned

function noun
functions

functional adjective
functionally

fund noun
funds

fundamental
adjective
fundamentally

funeral noun
funerals

fungus noun
fungi

funk verb
funks
funking
funked

funnel noun
funnels

funny adjective
funnier
funniest
funnily

★ **fur** noun
furs

furious adjective
furiously

furl verb
furls
furling
furled

furlong noun
furlongs

furnace noun
furnaces

furnish verb
furnishes
furnishing
furnished

furniture

furrow noun
furrows

furry adjective
furrier
furriest

☆ **further** adjective

✪ **further** verb
furthers
furthering
furthered

furthermore

✻ **furthest**

furtive adjective
furtively

fury noun
furies

fuse verb
fuses
fusing
fused

fuse noun
fuses

fuselage noun
fuselages

fusion noun
fusions

fuss verb
fusses
fussing
fussed

fuss noun
fusses

fussiness

fussy adjective
fussier
fussiest
fussily

futile adjective
futilely

futility

futon noun
futons

. . . .

★ **Fur** is the hair of animals. ! **fir.**
☆ You use **further** in e.g. *We need further information.* See **farther.**
✪ To **further** something is to make it progress.
✻ You use **furthest** in e.g. *Who has read the furthest?* See **farthest.**

future
fuzz
fuzziness *noun*
fuzzy *adjective*
  fuzzier
  fuzziest
  fuzzily

Gg

gabardine *noun*
  gabardines
gabble *verb*
  gabbles
  gabbling
  gabbled
gable *noun*
  gables
gabled
gadget *noun*
  gadgets
Gaelic
gag *verb*
  gags
  gagging
  gagged
gag *noun*
  gags
gaiety
gaily
gain *verb*
  gains
  gaining
  gained
gain *noun*
  gains
gala *noun*
  galas

galactic
galaxy *noun*
  galaxies
gale *noun*
  gales
gallant *adjective*
  gallantly
gallantry
★ galleon *noun*
  galleons
gallery *noun*
  galleries
galley *noun*
  galleys
☆ gallon *noun*
  gallons
gallop *verb*
  gallops
  galloping
  galloped
gallop *noun*
  gallops
gallows
galore
galvanize *verb*
  galvanizes
  galvanizing
  galvanized
gamble *verb*
  gambles
  gambling
  gambled
gamble *noun*
  gambles
gambler *noun*
  gamblers
game *noun*
  games
gamekeeper *noun*
  gamekeepers
gammon

gander *noun*
  ganders
gang *noun*
  gangs
gang *verb*
  gangs
  ganging
  ganged
gangplank *noun*
  gangplanks
gangster *noun*
  gangsters
gangway *noun*
  gangways
gaol *noun*
  use jail
gaoler *noun*
  use jailer
gap *noun*
  gaps
gape *verb*
  gapes
  gaping
  gaped
garage *noun*
  garages
garbage
garden *noun*
  gardens
gardener *noun*
  gardeners
gardening
gargle *verb*
  gargles
  gargling
  gargled
gargoyle *noun*
  gargoyles
garland *noun*
  garlands
garlic

★ A galleon is a type of ship. ! gallon.
☆ A gallon is a measurement of liquid. ! galleon.

garment noun
garments

garnish verb
garnishes
garnishing
garnished

garrison noun
garrisons

garter noun
garters

gas noun
gases

gas verb
gasses
gassing
gassed

gaseous

gash noun
gashes

gasket noun
gaskets

gasoline

gasometer noun
gasometers

gasp verb
gasps
gasping
gasped

gasp noun
gasps

gastric

gate noun
gates

⋆ **gateau** noun
gateaux

gateway noun
gateways

gather verb
gathers
gathering
gathered

gathering noun
gatherings

gaudy adjective
gaudier
gaudiest

gauge verb
gauges
gauging
gauged

gauge noun
gauges

gaunt

gauntlet noun
gauntlets

gauze

gave see **give**

gay adjective
gayer
gayest

gaze verb
gazes
gazing
gazed

gaze noun
gazes

gazetteer noun
gazetteers

gear noun
gears

geese see **goose**

Geiger counter
noun
Geiger counters

gel noun
gels

gelatine

gelding noun
geldings

gem noun
gems

gender noun
genders

gene noun
genes

genealogy noun
genealogies

general adjective
generally

general noun
generals

generalization
noun
generalizations

generalize verb
generalizes
generalizing
generalized

generate verb
generates
generating
generated

generation noun
generations

generator noun
generators

generosity

generous adjective
generously

genetic adjective
genetically

genetics plural noun

genial adjective
genially

genie noun
genies

genitals plural noun

genius noun
geniuses

gent noun
gents

⋆ **Gateau** is a French word used in English. It means 'a rich cream cake'.

gentle adjective
gentler
gentlest
gently

gentleman noun
gentlemen

gentlemanly

gentleness

genuine adjective
genuinely

genus noun
genera

geo-
geo- means 'earth',
e.g. geography (= the
study of the earth).

geographer

geographical
adjective
geographically

geography

geological adjective
geologically

geologist

geology

geometric adjective
geometrically

geometrical
adjective
geometrically

geometry

geranium noun
geraniums

gerbil noun
gerbils

germ noun
germs

germinate verb
germinates
germinating

germinated

germination

gesticulate verb
gesticulates
gesticulating
gesticulated

gesture noun
gestures

get verb
gets
getting
got

getaway noun
getaways

geyser noun
geysers

ghastly adjective
ghastlier
ghastliest

ghetto noun
ghettos

ghost noun
ghosts

ghostly adjective
ghostlier
ghostliest

ghoulish adjective
ghoulishly

giant noun
giants

giddiness

giddy adjective
giddier
giddiest
giddily

gift noun
gifts

gifted

gigantic adjective
gigantically

giggle verb
giggles
giggling
giggled

giggle noun
giggles

★ **gild** verb
gilds
gilding
gilded

gills plural noun

gimmick noun
gimmicks

gin

ginger

gingerbread

gingerly

gingery

gipsy noun use gypsy

giraffe noun
giraffes

girder noun
girders

girdle noun
girdles

girl noun
girls

girlfriend noun
girlfriends

girlhood

girlish

☆ **giro** noun
giros

girth noun
girths

gist

give verb
gives
giving
gave
given

★ To **gild** something is to cover it with gold. ! **guild**.
☆ A **giro** is a system of paying money. ! **gyro**.

given see give
giver noun
  givers
glacial
glacier noun
  glaciers
glad adjective
  gladder
  gladdest
  gladly
gladden verb
  gladdens
  gladdening
  gladdened
gladiator noun
  gladiators
gladness
glamorize verb
  glamorizes
  glamorizing
  glamorized
glamorous adjective
  glamorously
glamour
glance verb
  glances
  glancing
  glanced
glance noun
  glances
gland noun
  glands
glandular
glare verb
  glares
  glaring
  glared
glare noun
  glares
glass noun
  glasses

glassful noun
  glassfuls
glassy adjective
  glassier
  glassiest
glaze verb
  glazes
  glazing
  glazed
glaze noun
  glazes
glazier noun
  glaziers
gleam noun
  gleams
gleam verb
  gleams
  gleaming
  gleamed
glee
gleeful adjective
  gleefully
glen noun
  glens
glide verb
  glides
  gliding
  glided
glider noun
  gliders
glimmer verb
  glimmers
  glimmering
  glimmered
glimmer noun
  glimmers
glimpse verb
  glimpses
  glimpsing
  glimpsed

glimpse noun
  glimpses
glint verb
  glints
  glinting
  glinted
glint noun
  glints
glisten verb
  glistens
  glistening
  glistened
glitter verb
  glitters
  glittering
  glittered
gloat verb
  gloats
  gloating
  gloated
global adjective
  globally
globe noun
  globes
gloom
gloominess
gloomy adjective
  gloomier
  gloomiest
  gloomily
glorification
glorify verb
  glorifies
  glorifying
  glorified
glorious adjective
  gloriously
glory noun
  glories
gloss noun
  glosses

glossary noun
  glossaries
glossy adjective
  glossier
  glossiest
glove noun
  gloves
glow verb
  glows
  glowing
  glowed
glow noun
  glows
glower verb
  glowers
  glowering
  glowered
glow-worm noun
  glow-worms
glucose
glue noun
  glues
glue verb
  glues
  gluing
  glued
gluey adjective
  gluier
  gluiest
glum adjective
  glummer
  glummest
  glumly
glutton noun
  gluttons
gluttonous
gluttony
★ **gnarled**
★ **gnash** verb
  gnashes
  gnashing
  gnashed

★ **gnat** noun
  gnats
★ **gnaw** verb
  gnaws
  gnawing
  gnawed
★ **gnome** noun
  gnomes
go verb
  goes
  going
  went
  gone
go noun
  goes
goal noun
  goals
goalie noun
  goalies
goalkeeper noun
  goalkeepers
goalpost noun
  goalposts
goat noun
  goats
gobble verb
  gobbles
  gobbling
  gobbled
gobbledegook
goblet noun
  goblets
goblin noun
  goblins
☆ **God**
❂ **god** noun
  gods
godchild noun
  godchildren

goddess noun
  goddesses
godparent noun
  godparents
goggles plural noun
gold
golden
goldfinch noun
  goldfinches
goldfish noun
  goldfish
golf
golfer noun
  golfers
golfing
gondola noun
  gondolas
gondolier noun
  gondoliers
gone see go
gong noun
  gongs
good adjective
  better
  best
goodbye interjection
Good Friday
good-looking
good-natured
goodness
goods plural noun
goodwill
gooey adjective
  gooier
  gooiest
goose noun
  geese
gooseberry noun
  gooseberries

★ In these words beginning with **gn-** the 'g' is silent.
☆ You use a capital G when you mean the Christian, Jewish, and Muslim creator.
❂ You use a small g when you mean any male divine being.

gore verb
gores
goring
gored

gorge noun
gorges

gorgeous adjective
gorgeously

★ **gorilla** noun
gorillas

gorse

gory adjective
gorier
goriest

gosling noun
goslings

gospel noun
gospels

gossip verb
gossips
gossiping
gossiped

gossip noun
gossips

got see get

gouge verb
gouges
gouging
gouged

gourd noun
gourds

govern verb
governs
governing
governed

government noun
governments

governor noun
governors

gown noun
gowns

grab verb
grabs
grabbing
grabbed

grace noun
graces

graceful adjective
gracefully

gracefulness

gracious adjective
graciously

grade noun
grades

grade verb
grades
grading
graded

gradient noun
gradients

gradual adjective
gradually

graduate noun
graduates

graduate verb
graduates
graduating
graduated

graduation

graffiti plural noun

grain noun
grains

grainy adjective
grainier
grainiest

gram noun
grams

grammar noun
grammars

grammatical
adjective
grammatically

gramophone noun
gramophones

grand adjective
grander
grandest
grandly

grandad noun
grandads

grandchild noun
grandchildren

grandeur

grandfather noun
grandfathers

grandma noun
grandmas

grandmother noun
grandmothers

grandpa noun
grandpas

grandparent noun
grandparents

grandstand noun
grandstands

granite

granny noun
grannies

grant verb
grants
granting
granted

grant noun
grants

granulated

grape noun
grapes

grapefruit noun
grapefruit

grapevine noun
grapevines

graph noun
graphs

· ·

★ A gorilla is a large ape. ! guerrilla.

graphic adjective
graphically
graphics plural noun
graphite

-graphy
-graphy makes words
for subjects of study,
e.g. geography (= the
study of the earth). A
bibliography is a list
of books on a subject,
and the plural is
bibliographies.

grapple verb
grapples
grappling
grappled
grasp verb
grasps
grasping
grasped
grasp noun
grasps
grass noun
grasses
grasshopper noun
grasshoppers
grassy adjective
grassier
grassiest
★ **grate** verb
grates
grating
grated
☆ **grate** noun
grates
grateful adjective
gratefully
grating noun
gratings

gratitude
grave noun
graves
grave adjective
graver
gravest
gravely
gravel
gravelled
gravestone noun
gravestones
graveyard noun
graveyards
gravitation
gravitational
gravity
gravy
graze verb
grazes
grazing
grazed
graze noun
grazes
grease
greasy adjective
greasier
greasiest
great adjective
greater
greatest
greatly
greatness
greed
greediness
greedy adjective
greedier
greediest
greedily

green adjective and
noun
greener
greenest
greenery
greengage noun
greengages
greengrocer noun
greengrocers
greengrocery noun
greengroceries
greenhouse noun
greenhouses
greens plural noun
greet verb
greets
greeting
greeted
greeting noun
greetings
grenade noun
grenades
grew see grow
grey adjective and
noun
greyer
greyest
greyhound noun
greyhounds
grid noun
grids
grief
grievance noun
grievances
grieve verb
grieves
grieving
grieved
○ **grievous** adjective
grievously

★ To grate something is to shred it. ! **great**.
☆ A grate is a fireplace. ! **great**.
○ Note that this word does not end -ious.

grill verb
grills
grilling
grilled

grill noun
grills

grim adjective
grimmer
grimmest
grimly

grimace noun
grimaces

grime

grimness

grimy adjective
grimier
grimiest

grin noun
grins

grin verb
grins
grinning
grinned

grind verb
grinds
grinding
ground

grinder noun
grinders

grindstone noun
grindstones

grip verb
grips
gripping
gripped

grip noun
grips

★ **grisly** adjective
grislier
grisliest

gristle

gristly adjective
gristlier
gristliest

grit verb
grits
gritting
gritted

grit noun

gritty adjective
grittier
grittiest

☆ **grizzly** adjective

groan verb
groans
groaning
groaned

groan noun
groans

grocer noun
grocers

grocery noun
groceries

groggy adjective
groggier
groggiest

groin noun
groins

groom verb
grooms
grooming
groomed

groom noun
grooms

groove noun
grooves

grope verb
gropes
groping
groped

gross adjective
grosser
grossest

grossly

gross noun
gross

grossness

○ **grotesque** adjective
grotesquely

grotty adjective
grottier
grottiest

ground noun
grounds

ground see **grind**
grounded

grounds plural noun

groundsheet noun
groundsheets

groundsman noun
groundsmen

group noun
groups

group verb
groups
grouping
grouped

grouse verb
grouses
grousing
groused

grouse noun
grouse

grove noun
groves

grovel verb
grovels
grovelling
grovelled

grow verb
grows
growing
grew
grown

★ **Grisly** means 'revolting' or 'horrible'. **! grizzly.**
☆ You use **grizzly** in *grizzly bear*. **! grisly.**
○ **Grotesque** means 'strange' and 'ugly'. It sounds like 'grotesk'.

grower noun
grovers

growl verb
growls
growling
growled

growl noun
growls

grown-up noun
grown-ups

growth noun
growths

grub noun
grubs

grubby adjective
grubbier
grubbiest

grudge verb
grudges
grudging
grudged

grudge noun
grudges

grudgingly

gruelling

gruesome

gruff adjective
gruffer
gruffest
gruffly

grumble verb
grumbles
grumbling
grumbled

grumbler noun
grumblers

grumpiness

grumpy adjective
grumpier
grumpiest
grumpily

grunt verb
grunts
grunting
grunted

grunt noun
grunts

guarantee noun
guarantees

guarantee verb
guarantees
guaranteeing
guaranteed

guard verb
guards
guarding
guarded

guard noun
guards

guardian noun
guardians

guardianship

★ **guerrilla** noun
guerrillas

guess verb
guesses
guessing
guessed

guess noun
guesses

guesswork

guest noun
guests

guidance

guide verb
guides
guiding
guided

guide noun
guides

guidelines plural
noun

☆ **guild** noun
guilds

guillotine noun
guillotines

guilt

guilty adjective
guiltier
guiltiest

guinea noun
guineas

guinea pig noun
guinea pigs

guitar noun
guitars

guitarist

gulf noun
gulfs

gull noun
gulls

gullet noun
gullets

gullible

gully noun
gullies

gulp verb
gulps
gulping
gulped

gulp noun
gulps

gum noun
gums

gum verb
gums
gumming
gummed

gummy adjective
gummier
gummiest

gun noun
guns

★ A **guerrilla** is a member of a small army. ! **gorilla**.
☆ A **guild** is an organization of people. ! **gild**.

gun verb
guns
gunning
gunned

gunboat noun
gunboats

gunfire

gunman noun
gunmen

gunner noun
gunners

gunnery

gunpowder

gunshot noun
gunshots

★ **gurdwara** noun
gurdwaras

gurgle verb
gurgles
gurgling
gurgled

guru noun
gurus

☆ **Guru Granth Sahib**

gush verb
gushes
gushing
gushed

gust noun
gusts

gusty adjective
gustier
gustiest

gut noun
guts

gut verb
guts
gutting
gutted

gutter noun
gutters

guy noun
guys

guzzle verb
guzzles
guzzling
guzzled

gym noun
gyms

gymkhana noun
gymkhanas

gymnasium noun
gymnasiums

gymnast noun
gymnasts

gymnastics plural noun

gypsy noun
gypsies

○ **gyro** noun
gyros

gyroscope noun
gyroscopes

Hh

habit noun
habits

habitat noun
habitats

habitual adjective
habitually

hack verb
hacks
hacking
hacked

hacker noun
hackers

hacksaw noun
hacksaws

had see **has**

haddock noun
haddock

hadn't verb

hag noun
hags

haggard

haggis noun
haggises

haggle verb
haggles
haggling
haggled

✳ **haiku** noun
haiku

hail verb
hails
hailing
hailed

hail

hailstone noun
hailstones

✱ **hair** noun
hairs

hairbrush noun
hairbrushes

haircut noun
haircuts

hairdresser noun
hairdressers

hairpin noun
hairpins

hair-raising

hairstyle noun
hairstyles

. . . .

★ A Sikh place of worship.
☆ The holy book of Sikhs.
○ A gyro is type of compass. ! **giro**.
✳ A Japanese poem.
✱ **Hair** is the covering on the head. ! **hare**.

hairy adjective
hairier
hairiest

hake noun
hake

halal

half adjective and
noun
halves

half-baked

half-hearted
adjective
half-heartedly

half-life noun
half-lives

half-mast

★ **halfpenny** noun
halfpennies or
halfpence

half-term noun
half-terms

half-time noun
half-times

halfway

halibut noun
halibut

☆ **hall** noun
halls

hallo

○ **Halloween**

hallucination noun
hallucinations

halo noun
haloes

halt verb
halts
halting
halted

halt noun
halts

halter noun
halters

halting adjective
haltingly

halve verb
halves
halving
halved

halves see **half**

ham noun
hams

hamburger noun
hamburgers

hammer noun
hammers

hammer verb
hammers
hammering
hammered

hammock noun
hammocks

hamper verb
hampers
hampering
hampered

hamper noun
hampers

hamster noun
hamsters

hand noun
hands

hand verb
hands
handing
handed

handbag noun
handbags

handbook noun
handbooks

handcuffs plural
noun

handful noun
handfuls

handicap noun
handicaps

handicapped

handicraft noun
handicrafts

handiwork

handkerchief noun
handkerchiefs

handle noun
handles

handle verb
handles
handling
handled

handlebars plural
noun

handrail noun
handrails

handsome adjective
handsomer
handsomest
handsomely

hands-on

handstand noun
handstands

handwriting

handwritten

handy adjective
handier
handiest

handyman noun
handymen

hang verb
hangs
hanging
hung

. . . .

★ You use **halfpennies** when you mean several coins and **halfpence** for a sum of
money.

☆ A **hall** is a large space in a building. ! **haul**.

○ You will also see this word spelt *Hallowe'en*.

★ **hangar** noun
  hangars
☆ **hanger** noun
  hangers
hang-glider noun
  hang-gliders
hang-gliding
hangman noun
  hangmen
hangover noun
  hangovers
hank noun
  hanks
hanker verb
  hankers
  hankering
  hankered
hanky noun
  hankies
⊙ **Hanukkah**
haphazard adjective
  haphazardly
happen verb
  happens
  happening
  happened
happening noun
  happenings
happiness
happy adjective
  happier
  happiest
  happily
happy-go-lucky
✳ **harass** verb
  harasses
  harassing
  harassed
harassment
harbour noun
  harbours

harbour verb
  harbours
  harbouring
  harboured
hard adjective
  harder
  hardest
hard adverb
  harder
  hardest
hardboard
hard-boiled
hard disk noun
  hard disks
harden verb
  hardens
  hardening
  hardened
hardly
hardness
hardship noun
  hardships
hardware
hardwood noun
  hardwoods
hardy adjective
  hardier
  hardiest
✱ **hare** noun
  hares
hark verb
  harks
  harking
  harked
harm verb
  harms
  harming
  harmed
harm noun

harmful adjective
  harmfully
harmless adjective
  harmlessly
harmonic
harmonica noun
  harmonicas
harmonious
  adjective
  harmoniously
harmonization
harmonize verb
  harmonizes
  harmonizing
  harmonized
harmony noun
  harmonies
harness verb
  harnesses
  harnessing
  harnessed
harness noun
  harnesses
harp noun
  harps
harp verb
  harps
  harping
  harped
harpist noun
  harpists
harpoon noun
  harpoons
harpsichord noun
  harpsichords
harrow noun
  harrows
harsh adjective
  harsher
  harshest
  harshly

· ·

★ A **hangar** is a shed for aircraft. ! **hanger**.
☆ A **hanger** is a thing for hanging clothes on. ! **hangar**.
⊙ A Jewish festival.
✳ Note that there is only one r in **harass** and **harassment**.
✱ A **hare** is an animal like a large rabbit. ! **hair**.

harshness

harvest *noun*
harvests

harvest *verb*
harvests
harvesting
harvested

hash *noun*
hashes

hasn't *verb*

hassle *noun*
hassles

haste

hasten *verb*
hastens
hastening
hastened

hastiness

hasty *adjective*
hastier
hastiest
hastily

hatch *verb*
hatches
hatching
hatched

hatch *noun*
hatches

hatchback *noun*
hatchbacks

hatchet *noun*
hatchets

hate *verb*
hates
hating
hated

hate *noun*
hates

hateful *adjective*
hatefully

hatred

hat trick *noun*
hat tricks

haughtiness

haughty *adjective*
haughtier
haughtiest
haughtily

★ **haul** *verb*
hauls
hauling
hauled

haul *noun*
hauls

haunt *verb*
haunts
haunting
haunted

have *verb*
has
having
had

haven *noun*
havens

haven't *verb*

haversack *noun*
haversacks

hawk *noun*
hawks

hawk *verb*
hawks
hawking
hawked

hawker *noun*
hawkers

hawthorn *noun*
hawthorns

hay fever

haymaking

haystack *noun*
haystacks

hazard *noun*
hazards

hazardous

haze *noun*
hazes

hazel *noun*
hazels

haziness

hazy *adjective*
hazier
haziest
hazily

H-bomb *noun*
H-bombs

head *noun*
heads

head *verb*
heads
heading
headed

headache *noun*
headaches

headdress *noun*
headdresses

header *noun*
headers

heading *noun*
headings

headland *noun*
headlands

headlight *noun*
headlights

headline *noun*
headlines

headlong

headmaster *noun*
headmasters

headmistress *noun*
headmistresses

head-on

headphones

- -

★ To **haul** is to pull something heavy. ! hall

headquarters noun
headquarters

headteacher noun
headteachers

headway

heal verb
heals
healing
healed

healer noun
healers

health

healthiness

healthy adjective
healthier
healthiest
healthily

heap verb
heaps
heaping
heaped

heap noun
heaps

★ **hear** verb
hears
hearing
heard

hearing noun
hearings

hearse noun
hearses

heart noun
hearts

hearth noun
hearths

heartiness

heartless

hearty adjective
heartier
heartiest
heartily

heat verb
heats
heating
heated

heat noun
heats

heater noun
heaters

heath noun
heaths

heathen noun
heathens

heather

heatwave noun
heatwaves

☆ **heave** verb
heaves
heaving
heaved or hove

heaven

heavenly

heaviness

heavy adjective
heavier
heaviest
heavily

heavyweight noun
heavyweights

Hebrew

hectare noun
hectares

hectic adjective
hectically

he'd verb

hedge noun
hedges

hedge verb
hedges
hedging
hedged

hedgehog noun
hedgehogs

hedgerow noun
hedgerows

heed verb
heeds
heeding
heeded

heed noun

heedless

heel noun
heels

heel verb
heels
heeling
heeled

hefty adjective
heftier
heftiest

heifer noun
heifers

height noun
heights

heighten verb
heightens
heightening
heightened

○ **heir** noun
heirs

heiress noun
heiresses

held see **hold**

helicopter noun
helicopters

helium

helix noun
helices

hell

he'll verb

hellish adjective
hellishly

- - - - - - - - - - - - - - - -
★ You use **hear** in e.g. *I can't hear you.* ! **here**.
☆ You use **hove** in e.g. *the ship hove to.*
○ You do not pronounce the 'h' in **heir** (sounds like *air*).

hello

helm noun
helms

helmsman noun
helmsmen

helmet noun
helmets

helmeted

help verb
helps
helping
helped

help noun
helps

helper noun
helpers

helpful adjective
helpfully

helping noun
helpings

helpless adjective
helplessly

helter-skelter noun
helter-skelters

hem noun
hems

hem verb
hems
hemming
hemmed

hemisphere noun
hemispheres

hemp

hence

henceforth

herald noun
heralds

herald verb
heralds
heralding
heralded

heraldic

heraldry

herb noun
herbs

herbal

herbivore noun
herbivores

herd noun
herds

★ **herd** verb
herds
herding
herded

☆ **here**

hereditary

heredity

heritage noun
heritages

hermit noun
hermits

hermitage

hero noun
heroes

heroic adjective
heroically

⊙ **heroin** noun

✳ **heroine** noun
heroines

heroism

heron noun
herons

herring noun
herring
herrings

✴ **hers**

herself

he's verb

hesitant adjective
hesitantly

hesitate verb
hesitates
hesitating
hesitated

hesitation

hexagon noun
hexagons

hexagonal

hibernate verb
hibernates
hibernating
hibernated

hibernation

hiccup noun
hiccups

hide verb
hides
hiding
hidden
hid
hidden

hide-and-seek

hideous adjective
hideously

hideout noun
hideouts

hiding noun
hidings

hieroglyphics plural
noun

hi-fi noun
hi-fis

higgledy-piggledy

high adjective
higher
highest

highland adjective

highlands plural
noun

- -

★ A **herd** is a group of sheep. ! **heard**.

☆ You use **here** in e.g. *come here*. ! **hear**.

⊙ **Heroin** is a drug. ! **heroine**.

✳ A **heroine** is a woman or girl in a story. ! **heroin**.

✴ You use **hers** in e.g. *the book is hers*. Note that there is no apostrophe in this word.

highlander noun
highlanders
highlight noun
highlights
highlighter noun
highlighters
highly
Highness noun
Highnesses
high-rise
highway noun
highways
highwayman noun
highwaymen
hijack verb
hijacks
hijacking
hijacked
hijacker noun
hijackers
hike verb
hikes
hiking
hiked
hike noun
hikes
hiker noun
hikers
hilarious adjective
hilariously
hilarity
hill noun
hills
hillside noun
hillsides
hilly adjective
hillier
hilliest
hilt noun
hilts
himself

hind adjective
hind noun
hinds
hinder verb
hinders
hindering
hindered
Hindi
hindrance noun
hindrances
Hindu noun
Hindus
hinge noun
hinges
hinge verb
hinges
hinging
hinged
hint noun
hints
hint verb
hints
hinting
hinted
hip noun
hips
hippo noun
hippos
hippopotamus noun
hippopotamuses
hire verb
hires
hiring
hired
hiss verb
hisses
hissing
hissed
histogram noun
histograms

historian noun
historians
historic
historical adjective
historically
history noun
histories
hit verb
hits
hitting
hit
hit noun
hits
hitch verb
hitches
hitching
hitched
hitch noun
hitches
hitch-hike verb
hitch-hikes
hitch-hiking
hitch-hiked
hitch-hiker noun
hitch-hikers
hi-tech
hither
hitherto
hive noun
hives
hoard verb
hoards
hoarding
hoarded
★ **hoard** noun
hoards
hoarder noun
hoarders
hoarding noun
hoardings
hoar frost

. . . .

★ A **hoard** is a secret store. ! **horde**.

★ **hoarse** adjective
  hoarser
  hoarsest

hoax verb
  hoaxes
  hoaxing
  hoaxed

hoax noun
  hoaxes

hobble verb
  hobbles
  hobbling
  hobbled

hobby noun
  hobbies

hockey

hoe noun
  hoes

hoe verb
  hoes
  hoeing
  hoed

hog noun
  hogs

hog verb
  hogs
  hogging
  hogged

Hogmanay

hoist verb
  hoists
  hoisting
  hoisted

hold verb
  holds
  holding
  held

hold noun
  holds

holdall noun
  holdalls

holder noun
  holders

hold-up noun
  hold-ups

☆ **hole** noun
  holes

◍ **holey** adjective

✳ **Holi**

holiday noun
  holidays

holiness

hollow adjective and
  adverb

hollow verb
  hollows
  hollowing
  hollowed

hollow noun
  hollows

holly

holocaust noun
  holocausts

hologram noun
  holograms

holster noun
  holsters

✴ **holy** adjective
  holier
  holiest

home noun
  homes

home verb
  homes
  homing
  homed

homeless

homely

home-made

homesick

homesickness

homestead noun
  homesteads

homeward adjective

homewards
  adjective and adverb

homework

homing

homosexual
  adjective and noun
  homosexuals

honest adjective
  honestly

honesty

honey noun
  honeys

honeycomb noun
  honeycombs

honeymoon noun
  honeymoons

honeysuckle

honk verb
  honks
  honking
  honked

honk noun
  honks

honour verb
  honours
  honouring
  honoured

honour noun
  honours

honourable adjective
  honourably

hood noun
  hoods

-hood
-hood makes nouns,
e.g. **childhood**. Other
noun suffixes are
-dom, **-ment**, **-ness**,
and **-ship**.

★ A **hoarse** voice is rough or croaking. ! **horse**.
☆ A **hole** is a gap or opening. ! **whole**.
◍ **Holey** means 'full of holes'. ! **holy**.
✳ A Hindu festival.
✴ You use **holy** in e.g. *a holy man*. ! **holey**.

hooded

hoof *noun*
hoofs

hook *noun*
hooks

hook *verb*
hooks
hooking
hooked

hooligan *noun*
hooligans

hoop *noun*
hoops

hoopla

hooray

hoot *verb*
hoots
hooting
hooted

hoot *noun*
hoots

hooter *noun*
hooters

hop *verb*
hops
hopping
hopped

hop *noun*
hops

hope *verb*
hopes
hoping
hoped

hope *noun*
hopes

hopeful *adjective*
hopefully

hopeless *adjective*
hopelessly

hopscotch

★ **horde** *noun*
hordes

horizon *noun*
horizons

horizontal *adjective*
horizontally

hormone *noun*
hormones

horn *noun*
horns

hornet *noun*
hornets

horoscope *noun*
horoscopes

horrible *adjective*
horribly

horrid

horrific *adjective*
horrifically

horrify *verb*
horrifies
horrifying
horrified

horror *noun*
horrors

horse *noun*
horses

horseback

horseman *noun*
horsemen

horsemanship

horsepower *noun*
horsepower

horseshoe *noun*
horseshoes

horsewoman *noun*
horsewomen

horticulture

hose *noun*
hoses

hospitable *adjective*
hospitably

hospital *noun*
hospitals

hospitality

host *noun*
hosts

hostage *noun*
hostages

hostel *noun*
hostels

hostess *noun*
hostesses

hostile

hostility *noun*
hostilities

hot *adjective*
hotter
hottest
hotly

hot *verb*
hots
hotting
hotted

hotel *noun*
hotels

hothouse *noun*
hothouses

hotpot *noun*
hotpots

hound *noun*
hounds

hound *verb*
hounds
hounding
hounded

☆ **hour** *noun*
hours

hourglass *noun*
hourglasses

★ A **horde** is a large crowd. ! **hoard**.
☆ An **hour** is a measure of time. ! **our**.

hourly *adjective* and *adverb*

house *noun*
houses

house *verb*
houses
housing
housed

houseboat *noun*
houseboats

household *noun*
households

householder *noun*
householders

housekeeper *noun*
housekeepers

housekeeping

housewife *noun*
housewives

housework

housing *noun*
housings

hove see heave

hover *verb*
hovers
hovering
hovered

hovercraft *noun*
hovercraft

however

howl *verb*
howls
howling
howled

howl *noun*
howls

howler *noun*
howlers

hub *noun*
hubs

huddle *verb*
huddles
huddling
huddled

hue *noun*
hues

huff

hug *verb*
hugs
hugging
hugged

hug *noun*
hugs

huge *adjective*
huger
hugest
hugely

hugeness

hulk *noun*
hulks

hulking

hull *noun*
hulls

hullabaloo *noun*
hullabaloos

hullo

hum *verb*
hums
humming
hummed

hum *noun*
hums

human *adjective* and *noun*
humans

humane *adjective*
humanely

humanitarian

humanity *noun*
humanities

humble *adjective*
humbler
humblest
humbly

humid

humidity

humiliate *verb*
humiliates
humiliating
humiliated

humiliation

humility

hummingbird *noun*
hummingbirds

humorous *adjective*
humorously

humour *noun*

humour *verb*
humours
humouring
humoured

hump *noun*
humps

hump *verb*
humps
humping
humped

humpback

humus

hunch *verb*
hunches
hunching
hunched

hunch *noun*
hunches

hunchback *noun*
hunchbacks

hunchbacked

hundred *noun*
hundreds

hundredth

hundredweight noun
hundredweights

hung see **hang**

hunger

hungry adjective
hungrier
hungriest
hungrily

hunk noun
hunks

hunt verb
hunts
hunting
hunted

hunt noun
hunts

hunter noun
hunters

hurdle noun
hurdles

hurdler noun
hurdlers

hurdling

hurl verb
hurls
hurling
hurled

hurrah or **hurray**

hurricane noun
hurricanes

hurriedly

hurry verb
hurries
hurrying
hurried

hurry noun
hurries

hurt verb
hurts
hurting
hurt

hurt noun

hurtle verb
hurtles
hurtling
hurtled

husband noun
husbands

hush verb
hushes
hushing
hushed

hush noun

husk noun
husks

huskiness

husky adjective
huskier
huskiest
huskily

husky noun
huskies

hustle verb
hustles
hustling
hustled

hutch noun
hutches

hyacinth noun
hyacinths

hybrid noun
hybrids

hydrangea noun
hydrangeas

hydrant noun
hydrants

hydraulic adjective
hydraulically

hydroelectric

hydrofoil noun
hydrofoils

hydrogen

hydrophobia

hyena noun
hyenas

hygiene

hygienic adjective
hygienically

hymn noun
hymns

hyperactive

hypermarket noun
hypermarkets

hyphen noun
hyphens

hyphenated

hypnosis

hypnotism

hypnotist

hypnotize verb
hypnotizes
hypnotizing
hypnotized

hypocrisy

hypocrite noun
hypocrites

hypocritical
adjective
hypocritically

hypodermic

hypotenuse noun
hypotenuses

hypothermia

hypothesis noun
hypotheses

hypothetical
adjective
hypothetically

hysteria

hysterical adjective
hysterically

hysterics plural noun

Ii

-i
Most nouns ending in -i, e.g. **ski**, **taxi**, have plurals ending in -is, e.g. **skis**, **taxis**.

-ible
See the note at -able.

-ic and -ically
Most adjectives ending in -ic have adverbs ending in -ically, e.g. **heroic** - **heroically**, **scientific** - **scientifically**. An exception is **public**, which has an adverb - **publicly**.

ice noun
  ices
ice verb
  ices
  icing
  iced
iceberg noun
  icebergs
ice cream noun
  ice creams
icicle noun
  icicles
icing
icon noun
  icons
icy adjective
  icier
  iciest
  icily

I'd verb
idea noun
  ideas
ideal adjective
  ideally
ideal noun
  ideals
identical adjective
  identically
identification
identify verb
  identifies
  identifying
  identified
identity noun
  identities
idiocy noun
  idiocies
idiom noun
  idioms
idiomatic
idiot noun
  idiots
idiotic adjective
  idiotically
★ **idle** adjective
  idler
  idlest
  idly
idle verb
  idles
  idling
  idled
☆ **idol** noun
  idols
idolatry
idolize verb
  idolizes
  idolizing
  idolized

-ie-
See the note at -ei-.

igloo noun
  igloos
igneous
ignite verb
  ignites
  igniting
  ignited
ignition
ignorance
ignorant
ignore verb
  ignores
  ignoring
  ignored
I'll verb
ill
illegal adjective
  illegally
illegible adjective
  illegibly
illegitimate
illiteracy
illiterate
illness noun
  illnesses
illogical adjective
  illogically
illuminate verb
  illuminates
  illuminating
  illuminated
illumination noun
  illuminations
illusion noun
  illusions

★ **Idle** means 'lazy'. ! **idol**.
☆ An **idol** is someone people admire. ! **idle**.

illustrate verb
illustrates
illustrating
illustrated

illustration noun
illustrations

illustrious

I'm verb

image noun
images

imagery

imaginable

imaginary

imagination noun
imaginations

imaginative adjective
imaginatively

imagine verb
imagines
imagining
imagined

★ **imam** noun
imams

imbecile noun
imbeciles

imitate verb
imitates
imitating
imitated

imitation noun
imitations

imitator noun
imitators

immature

immaturity

immediate adjective
immediately

immense adjective
immensely

immensity

immerse verb
immerses
immersing
immersed

immersion

immigrant noun
immigrants

immigrate verb
immigrates
immigrating
immigrated

immigration

immobile

immobility

immobilize verb
immobilizes
immobilizing
immobilized

immoral adjective
immorally

immorality

immortal

immortality

immune

immunity noun
immunities

immunization

immunize verb
immunizes
immunizing
immunized

imp noun
imps

impish

impact noun
impacts

impair verb
impairs
impairing
impaired

impale verb
impales
impaling
impaled

impartial adjective
impartially

impartiality

impassable

impatience

impatient adjective
impatiently

impede verb
impedes
impeding
impeded

imperative

imperceptible adjective
imperceptibly

imperfect adjective
imperfectly

imperfection noun
imperfections

imperial

impersonal adjective
impersonally

impersonate verb
impersonates
impersonating
impersonated

impersonation noun
impersonations

impersonator noun
impersonators

impertinence

impertinent adjective
impertinently

★ A Muslim religious leader.

implement *verb*
implements
implementing
implemented

implement *noun*
implements

implication *noun*
implications

implore *verb*
implores
imploring
implored

imply *verb*
implies
implying
implied

impolite *adjective*
impolitely

import *verb*
imports
importing
imported

import *noun*
imports

importance

important *adjective*
importantly

importer *noun*
importers

impose *verb*
imposes
imposing
imposed

imposition *noun*
impositions

impossibility

impossible *adjective*
impossibly

impostor *noun*
impostors

impracticable

impractical

impress *verb*
impresses
impressing
impressed

impression *noun*
impressions

impressive *adjective*
impressively

imprison *verb*
imprisons
imprisoning
imprisoned

imprisonment

improbability

improbable *adjective*
improbably

impromptu

improper *adjective*
improperly

impropriety *noun*
improprieties

improve *verb*
improves
improving
improved

improvement *noun*
improvements

improvisation *noun*
improvisations

improvise *verb*
improvises
improvising
improvised

impudence

impudent *adjective*
impudently

impulse *noun*
impulses

impulsive *adjective*
impulsively

impure

impurity *adjective*
impurities

in-
in- makes words with the meaning 'not', e.g. *inedible, infertile.* There is a fixed number of these, and you cannot freely add *in-* as you can with *un-. in-* changes to *il-* or *im-* before certain sounds, e.g. **illogical, impossible.**

inability

inaccessible

inaccuracy *noun*
inaccuracies

inaccurate *adjective*
inaccurately

inaction

inactive

inactivity

inadequacy

inadequate *adjective*
inadequately

inanimate

inappropriate
adjective
inappropriately

inattention

inattentive

inaudible *adjective*
inaudibly

incapable

incapacity

incendiary

incense *noun*

incense verb
incenses
incensing
incensed

incentive noun
incentives

incessant adjective
incessantly

inch noun
inches

incident noun
incidents

incidental adjective
incidentally

incinerator noun
incinerators

inclination noun
inclinations

incline verb
inclines
inclining
inclined

incline noun
inclines

include verb
includes
including
included

inclusion

inclusive

income noun
incomes

incompatible

incompetence

incompetent
adjective
incompetently

incomplete adjective
incompletely

incomprehensible
adjective
incomprehensibly

incongruity

incongruous
adjective
incongruously

inconsiderate
adjective
inconsiderately

inconsistency noun
inconsistencies

inconsistent
adjective
inconsistently

inconspicuous
adjective
inconspicuously

inconvenience

inconvenient
adjective
inconveniently

incorporate verb
incorporates
incorporating
incorporated

incorporation

incorrect adjective
incorrectly

increase verb
increases
increasing
increased

increase noun
increases

increasingly

incredible adjective
incredibly

incredulity

incredulous

incubate verb
incubates
incubating
incubated

incubation

incubator noun
incubators

indebted

indecency

indecent adjective
indecently

indeed

indefinite adjective
indefinitely

indelible adjective
indelibly

indent verb
indents
indenting
indented

indentation

independence

independent
adjective
independently

index noun
indexes

Indian adjective and
noun
Indians

indicate verb
indicates
indicating
indicated

indication noun
indications

indicative

indicator noun
indicators

indifference

indifferent adjective
indifferently

indigestible

indigestion

in

indignant *adjective*
indignantly
indignation
indigo
indirect *adjective*
indirectly
indispensable
adjective
indispensably
indistinct *adjective*
indistinctly
indistinguishable
individual *adjective*
individually
individual *noun*
individuals
individuality
indoctrinate *verb*
indoctrinates
indoctrinating
indoctrinated
indoctrination
indoor *adjective*
indoors *adverb*
induce *verb*
induces
inducing
induced
inducement *noun*
inducements
indulge *verb*
indulges
indulging
indulged
indulgence *noun*
indulgences
indulgent
industrial
industrialist *noun*
industrialists

industrialization
industrialize *verb*
industrializes
industrializing
industrialized
industrious *adjective*
industriously
industry *noun*
industries
ineffective *adjective*
ineffectively
ineffectual *adjective*
ineffectually
inefficiency *noun*
inefficiencies
inefficient *adjective*
inefficiently
inequality *noun*
inequalities
inert
inertia
inevitability
inevitable *adjective*
inevitably
inexhaustible
inexpensive *adjective*
inexpensively
inexperience
inexperienced
inexplicable *adjective*
inexplicably
infallibility
infallible *adjective*
infallibly
infamous *adjective*
infamously
infamy
infancy
infant *noun*
infants

infantile
infantry
infect *verb*
infects
infecting
infected
infection *noun*
infections
infectious *adjective*
infectiously
infer *verb*
infers
inferring
inferred
inference *noun*
inferences
inferior *adjective* and
noun
inferiors
inferiority
infernal *adjective*
infernally
inferno *noun*
infernos
infested
infiltrate *verb*
infiltrates
infiltrating
infiltrated
infiltration
infinite *adjective*
infinitely
infinitive *noun*
infinitives
infinity
infirm
infirmary *noun*
infirmaries
infirmity

inflame verb
 inflames
 inflaming
 inflamed
inflammable
inflammation noun
 inflammations
inflammatory
inflatable
inflate verb
 inflates
 inflating
 inflated
inflation
inflect verb
 inflects
 inflecting
 inflected
inflection noun
 inflections
inflexibility
inflexible adjective
 inflexibly
inflict verb
 inflicts
 inflicting
 inflicted
influence verb
 influences
 influencing
 influenced
influence noun
 influences
influential adjective
 influentially
influenza
inform verb
 informs
 informing
 informed
informal adjective
 informally

informality
informant noun
 informants
information
informative
informed
informer noun
 informers
infrequency
infrequent adjective
 infrequently
infuriate verb
 infuriates
 infuriating
 infuriated

-ing
-ing makes present
participles and nouns,
e.g. hunt - hunting.
You normally drop an
e at the end, e.g.
change - changing,
smoke - smoking. An
exception is ageing.
Words ending in a
consonant following a
single vowel double
the consonant, e.g.
run - running.

ingenious adjective
 ingeniously
ingenuity
ingot noun
 ingots
ingrained
ingredient noun
 ingredients
inhabit verb
 inhabits
 inhabiting
 inhabited

inhabitant noun
 inhabitants
inhale verb
 inhales
 inhaling
 inhaled
inhaler noun
 inhalers
inherent adjective
 inherently
inherit verb
 inherits
 inheriting
 inherited
inheritance
inhibited
inhospitable adjective
 inhospitably
inhuman
inhumanity
initial adjective
 initially
initial noun
 initials
initiate verb
 initiates
 initiating
 initiated
initiation
initiative noun
 initiatives
inject verb
 injects
 injecting
 injected
injection noun
 injections
injure verb
 injures
 injuring
 injured

in

injurious adjective
injuriously

injury noun
injuries

injustice noun
injustices

ink noun
inks

inkling noun
inklings

inky adjective
inkier
inkiest

inland

inlet noun
inlets

inn noun
inns

innkeeper noun
innkeepers

inner

innermost

innings noun
innings

innocence

innocent adjective
innocently

innocuous adjective
innocuously

innovation noun
innovations

innovative

innovator noun
innovators

innumerable

inoculate verb
inoculates
inoculating
inoculated

inoculation

input verb
inputs
inputting
input

input noun
inputs

inquest noun
inquests

inquire verb
inquires
inquiring
inquired

★ **inquiry** noun
inquiries

inquisitive adjective
inquisitively

insane adjective
insanely

insanitary

insanity

inscribe verb
inscribes
inscribing
inscribed

inscription noun
inscriptions

insect noun
insects

insecticide noun
insecticides

insecure adjective
insecurely

insecurity

insensitive adjective
insensitively

insensitivity

inseparable
adjective
inseparably

insert verb
inserts
inserting
inserted

insertion noun
insertions

inshore adjective and
adverb

inside noun
insides

inside adverb,
adjective, and
preposition

insight noun
insights

insignificance

insignificant
adjective
insignificantly

insincere adjective
insincerely

insincerity

insist verb
insists
insisting
insisted

insistence

insistent adjective
insistently

insolence

insolent adjective
insolently

insolubility

insoluble adjective
insolubly

insomnia

inspect verb
inspects
inspecting
inspected

. . . .

★ An **inquiry** is an official investigation. ! **enquiry.**

inspection noun
inspections
inspector noun
inspectors
inspiration
inspire verb
inspires
inspiring
inspired
install verb
installs
installing
installed
installation noun
installations
instalment noun
instalments
instance noun
instances
instant adjective
instantly
instant noun
instants
instantaneous
adjective
instantaneously
instead
instep noun
insteps
instinct noun
instincts
instinctive adjective
instinctively
institute verb
institutes
instituting
instituted
institute noun
institutes
institution noun
institutions

instruct verb
instructs
instructing
instructed
instruction noun
instructions
instrument noun
instruments
instrumental
insufficient adjective
insufficiently
insulate verb
insulates
insulating
insulated
insulation
insulin
insult verb
insults
insulting
insulted
insult noun
insults
insurance
insure verb
insures
insuring
insured
intact
intake noun
intakes
integer noun
integers
integral adjective
integrally
integrate verb
integrates
integrating
integrated
integration
integrity

intellect noun
intellects
intellectual adjective
intellectually
intellectual noun
intellectuals
intelligence
intelligent adjective
intelligently
intelligibility
intelligible adjective
intelligibly
intend verb
intends
intending
intended
intense adjective
intensely
intensification
intensify verb
intensifies
intensifying
intensified
intensity noun
intensities
intensive adjective
intensively
intent adjective
intently
intent noun
intents
intention noun
intentions
intentional adjective
intentionally
interact verb
interacts
interacting
interacted
interaction

interactive

intercept *verb*
  intercepts
  intercepting
  intercepted

interception

interchange *noun*
  interchanges

interchangeable
  adjective
  interchangeably

intercom *noun*
  intercoms

intercourse

interest *verb*
  interests
  interesting
  interested

interest *noun*
  interests

interface *noun*
  interfaces

interfere *verb*
  interferes
  interfering
  interfered

interference

interior *noun*
  interiors

interjection *noun*
  interjections

interlock *verb*
  interlocks
  interlocking
  interlocked

interlude *noun*
  interludes

intermediate

interminable
  adjective
  interminably

intermission *noun*
  intermissions

intermittent
  adjective
  intermittently

intern *verb*
  interns
  interning
  interned

internal *adjective*
  internally

international
  adjective
  internationally

internee

internment

internet

interplanetary

interpret *verb*
  interprets
  interpreting
  interpreted

interpretation *noun*
  interpretations

interpreter *noun*
  interpreters

interrogate *verb*
  interrogates
  interrogating
  interrogated

interrogation

interrogative

interrogator *noun*
  interrogators

interrupt *verb*
  interrupts
  interrupting
  interrupted

interruption *noun*
  interruptions

intersect *verb*
  intersects
  intersecting
  intersected

intersection *noun*
  intersections

interval *noun*
  intervals

intervene *verb*
  intervenes
  intervening
  intervened

intervention *noun*
  interventions

interview *noun*
  interviews

interview *verb*
  interviews
  interviewing
  interviewed

interviewer *noun*
  interviewers

intestinal

intestine

intimacy

intimate *adjective*
  intimately

intimate *verb*
  intimates
  intimating
  intimated

intimation *noun*
  intimations

intimidate *verb*
  intimidates
  intimidating
  intimidated

intimidation

into *preposition*

intolerable *adjective*
  intolerably

intolerance

intolerant adjective
intolerantly

intonation noun
intonations

intoxicate verb
intoxicates
intoxicating
intoxicated

intoxication

intransitive

intrepid adjective
intrepidly

intricacy noun
intricacies

intricate adjective
intricately

intrigue verb
intrigues
intriguing
intrigued

introduce verb
introduces
introducing
introduced

introduction noun
introductions

introductory

intrude verb
intrudes
intruding
intruded

intruder noun
intruders

intrusion noun
intrusions

intrusive adjective
intrusively

intuition

intuitive adjective
intuitively

Inuit noun
Inuit or Inuits

inundate verb
inundates
inundating
inundated

inundation noun
inundations

invade verb
invades
invading
invaded

invader noun
invaders

invalid noun
invalids

invalid adjective
invalidly

invaluable

invariable adjective
invariably

invasion noun
invasions

invent verb
invents
inventing
invented

invention noun
inventions

inventive adjective
inventively

inventor noun
inventors

inverse noun and
adjective
inversely

inversion noun
inversions

invert verb
inverts
inverting
inverted

invertebrate noun
invertebrates

invest verb
invests
investing
invested

investigate verb
investigates
investigating
investigated

investigation noun
investigations

investigator noun
investigators

investiture noun
investitures

investment noun
investments

investor noun
investors

invigilate verb
invigilates
invigilating
invigilated

invigilation

invigilator noun
invigilators

invigorate verb
invigorates
invigorating
invigorated

invincible

invisibility

invisible adjective
invisibly

invitation noun
invitations

invite verb
invites
inviting
invited

invoice *noun*
invoices

involuntary

involve *verb*
involves
involving
involved

involvement

inward *adjective*
inwardly

inwards *adverb*

iodine

ion *noun*
ions

iris *noun*
irises

iron *noun*
irons

iron *verb*
irons
ironing
ironed

ironic *adjective*
ironically

ironmonger *noun*
ironmongers

ironmongery

irony *noun*
ironies

irrational *adjective*
irrationally

irregular *adjective*
irregularly

irregularity *noun*
irregularities

irrelevance

irrelevant *adjective*
irrelevantly

irresistible *adjective*
irresistibly

irresponsible *adjective*
irresponsibly

irresponsibility

irreverence

irreverent *adjective*
irreverently

irrigate *verb*
irrigates
irrigating
irrigated

irrigation

irritability

irritable *adjective*
irritably

irritant

irritate *verb*
irritates
irritating
irritated

irritation *noun*
irritations

-ish
-ish makes words meaning 'rather' or 'fairly', e.g. soft - softish. You normally drop an e at the end, e.g. blue - bluish. Words ending in a consonant following a single vowel double the consonant, e.g. **fat - fattish.**

Islam

Islamic

island *noun*
islands

islander *noun*
islanders

★ **isle** *noun*
isles

isn't *verb*

isobar *noun*
isobars

isolate *verb*
isolates
isolating
isolated

isolation

isosceles *adjective*

isotope *noun*
isotopes

issue *verb*
issues
issuing
issued

issue *noun*
issues

isthmus *noun*
isthmuses

italics

itch *verb*
itches
itching
itched

itch *noun*
itches

itchy *adjective*
itchier
itchiest

item *noun*
items

itinerary *noun*
itineraries

it'll *verb*

☆ **its**

○ **it's** *verb*

itself

★ An isle is a small island. ! aisle.
☆ You use its in e.g. the cat licked its paw. ! it's.
○ You use it's in it's (= it is) raining and it's (= it has) been raining. ! its.

I've *verb*

ivory *adjective* and *noun*
  ivories

ivy

> **-ize and -ise**
> You can use *-ize* or *-ise* at the end of many verbs, e.g. **realize** or **realise**, **privatize** or **privatise**. This book prefers *-ize*, but some words have to be spelt *-ise*, e.g. **advertise**, **exercise**, **supervise**. Check each spelling if you are not sure.

Jj

jab *verb*
  jabs
  jabbing
  jabbed

jab *noun*
  jabs

jabber *verb*
  jabbers
  jabbering
  jabbered

jack *noun*
  jacks

jack *verb*
  jacks
  jacking
  jacked

jackal *noun*
  jackals

jackass *noun*
  jackasses

jackdaw *noun*
  jackdaws

jacket *noun*
  jackets

jack-in-the-box *noun*
  jack-in-the-boxes

jackknife *verb*
  jackknifes
  jackknifing
  jackknifed

jackpot *noun*
  jackpots

jacuzzi *noun*
  jacuzzis

jade

jaded

jagged

jaguar *noun*
  jaguars

jail *noun*
  jails

jail *verb*
  jails
  jailing
  jailed

jailer *noun*
  jailers

★ **Jain** *noun*
  Jains

jam *noun*
  jams

jam *verb*
  jams
  jamming
  jammed

jamboree *noun*
  jamborees

jammy *adjective*
  jammier
  jammiest

jangle *verb*
  jangles
  jangling
  jangled

January *noun*
  Januaries

jar *noun*
  jars

jar *verb*
  jars
  jarring
  jarred

jaundice

jaunt *noun*
  jaunts

jauntiness

jaunty *adjective*
  jauntier
  jauntiest
  jauntily

javelin *noun*
  javelins

jaw *noun*
  jaws

jay *noun*
  jays

jazz

jazzy *adjective*
  jazzier
  jazziest

jealous *adjective*
  jealously

jealousy

jeans

Jeep *noun*
  Jeeps

★ A member of an Indian religion.

jeer verb
jeers
jeering
jeered
jellied
jelly noun
jellies
jellyfish noun
jellyfish
jerk verb
jerks
jerking
jerked
jerk noun
jerks
jerky adjective
jerkier
jerkiest
jerkily
jersey noun
jerseys
jest verb
jests
jesting
jested
jest noun
jests
jester noun
jesters
jet noun
jets
jet verb
jets
jetting
jetted
jet-propelled
jetty noun
jetties
Jew noun
Jews

jewel noun
jewels
jewelled
jeweller noun
jewellers
jewellery
Jewish
jib noun
jibs
jiffy noun
jiffies
jig noun
jigs
jig verb
jigs
jigging
jigged
jigsaw noun
jigsaws
jingle verb
jingles
jingling
jingled
jingle noun
jingles
job noun
jobs
jobcentre noun
jobcentres
jockey noun
jockeys
jodhpurs plural noun
jog verb
jogs
jogging
jogged
jogger noun
joggers
jogtrot noun
jogtrots

join verb
joins
joining
joined
join noun
joins
joiner noun
joiners
joinery
joint noun
joints
joint adjective
jointly
joist noun
joists
jojoba
joke verb
jokes
joking
joked
joke noun
jokes
joker noun
jokers
jollity
jolly adjective
jollier
jolliest
jolly adverb
jolly verb
jollies
jollying
jollied
jolt verb
jolts
jolting
jolted
jolt noun
jolts

jostle verb
jostles
jostling
jostled

jot verb
jots
jotting
jotted

jot noun
jots

jotter noun
jotters

joule noun
joules

journal noun
journals

journalism

journalist noun
journalists

journey noun
journeys

journey verb
journeys
journeying
journeyed

joust verb
jousts
jousting
jousted

jovial adjective
jovially

joviality

joy noun
joys

joyful adjective
joyfully

joyous adjective
joyously

joyride noun
joyrides

joystick noun
joysticks

jubilant adjective
jubilantly

jubilation

jubilee noun
jubilees

Judaism

judge verb
judges
judging
judged

judge noun
judges

judgement noun
judgements

judicial adjective
judicially

judicious adjective
judiciously

judo

jug noun
jugs

juggernaut noun
juggernauts

juggle verb
juggles
juggling
juggled

juggler noun
jugglers

★ **juice** noun
juices

juicy adjective
juicier
juiciest

jukebox noun
jukeboxes

July noun
Julys

jumble verb
jumbles
jumbling
jumbled

jumble noun

jumbo jet noun
jumbo jets

jump verb
jumps
jumping
jumped

jump noun
jumps

jumper noun
jumpers

jumpy adjective
jumpier
jumpiest

junction noun
junctions

June noun
Junes

jungle noun
jungles

jungly adjective
junglier
jungliest

junior adjective and noun
juniors

junk noun
junks

junket noun
junkets

juror noun
jurors

jury noun
juries

just adjective
justly

- -

★ **Juice** is the liquid from fruit. ! **deuce.**

just adverb
justice noun
  justices
justifiable adjective
  justifiably
justification
justify verb
  justifies
  justifying
  justified
jut verb
  juts
  jutting
  jutted
juvenile

Kk

kaleidoscope noun
  kaleidoscopes
kangaroo noun
  kangaroos
karaoke
karate
kayak noun
  kayaks
kebab noun
  kebabs
keel noun
  keels
keel verb
  keels
  keeling
  keeled
keen adjective
  keener
  keenest
  keenly

keenness
keep verb
  keeps
  keeping
  kept
keep noun
  keeps
keeper noun
  keepers
keg noun
  kegs
kennel noun
  kennels
kept see **keep**
★ **kerb** noun
  kerbs
kerbstone noun
  kerbstones
☆ **kernel** noun
  kernels
kestrel noun
  kestrels
ketchup
kettle noun
  kettles
kettledrum noun
  kettledrums
⊙ **key** noun
  keys
keyboard noun
  keyboards
keyhole noun
  keyholes
keynote noun
  keynotes
khaki
kibbutz noun
  kibbutzim

kick verb
  kicks
  kicking
  kicked
kick noun
  kicks
kick-off noun
  kick-offs
kid noun
  kids
kid verb
  kids
  kidding
  kidded
kidnap verb
  kidnaps
  kidnapping
  kidnapped
kidnapper noun
  kidnappers
kidney noun
  kidneys
kill verb
  kills
  killing
  killed
killer noun
  killers
kiln noun
  kilns
kilo noun
  kilos
kilogram noun
  kilograms
kilometre noun
  kilometres
kilowatt noun
  kilowatts
kilt noun
  kilts
kin

- -

★ A kerb is the edge of a pavement. ! **curb**.
☆ Kernel is part of a nut. ! **colonel**.
⊙ A key is a device for opening a lock. ! **quay**.

kind adjective
kinder
kindest
kindly

kind noun
kinds

kindergarten noun
kindergartens

kind-hearted

kindle verb
kindles
kindling
kindled

kindliness

kindling

kindly adjective
kindlier
kindliest

kindness

kinetic

king noun
kings

kingdom noun
kingdoms

kingfisher noun
kingfishers

kingly

kink noun
kinks

kinky adjective
kinkier
kinkiest

kiosk noun
kiosks

kipper noun
kippers

kiss verb
kisses
kissing
kissed

kiss noun
kisses

kit noun
kits

kitchen noun
kitchens

kite noun
kites

kitten noun
kittens

kitty noun
kitties

kiwi noun
kiwis

knack

knapsack noun
knapsacks

knave noun
knaves

★ **knead** verb
kneads
kneading
kneaded

knee noun
knees

kneecap noun
kneecaps

kneel verb
kneels
kneeling
knelt

☆ **knew** see **know**

knickers plural noun

knife noun
knives

knife verb
knifes
knifing
knifed

○ **knight** noun
knights

knight verb
knights
knighting
knighted

knighthood noun
knighthoods

knit verb
knits
knitting
knitted

knives see **knife**

knob noun
knobs

knobbly adjective
knobblier
knobbliest

knock verb
knocks
knocking
knocked

knock noun
knocks

knocker noun
knockers

knockout noun
knockouts

knot noun
knots

knot verb
knots
knotting
knotted

knotty adjective
knottier
knottiest

know verb
knows
knowing
knew
known

. . . .

★ To **knead** is to work a mixture into a dough. ! **need**.
☆ **Knew** is the past tense of know. ! **new**.
○ A **knight** is a soldier in old times. ! **night**.

know-all *noun*
know-alls
know-how
knowing *adjective*
knowingly
knowledge
knowledgeable *adjective*
knowledgeably
knuckle *noun*
knuckles
koala *noun*
koalas
kookaburra *noun*
kookaburras
Koran
kosher
kung fu

Ll

label *noun*
labels
label *verb*
labels
labelling
labelled
laboratory *noun*
laboratories
laborious *adjective*
laboriously
labour *noun*
labours
labourer *noun*
labourers
Labrador *noun*
Labradors

laburnum *noun*
laburnums
labyrinth *noun*
labyrinths
lace *noun*
laces
lace *verb*
laces
lacing
laced
lack *verb*
lacks
lacking
lacked
lack *noun*
lacquer
lacrosse
lad *noun*
lads
ladder *noun*
ladders
laden
ladle *noun*
ladles
lady *noun*
ladies
ladybird *noun*
ladybirds
ladylike
ladyship *noun*
ladyships
lag *verb*
lags
lagging
lagged
lager *noun*
lagers
lagoon *noun*
lagoons
laid see **lay**

lain see **lie**
lair *noun*
lairs
lake *noun*
lakes
lama *noun*
lamas
lamb *noun*
lambs
lame *adjective*
lamer
lamest
lamely
lameness
lament *verb*
laments
lamenting
lamented
lament *noun*
laments
lamentation *noun*
lamentations
laminated
lamp *noun*
lamps
lamp-post *noun*
lamp-posts
lampshade *noun*
lampshades
lance *noun*
lances
lance corporal *noun*
lance corporals
land *noun*
lands
land *verb*
lands
landing
landed

landing noun
landings

landlady noun
landladies

landlord noun
landlords

landmark noun
landmarks

landowner noun
landowners

landscape noun
landscapes

landslide noun
landslides

lane noun
lanes

language noun
languages

lankiness

lanky adjective
lankier
lankiest

lantern noun
lanterns

lap verb
laps
lapping
lapped

lap noun
laps

lapel noun
lapels

lapse verb
lapses
lapsing
lapsed

lapse noun
lapses

laptop noun
laptops

lapwing noun
lapwings

larch noun
larches

lard

larder noun
larders

large adjective
larger
largest
largely

largeness

lark noun
larks

lark verb
larks
larking
larked

larva noun
larvae

lasagne noun
lasagnes

laser noun
lasers

lash verb
lashes
lashing
lashed

lash noun
lashes

lass noun
lasses

lasso noun
lassos

lasso verb
lassoes
lassoing
lassoed

last adjective and
adverb
lastly

last verb
lasts
lasting
lasted

last noun

latch noun
latches

late adjective and
adverb
later
latest

lately

lateness

latent

lateral adjective
laterally

lathe noun
lathes

lather noun
lathers

Latin

latitude noun
latitudes

latter adjective
latterly

lattice noun
lattices

laugh verb
laughs
laughing
laughed

laugh noun
laughs

laughable adjective
laughably

laughter

launch verb
launches
launching
launched

launch *noun*
launches
launder *verb*
launders
laundering
laundered
launderette *noun*
launderettes
laundry *noun*
laundries
laurel *noun*
laurels
lava
lavatory *noun*
lavatories
lavender
lavish *adjective*
lavishly
law *noun*
laws
lawcourt *noun*
lawcourts
lawful *adjective*
lawfully
lawless *adjective*
lawlessly
lawn *noun*
lawns
lawnmower *noun*
lawnmowers
lawsuit *noun*
lawsuits
lawyer *noun*
lawyers
lax *adjective*
laxly
laxative *noun*
laxatives
lay *verb*
lays
laying
laid

lay see lie
layabout *noun*
layabouts
layer *noun*
layers
layman *noun*
laymen
layout *noun*
layouts
laze *verb*
lazes
lazing
lazed
laziness
lazy *adjective*
lazier
laziest
lazily
lead *verb*
leads
leading
led
★ **lead** *noun*
leads
leader *noun*
leaders
leadership
leaf *noun*
leaves
leaflet *noun*
leaflets
leafy *adjective*
leafier
leafiest
league *noun*
leagues
leak *verb*
leaks
leaking
leaked

☆ **leak** *noun*
leaks
leakage *noun*
leakages
leaky *adjective*
leakier
leakiest
lean *verb*
leans
leaning
leaned *or* leant
lean *adjective*
leaner
leanest
leap *verb*
leaps
leaping
leapt
leaped
leap *noun*
leaps
leapfrog
leap year *noun*
leap years
learn *verb*
learns
learning
learnt *or* learned
◉ **learned** *adjective*
learner *noun*
learners
lease *noun*
leases
leash *noun*
leashes
least *adjective* and *noun*
leather *noun*
leathers

★ A **lead** (pronounced *leed*) is a cord for leading a dog. **Lead** (pronounced *led*) is a metal.
☆ A **leak** is a hole or crack that liquid or gas can get through. ! **leek**.
◉ Pronounced *ler-nid*.

leathery

leave *verb*
 leaves
 leaving
 left

leave *noun*

leaves see **leaf**

lectern *noun*
 lecterns

lecture *verb*
 lectures
 lecturing
 lectured

lecture *noun*
 lectures

lecturer *noun*
 lecturers

led see **lead**

ledge *noun*
 ledges

lee

★ **leek** *noun*
 leeks

leer *verb*
 leers
 leering
 leered

leeward

left *adjective* and
 noun

left see **leave**

left-handed

leftovers *plural noun*

leg *noun*
 legs

legacy *noun*
 legacies

legal *adjective*
 legally

legality

legalize *verb*
 legalizes
 legalizing
 legalized

legend *noun*
 legends

legendary

legibility

legible *adjective*
 legibly

legion *noun*
 legions

legislate *verb*
 legislates
 legislating
 legislated

legislation

legislator *noun*
 legislators

legitimacy

legitimate *adjective*
 legitimately

leisure

leisurely

lemon *noun*
 lemons

lemonade *noun*
 lemonades

lend *verb*
 lends
 lending
 lent

length *noun*
 lengths

lengthen *verb*
 lengthens
 lengthening
 lengthened

lengthways *adverb*
lengthwise *adverb*
lengthy *adjective*
 lengthier
 lengthiest
 lengthily

lenience

lenient *adjective*
 leniently

lens *noun*
 lenses

☆ **Lent**

lent see **lend**

lentil *noun*
 lentils

leopard *noun*
 leopards

leotard *noun*
 leotards

leper *noun*
 lepers

leprosy

less

○ **lessen** *verb*
 lessens
 lessening
 lessened

lesser

✻ **lesson** *noun*
 lessons

lest *conjunction*

let *verb*
 lets
 letting
 let

. . . .

★ A **leek** is a vegetable. ! **leak**.
☆ **Lent** is the Christian time of fasting. ! **lent**.
○ To **lessen** something is to make it less. **lesson**.
✻ A **lesson** is a period of learning. ! **lessen**.

-let
-let makes nouns meaning 'a small version of', e.g. booklet, piglet. It also makes words for pieces of jewellery, e.g. anklet (worn on the ankle), bracelet (from a French word bras meaning 'arm')

lethal adjective
lethally

let's verb

letter noun
letters

letter box noun
letter boxes

lettering

lettuce noun
lettuces

leukaemia

level verb
levels
levelling
levelled

level adjective and noun
levels

lever noun
levers

leverage

liability noun
liabilities

liable

liar noun
liars

liberal adjective
liberally

liberate verb
liberates
liberating
liberated

liberation

liberty noun
liberties

librarian noun
librarians

librarianship

library noun
libraries

licence noun
licences

license verb
licenses
licensing
licensed

lichen noun
lichens

lick verb
licks
licking
licked

lick noun
licks

lid noun
lids

★ **lie** verb
lies
lying
lay
lain

☆ **lie** verb
lies
lying
lied

lie noun
lies

lieutenant noun
lieutenants

life noun
lives

lifebelt noun
lifebelts

lifeboat noun
lifeboats

life cycle noun
life cycles

lifeguard noun
lifeguards

lifeless adjective
lifelessly

lifelike

lifelong

lifestyle noun
lifestyles

lifetime noun
lifetimes

lift verb
lifts
lifting
lifted

lift noun
lifts

lift-off noun
lift-offs

light adjective
lighter
lightest
lightly

light verb
lights
lighting
lit or lighted

light noun
lights

lighten verb
lightens
lightening
lightened

★ As in to lie on the bed.
☆ Meaning 'to say something untrue'.

lighter noun
lighters

lighthouse noun
lighthouses

lighting

lightning

lightweight

like verb
likes
liking
liked

like preposition

likeable

likely adjective
likelier
likeliest

liken verb
likens
likening
likened

likeness noun
likenesses

likewise

liking noun
likings

lilac noun
lilacs

lily noun
lilies

limb noun
limbs

limber verb
limbers
limbering
limbered

lime noun
limes

limelight

limerick noun
limericks

limestone

limit noun
limits

limit verb
limits
limiting
limited

limitation noun
limitations

limited

limitless

limp adjective
limper
limpest
limply

limp verb
limps
limping
limped

limp noun
limps

limpet noun
limpets

line noun
lines

line verb
lines
lining
lined

linen

liner noun
liners

linesman noun
linesmen

-ling
-ling makes words for
small things, e.g.
duckling.

linger verb
lingers
lingering
lingered

lingerie

linguist noun
linguists

linguistic

linguistics

lining noun
linings

link verb
links
linking
linked

link noun
links

lino

linoleum

lint

lion noun
lions

lioness noun
lionesses

lip noun
lips

lip-read verb
lip-reads
lip-reading
lip-read

lipstick noun
lipsticks

liquid adjective and
noun
liquids

liquidizer noun
liquidizers

liquor noun
liquors

liquorice

lisp noun
lisps

lisp verb
lisps
lisping
lisped

list noun
lists

list verb
lists
listing
listed

listen verb
listens
listening
listened

listener noun
listeners

listless adjective
listlessly

lit see light

literacy

literal adjective
literally

literary

literate

literature

litmus

litre noun
litres

litter noun
litters

litter verb
litters
littering
littered

★ **little** adjective and
adverb
less
least

live verb
lives
living
lived

live adjective

livelihood noun
livelihoods

liveliness

lively adjective
livelier
liveliest

liver noun
livers

livery noun
liveries

lives see life

livestock

livid

living noun
livings

lizard noun
lizards

llama noun
llamas

load verb
loads
loading
loaded

load noun
loads

loaf noun
loaves

loaf verb
loafs
loafing
loafed

loafer noun
loafers

loam

loamy adjective
loamier
loamiest

☆ **loan** noun
loans

loan verb
loans
loaning
loaned

○ **loath** adjective

✳ **loathe** verb
loathes
loathing
loathed

loathsome

loaves see loaf

lob verb
lobs
lobbing
lobbed

lobby noun
lobbies

lobby verb
lobbies
lobbying
lobbied

lobe noun
lobes

lobster noun
lobsters

local adjective
locally

local noun
locals

locality noun
localities

locate verb
locates
locating
located

★ You can also use **littler** and **littlest** when you are talking about size.
☆ A **loan** is a thing that is lent to someone. ! **lone**.
○ **Loath** means 'unwilling'. ! **loathe**.
✳ To **loathe** is to dislike very much. ! **loath**.

location noun
locations

★ **loch** noun
lochs

☆ **lock** noun
locks

lock verb
locks
locking
locked

locker noun
lockers

locket noun
lockets

locomotive noun
locomotives

locust noun
locusts

lodge noun
lodges

lodge verb
lodges
lodging
lodged

lodger noun
lodgers

lodgings plural noun

loft noun
lofts

lofty adjective
loftier
loftiest
loftily

log noun
logs

log verb
logs
logging
logged

logarithm noun
logarithms

logbook noun
logbooks

logic

logical adjective
logically

logo noun
logos

-logy
-logy makes words for
subjects of study, e.g.
archaeology (= the
study of ancient
remains). Most of
these words end in
-ology, but an
important exception
is **genealogy**. Some
words have plurals,
e.g. **genealogies**.

loiter verb
loiters
loitering
loitered

loiterer noun
loiterers

loll verb
lolls
lolling
lolled

lollipop noun
lollipops

lolly noun
lollies

○ **lone**

loneliness

lonely adjective
lonelier
loneliest

long adjective and
adverb
longer
longest

long verb
longs
longing
longed

longitude noun
longitudes

longitudinal
adjective
longitudinally

loo noun
loos

look verb
looks
looking
looked

look noun
looks

lookout noun
lookouts

loom noun
looms

loom verb
looms
looming
loomed

loop noun
loops

loop verb
loops
looping
looped

loophole noun
loopholes

loose adjective
looser
loosest
loosely

loose verb
looses
loosing
loosed

. . . .

★ A **loch** is a lake in Scotland. ! **lock**.
☆ A **lock** is a mechanism for keeping something closed. ! **loch**.
○ **Lone** means 'alone'. ! **loan**.

lo - lu

loosen verb
loosens
loosening
loosened

looseness

loot verb
loots
looting
looted

loot noun

looter noun
looters

lopsided

lord noun
lords

lordly

lordship

lorry noun
lorries

lose verb
loses
losing
lost

loser noun
losers

loss noun
losses

lot noun
lots

lotion noun
lotions

lottery noun
lotteries

lotto

loud adjective
louder
loudest
loudly

loudness

loudspeaker noun
loudspeakers

lounge noun
lounges

lounge verb
lounges
lounging
lounged

louse noun
lice

lousy adjective
lousier
lousiest
lousily

lout noun
louts

lovable adjective
lovably

love verb
loves
loving
loved

love noun
loves

loveliness

lovely adjective
lovelier
loveliest

lover noun
lovers

loving adjective
lovingly

low adjective
lower
lowest

low verb
lows
lowing
lowed

lower verb
lowers
lowering
lowered

lowland adjective

lowlands plural
nouns

lowlander noun
lowlanders

lowliness

lowly adjective
lowlier
lowliest

lowness

loyal adjective
loyally

loyalty noun
loyalties

lozenge noun
lozenges

lubricant noun
lubricants

lubricate verb
lubricates
lubricating
lubricated

lubrication

lucid adjective
lucidly

lucidity

luck

lucky adjective
luckier
luckiest
luckily

ludicrous adjective
ludicrously

ludo

lug verb
lugs
lugging
lugged

luggage

lukewarm

lull verb
lulls
lulling
lulled

lull noun
lulls

lullaby noun
lullabies

lumber verb
lumbers
lumbering
lumbered

lumber noun

lumberjack noun
lumberjacks

luminosity

luminous

lump noun
lumps

lump verb
lumps
lumping
lumped

lumpy adjective
lumpier
lumpiest

lunacy noun
lunacies

lunar

lunatic noun
lunatics

lunch noun
lunches

lung noun
lungs

lunge verb
lunges
lunging or lungeing
lunged

lupin noun
lupins

lurch verb
lurches
lurching
lurched

lurch noun
lurches

lure verb
lures
luring
lured

lurk verb
lurks
lurking
lurked

luscious adjective
lusciously

lush adjective
lusher
lushest
lushly

lushness

lust noun
lusts

lustful adjective
lustfully

lustre noun
lustres

lustrous

lute noun
lutes

luxury noun
luxuries

luxurious adjective
luxuriously

Lycra

-ly
-ly makes adverbs from adjectives, e.g. **slow - slowly**. When the adjective ends in -y following a consonant, you change the y to i, e.g. **happy - happily**. -ly is also used to make some adjectives, e.g. **lovely**, and some words that are adjectives and adverbs, e.g. **kindly, hourly**.

lying see lie

lynch verb
lynches
lynching
lynched

lyre noun
lyres

lyric noun
lyrics

lyrical adjective
lyrically

lyrics plural noun

Mm

ma noun
mas

mac noun
macs

macabre

macaroni

machine noun
machines

machinery

mackerel *noun*
  mackerel

mackintosh *noun*
  mackintoshes

mad *adjective*
  madder
  maddest
  madly

madam

madden *verb*
  maddens
  maddening
  maddened

★ made see make

madman *noun*
  madmen

madness

magazine *noun*
  magazines

maggot *noun*
  maggots

magic *noun* and
  adjective

magical *adjective*
  magically

magician *noun*
  magicians

magistrate *noun*
  magistrates

magma

magnesium

magnet *noun*
  magnets

magnetism

magnetic *adjective*
  magnetically

magnetize *verb*
  magnetizes
  magnetizing
  magnetized

magnificent
  adjective
  magnificently

magnificence

magnification

magnifier

magnify *verb*
  magnifies
  magnifying
  magnified

magnitude *noun*
  magnitudes

magnolia *noun*
  magnolias

magpie *noun*
  magpies

mahogany

☆ maid *noun*
  maids

maiden *noun*
  maidens

○ mail *noun*

mail *verb*
  mails
  mailing
  mailed

maim *verb*
  maims
  maiming
  maimed

✳ main *adjective*
  mainly

mainland

mainly

mains *plural noun*

maintain *verb*
  maintains
  maintaining
  maintained

maintenance

maisonette *noun*
  maisonettes

maize

majestic *adjective*
  majestically

majesty *noun*
  majesties

major *adjective*

major *noun*
  majors

majority *noun*
  majorities

make *verb*
  makes
  making
  made

make *noun*
  makes

make-believe

maker *noun*
  makers

make-up

maladjusted

malaria

✱ male *adjective* and
  noun
  males

malevolence

malevolent *adjective*
  malevolently

malice

malicious *adjective*
  maliciously

mallet *noun*
  mallets

malnourished

malnutrition

malt

malted

. . . .

★ You use made in e.g. *I made a cake.* ! maid.
☆ A maid is a female servant. ! made.
○ Mail is letters and parcels sent by post. ! male.
✳ Main means 'most important'. ! mane.
✱ A male is a man or an animal of the same gender as a man. ! mail.

mammal *noun*
mammals

mammoth *adjective and noun*
mammoths

man *noun*
men

man *verb*
mans
manning
manned

manage *verb*
manages
managing
managed

manageable

management

manager *noun*
managers

manageress *noun*
manageresses

★ **mane** *noun*
manes

manger *noun*
mangers

mangle *verb*
mangles
mangling
mangled

mango *noun*
mangoes

manhandle *verb*
manhandles
manhandling
manhandled

manhole *noun*
manholes

mania *noun*
manias

maniac *noun*
maniacs

manic *adjective*
manically

manifesto *noun*
manifestos

manipulate *verb*
manipulates
manipulating
manipulated

manipulation

manipulator

mankind

manliness

manly *adjective*
manlier
manliest

☆ **manner** *noun*
manners

manoeuvrable

manoeuvre *verb*
manoeuvres
manoeuvring
manoeuvred

manoeuvre *noun*
manoeuvres

man-of-war *noun*
men-of-war

⊙ **manor** *noun*
manors

mansion *noun*
mansions

manslaughter

mantelpiece *noun*
mantelpieces

mantle *noun*
mantles

manual *adjective*
manually

manual *noun*
manuals

manufacture *verb*
manufactures
manufacturing
manufactured

manufacture *noun*

manufacturer *noun*
manufacturers

manure

manuscript *noun*
manuscripts

Manx

many *adjective and noun*
more
most

Maori *noun*
Maoris

map *noun*
maps

map *verb*
maps
mapping
mapped

maple *noun*
maples

mar *verb*
mars
marring
marred

marathon *noun*
marathons

marauder *noun*
marauders

marauding

marble *noun*
marbles

March *noun*
Marches

★ A mane is the long piece of hair on a horse or lion. ! main.
☆ You use manner in e.g. *a friendly manner*. ! manor.
⊙ A manor is a big house in the country. ! manner.

march *verb*
marches
marching
marched

march *noun*
marches

marcher *noun*
marchers

★ **mare** *noun*
mares

margarine

margin *noun*
margins

marginal *adjective*
marginally

marigold *noun*
marigolds

marijuana

marina *noun*
marinas

marine *adjective* and *noun*
marines

mariner *noun*
mariners

marionette *noun*
marionettes

mark *verb*
marks
marking
marked

mark *noun*
marks

market *noun*
markets

market *verb*
markets
marketing
marketed

marksman *noun*
marksmen

marksmanship

marmalade

maroon *verb*
maroons
marooning
marooned

maroon *adjective* and *noun*

marquee *noun*
marquees

marriage *noun*
marriages

marrow *noun*
marrows

marry *verb*
marries
marrying
married

marsh *noun*
marshes

marshal *noun*
marshals

marshmallow *noun*
marshmallows

marshy *adjective*
marshier
marshiest

marsupial *noun*
marsupials

martial

Martian *noun*
Martians

martin *noun*
martins

martyr *noun*
martyrs

martyrdom

marvel *verb*
marvels
marvelling
marvelled

marvel *noun*
marvels

marvellous *adjective*
marvellously

Marxism

Marxist

marzipan

mascot *noun*
mascots

masculine

masculinity

mash *verb*
mashes
mashing
mashed

mash *noun*

mask *noun*
masks

mask *verb*
masks
masking
masked

☆ **Mason** *noun*
Masons

○ **mason** *noun*
masons

masonry

✳ **Mass** *noun*
Masses

mass *noun*
masses

mass *verb*
masses
massing
massed

massacre *verb*
massacres
massacring
massacred

. . . .

★ A mare is a female horse. ! mayor.
☆ You use a capital M when you mean a member of the Freemasons.
○ Use a small m when you mean someone who builds with stone.
✳ Use a capital M when you mean the Roman Catholic service.

massacre noun
massacres

massage verb
massages
massaging
massaged

massage noun

massive adjective
massively

mast noun
masts

master noun
masters

master verb
masters
mastering
mastered

masterly

mastermind noun
masterminds

masterpiece noun
masterpieces

mastery

★ **mat** noun
mats

matador noun
matadors

match verb
matches
matching
matched

match noun
matches

mate noun
mates

mate verb
mates
mating
mated

material noun
materials

materialistic

maternal adjective
maternally

maternity

mathematical adjective
mathematically

mathematician noun
mathematicians

mathematics

maths

matinée noun
matinées

matrimonial

matrimony

matrix noun
matrices

matron noun
matrons

☆ **matt**

matted

matter verb
matters
mattering
mattered

matter noun
matters

matting

mattress noun
mattresses

mature

maturity

mauve

maximum adjective
and noun
maxima or
maximums

May noun
Mays

may verb
might

may

maybe

May Day

◘ **mayday** noun
maydays

mayonnaise

✳ **mayor** noun
mayors

mayoress noun
mayoresses

maypole noun
maypoles

maze noun
mazes

meadow noun
meadows

meagre

meal noun
meals

mean adjective
meaner
meanest
meanly

mean verb
means
meaning
meant

meander verb
meanders
meandering
meandered

meaning noun
meanings

meaningful adjective
meaningfully

meaningless adjective
meaninglessly

. . . .

★ A mat is a covering for a floor. ! matt.
☆ Matt means 'not shiny'. ! mat.
◘ An international radio signal.
✳ You use mayor in e.g. the Mayor of London. ! mare.

meanness
means plural noun
meantime
meanwhile
measles plural noun
measly adjective
 measlier
 measliest
measure verb
 measures
 measuring
 measured
measure noun
 measures
measurement noun
 measurements
★ **meat** noun
 meats
meaty adjective
 meatier
 meatiest
mechanic noun
 mechanics
mechanical
 adjective
 mechanically
mechanics
mechanism noun
 mechanisms
medal noun
 medals
medallist noun
 medallists
meddle verb
 meddles
 meddling
 meddled
meddler noun
 meddlers
meddlesome

media plural noun
median noun
 medians
medical adjective
 medically
medicine noun
 medicines
medicinal
medieval
mediocre
mediocrity
meditate verb
 meditates
 meditating
 meditated
meditation
Mediterranean
medium adjective
medium noun
 media or mediums
meek adjective
 meeker
 meekest
 meekly
meekness
☆ **meet** verb
 meets
 meeting
 met
meeting noun
 meetings
megaphone noun
 megaphones
melancholy
mellow adjective
 mellower
 mellowest
melodious adjective
 melodiously

melodrama noun
 melodramas
melodramatic
 adjective
 melodramatically
melody noun
 melodies
melodic
melon noun
 melons
melt verb
 melts
 melting
 melted
member noun
 members
membership
**Member of
Parliament** noun
 Members of
Parliament
membrane noun
 membranes
memoirs plural noun
memorable
 adjective
 memorably
memorial noun
 memorials
memorize verb
 memorizes
 memorizing
 memorized
memory noun
 memories
men see man
menace verb
 menaces
 menacing
 menaced

. . . .

★ **Meat** is the flesh of an animal. **! meet.**
☆ People **meet** when they come together. **! meat.**

menace noun
menaces

menagerie noun
menageries

mend verb
mends
mending
mended

mender noun
menders

menstrual

menstruation

> **-ment**
> -ment makes nouns
> from adjectives e.g.
> contentment. There
> is a fixed number of
> these, and you cannot
> freely add -ment as
> you can with -ness.
> When the adjective
> ends in -y following a
> consonant, you
> change the y to i, e.g.
> merry - merriment.

mental adjective
mentally

mention verb
mentions
mentioning
mentioned

mention noun
mentions

menu noun
menus

mercenary adjective
and noun
mercenaries

merchandise

merchant noun
merchants

merciful adjective
mercifully

merciless adjective
mercilessly

mercury

mercy noun
mercies

mere adjective

mere noun
meres

merely adverb

merge verb
merges
merging
merged

merger noun
mergers

meridian noun
meridians

meringue noun
meringues

merit noun
merits

merit verb
merits
meriting
merited

mermaid noun
mermaids

merriment

merry adjective
merrier
merriest
merrily

merry-go-round
noun
merry-go-rounds

mesh noun
meshes

mess noun
messes

mess verb
messes
messing
messed

message noun
messages

messenger noun
messengers

Messiah

messiness

messy adjective
messier
messiest
messily

met see meet

★ **metal** noun
metals

metallic

metallurgical

metallurgist

metallurgy

metamorphosis
noun
metamorphoses

metaphor noun
metaphors

metaphorical
adjective
metaphorically

meteor noun
meteors

meteoric

meteorite noun
meteorites

meteorological

meteorologist

meteorology

☆ **meter** noun
meters

methane

. . . .
★ Metal is a hard substance used to make things. ! **mettle**.
☆ A meter is a device that shows how much of something has been used. ! **metre**.

method *noun*
methods

methodical *adjective*
methodically

Methodist *noun*
Methodists

meths

methylated spirit

meticulous *adjective*
meticulously

★ **metre** *noun*
metres

metric *adjective*

metrical *adjective*
metrically

metronome *noun*
metronomes

☆ **mettle**

mew *verb*
mews
mewing
mewed

miaow *verb*
miaows
miaowing
miaowed

mice see mouse

micro-
micro- makes words
meaning 'small', e.g.
microwave. When the
word begins with a
vowel you add a
hyphen, e.g.
micro-organism.

microbe *noun*
microbes

microchip *noun*
microchips

microcomputer
noun
microcomputers

microfilm *noun*
microfilms

microphone *noun*
microphones

microprocessor
noun
microprocessors

microscope *noun*
microscopes

microscopic
adjective
microscopically

microwave *noun*
microwaves

microwave *verb*
microwaves
microwaving
microwaved

⊙ **mid**

midday

middle *noun*
middles

Middle Ages

Middle East

midge *noun*
midges

midget *noun*
midgets

midland *adjective*

midnight

midst

midsummer

midway

midwife *noun*
midwives

midwifery

✳ **might** *noun*

might see may
mightiness

mighty *adjective*
mightier
mightiest
mightily

migraine *noun*
migraines

migrant *noun*
migrants

migrate *verb*
migrates
migrating
migrated

migration *noun*
migrations

migratory

mike *noun*
mikes

mild *adjective*
milder
mildest
mildly

mildness

mile *noun*
miles

mileage *noun*
mileages

milestone *noun*
milestones

militancy

militant

militarism

militaristic

military

milk *noun*

milk *verb*
milks
milking
milked

. . . .

★ A metre is a unit of length. ! meter.
☆ As in to be on your mettle. ! metal.
⊙ You use a hyphen, e.g. mid-August.
✳ **Might** means 'force' or 'strength'. ! mite.

milkman noun
milkmen

milky adjective
milkier
milkiest

Milky Way

mill noun
mills

mill verb
mills
milling
milled

millennium noun
millenniums

miller noun
millers

millet

milligram noun
milligrams

millilitre noun
millilitres

millimetre noun
millimetres

million noun
millions

millionth

millionaire noun
millionaires

millstone noun
millstones

milometer noun
milometers

mime verb
mimes
miming
mimed

mime noun
mimes

mimic verb
mimics
mimicking
mimicked

mimic noun
mimics

mimicry

minaret noun
minarets

mince verb
minces
mincing
minced

mince noun

mincemeat

mincer noun
mincers

mind noun
minds

mind verb
minds
minding
minded

mindless adjective
mindlessly

mine adjective

mine verb
mines
mining
mined

mine noun
mines

minefield noun
minefields

miner noun
miners

mineral noun
minerals

mingle verb
mingles
mingling
mingled

mini-
mini- makes words
meaning 'small', e.g.
miniskirt. You do not
normally need a
hyphen.

mingy adjective
mingier
mingiest

miniature adjective
and noun
miniatures

minibus noun
minibuses

minim noun
minims

minimal adjective
minimally

minimize verb
minimizes
minimizing
minimized

minimum adjective
and noun
minima or minimums

minister noun
ministers

ministry noun
ministries

mink noun
minks

minnow noun
minnows

minor adjective and
noun
minors

minority noun
minorities

minstrel noun
minstrels

mi

mint noun
mints
mint verb
mints
minting
minted
minus preposition
minute adjective
minutely
minute noun
minutes
miracle noun
miracles
miraculous adjective
miraculously
mirage noun
mirages
mirror noun
mirrors
mirth
misbehave verb
misbehaves
misbehaving
misbehaved
misbehaviour
miscarriage noun
miscarriages
miscellaneous
miscellany noun
miscellanies
mischief
mischievous
adjective
mischievously
miser noun
misers
miserable adjective
miserably
miserly
misery noun
miseries

misfire verb
misfires
misfiring
misfired
misfit noun
misfits
misfortune noun
misfortunes
mishap noun
mishaps
misjudge verb
misjudges
misjudging
misjudged
mislay verb
mislays
mislaying
mislaid
mislead verb
misleads
misleading
misled
misprint noun
misprints
miss verb
misses
missing
missed
miss noun
misses
missile noun
missiles
missing
mission noun
missions
missionary noun
missionaries
misspell verb
misspells
misspelling
misspelt or
misspelled

★ **mist** noun
mists
mistake noun
mistakes
mistake verb
mistakes
mistaking
mistook
mistaken
mister
mistiness
mistletoe
mistreat verb
mistreats
mistreating
mistreated
mistreatment
mistress noun
mistresses
mistrust verb
mistrusts
mistrusting
mistrusted
misty adjective
mistier
mistiest
mistily
misunderstand verb
misunderstands
misunderstanding
misunderstood
misunderstanding
noun
misunderstandings
misuse verb
misuses
misusing
misused
misuse noun
misuses

- -

★ **Mist** is damp air that is difficult to see through. ! **missed.**

★ **mite** *noun*
mites

mitre *noun*
mitres

mitten *noun*
mittens

mix *verb*
mixes
mixing
mixed

mixer *noun*
mixers

mixture *noun*
mixtures

mix-up *noun*
mix-ups

moan *verb*
moans
moaning
moaned

moan *noun*
moans

moat *noun*
moats

mob *noun*
mobs

mob *verb*
mobs
mobbing
mobbed

mobile *adjective* and
noun
mobiles

mobility

mobilization

mobilize *verb*
mobilizes
mobilizing
mobilized

moccasin *noun*
moccasins

mock *adjective*

mock *verb*
mocks
mocking
mocked

mockery *noun*
mockeries

mock-up *noun*
mock-ups

mode *noun*
modes

model *noun*
models

model *verb*
models
modelling
modelled

modem *noun*
modems

moderate *adjective*
moderately

moderate *verb*
moderates
moderating
moderated

moderation

modern

modernity

modernization

modernize *verb*
modernizes
modernizing
modernized

modest *adjective*
modestly

modesty

modification *noun*
modifications

modify *verb*
modifies
modifying
modified

module *noun*
modules

moist *adjective*
moister
moistest

moisture

moisten *verb*
moistens
moistening
moistened

molar *noun*
molars

mole *noun*
moles

molecular

molecule *noun*
molecules

molehill *noun*
molehills

molest *verb*
molests
molesting
molested

mollusc *noun*
molluscs

molten

moment *noun*
moments

momentary
adjective
momentarily

momentous
adjective
momentously

momentum

monarch *noun*
monarchs

monarchy *noun*
monarchies

• •

★ A mite is a tiny insect. ! might.

monastery noun
monasteries

monastic

Monday noun
Mondays

money

mongoose noun
mongooses

mongrel noun
mongrels

monitor verb
monitors
monitoring
monitored

monitor noun
monitors

monk noun
monks

monkey noun
monkeys

monogram noun
monograms

monologue noun
monologues

monopolize verb
monopolizes
monopolizing
monopolized

monopoly noun
monopolies

monorail noun
monorails

monotonous
adjective
monotonously

monotony

monsoon noun
monsoons

monster noun
monsters

monstrosity noun
monstrosities

monstrous adjective
monstrously

month noun
months

monthly adjective
and adverb

monument noun
monuments

monumental
adjective
monumentally

moo verb
moos
mooing
mooed

mood noun
moods

moodiness

moody adjective
moodier
moodiest
moodily

moon noun
moons

moonlight

moonlit

★ **moor** verb
moors
mooring
moored

☆ **moor** noun
moors

moorhen noun
moorhens

mooring noun
moorings

◎ **moose** noun
moose

mop noun
mops

mop verb
mops
mopping
mopped

mope verb
mopes
moping
moped

moped noun
mopeds

moraine noun
moraines

moral adjective
morally

moral noun
morals

morale

morality

morals plural noun

morbid adjective
morbidly

✳ **more** adjective,
adverb, and noun

moreover

Mormon noun
Mormons

morning noun
mornings

moron noun
morons

moronic adjective
moronically

morose adjective
morosely

morphine

morris dance noun
morris dances

Morse code

. . . .

★ To moor a boat is to tie it up. ! more.
☆ A moor is an area of rough land. ! more.
◎ A moose is an American elk. ! mouse, mousse.
✳ You use more in e.g. I'd like more to eat. ! moor.

morsel *noun*
morsels
mortal *adjective*
mortally
mortality
mortar
mortgage *noun*
mortgages
mortuary *noun*
mortuaries
mosaic *noun*
mosaics
mosque *noun*
mosques
mosquito *noun*
mosquitoes
moss *noun*
mosses
mossy *adjective*
mossier
mossiest
most *adjective,*
adverb, and noun
mostly *adverb*
motel *noun*
motels
moth *noun*
moths
mother *noun*
mothers
motherhood
mother-in-law *noun*
mothers-in-law
motherly
motion *noun*
motions
motionless
motivate *verb*
motivates
motivating
motivated

motive *noun*
motives
motor *noun*
motors
motorbike *noun*
motorbikes
motor boat *noun*
motor boats
motor car *noun*
motor cars
motorcycle *noun*
motorcycles
motorcyclist *noun*
motorcyclists
motorist *noun*
motorists
motorway *noun*
motorways
mottled
motto *noun*
mottoes
mould *verb*
moulds
moulding
moulded
mould *noun*
moulds
mouldy *adjective*
mouldier
mouldiest
moult *verb*
moults
moulting
moulted
mound *noun*
mounds
mount *verb*
mounts
mounting
mounted

mount *noun*
mounts
mountain *noun*
mountains
mountaineer *noun*
mountaineers
mountaineering
mountainous
mourn *verb*
mourns
mourning
mourned
mourner *noun*
mourners
mournful *adjective*
mournfully
★ **mouse** *noun*
mice
mousetrap *noun*
mousetraps
☆ **mousse** *noun*
mousses
moustache *noun*
moustaches
mousy *adjective*
mousier
mousiest
mouth *noun*
mouths
mouthful *noun*
mouthfuls
mouthpiece *noun*
mouthpieces
movable
move *verb*
moves
moving
moved
move *noun*
moves

★ A **mouse** is a small animal. ! **moose, mousse.**
☆ A **mousse** is a creamy pudding. ! **moose, mouse.**

movement noun
movements

movie noun
movies

mow verb
mows
mowing
mowed
mown

mower noun
mowers

much adjective,
adverb, and noun

muck noun

muck verb
mucks
mucking
mucked

mucky adjective
muckier
muckiest

mud

muddle verb
muddles
muddling
muddled

muddle noun
muddles

muddler noun
muddlers

muddy adjective
muddier
muddiest

mudguard noun
mudguards

muesli

★ **muezzin** noun
muezzins

muffle verb
muffles
muffling
muffled

mug noun
mugs

mug verb
mugs
mugging
mugged

mugger noun
muggers

muggy adjective
muggier
muggiest

mule noun
mules

multi-
multi- makes words
with the meaning
'many', e.g.
multicultural. You do
not normally need a
hyphen.

multiple adjective
and noun
multiples

multiplication

multiply verb
multiplies
multiplying
multiplied

multiracial

multitude noun
multitudes

mumble verb
mumbles
mumbling
mumbled

mummify verb
mummifies
mummifying
mummified

mummy noun
mummies

mumps

munch verb
munches
munching
munched

mundane

municipal

mural noun
murals

murder verb
murders
murdering
murdered

murder noun
murders

murderer noun
murderers

murderous adjective
murderously

murky adjective
murkier
murkiest

murmur verb
murmurs
murmuring
murmured

murmur noun
murmurs

☆ **muscle** noun
muscles

muscle verb
muscles
muscling
muscled

muscular

museum noun
museums

mushroom noun
mushrooms

★ A man who calls Muslims to prayer.
☆ A muscle is a part of the body. ! mussel.

mushroom verb
mushrooms
mushrooming
mushroomed

music

musical adjective
musically

musical noun
musicals

musician noun
musicians

musket noun
muskets

musketeer noun
musketeers

Muslim noun
Muslims

muslin

★ **mussel** noun
mussels

must

mustard

muster verb
musters
mustering
mustered

mustiness

musty adjective
mustier
mustiest

mutation noun
mutations

mute adjective
mutely

mute noun
mutes

muted

mutilate verb
mutilates
mutilating
mutilated

mutilation

mutineer noun
mutineers

mutiny noun
mutinies

mutinous adjective
mutinously

mutiny verb
mutinies
mutinying
mutinied

mutter verb
mutters
muttering
muttered

mutton

mutual adjective
mutually

muzzle verb
muzzles
muzzling
muzzled

muzzle noun
muzzles

myself

mysterious adjective
mysteriously

mystery noun
mysteries

mystification

mystify verb
mystifies
mystifying
mystified

myth noun
myths

mythical

mythological
adjective

mythology

Nn

nab verb
nabs
nabbing
nabbed

nag verb
nags
nagging
nagged

nag noun
nags

nail noun
nails

nail verb
nails
nailing
nailed

naive adjective
naively

naivety

naked

nakedness

name noun
names

name verb
names
naming
named

nameless

namely

nanny noun
nannies

nap noun
naps

napkin noun
napkins

. . . .

★ A **mussel** is a shellfish. **!** **muscle**.

nappy noun
nappies

narcissus noun
narcissi

narcotic noun
narcotics

narrate verb
narrates
narrating
narrated

narration noun
narrations

narrative noun
narratives

narrator noun
narrators

narrow adjective
narrower
narrowest
narrowly

nasal adjective
nasally

nastiness

nasturtium noun
nasturtiums

nasty adjective
nastier
nastiest
nastily

nation noun
nations

national adjective
nationally

nationalism

nationalist

nationality noun
nationalities

nationalization

nationalize verb
nationalizes
nationalizing
nationalized

nationwide adjective

native adjective and noun
natives

Native American noun
Native Americans

nativity noun
nativities

natural adjective
naturally

natural noun
naturals

naturalist noun
naturalists

naturalization

naturalize verb
naturalizes
naturalizing
naturalized

nature noun
natures

naughtiness

naughty adjective
naughtier
naughtiest
naughtily

nausea

nautical

★ **naval** adjective

nave noun
naves

☆ **navel** noun
navels

navigable

navigate verb
navigates
navigating
navigated

navigation

navigator noun
navigators

navy noun
navies

Nazi noun
Nazis

Nazism

near adjective and adverb
nearer
nearest

near preposition

near verb
nears
nearing
neared

nearby

nearly

neat adjective
neater
neatest
neatly

neatness

necessarily

necessary

necessity noun
necessities

neck noun
necks

neckerchief noun
neckerchiefs

necklace noun
necklaces

nectar

nectarine noun
nectarines

need verb
needs
needing
needed

★ **Naval** means 'to do with a navy'. ! navel.
☆ A **navel** is a small hollow in your stomach. ! naval.

* **need** *noun*
  needs
needle *noun*
  needles
needless *adjective*
  needlessly
needlework
needy *adjective*
  needier
  neediest
negative *adjective*
  negatively
negative *noun*
  negatives
neglect *verb*
  neglects
  neglecting
  neglected
neglect *noun*
neglectful *adjective*
  neglectfully
negligence
negligent *adjective*
  negligently
negligible *adjective*
  negligibly
negotiate *verb*
  negotiates
  negotiating
  negotiated
negotiation *noun*
  negotiations
negotiator *noun*
  negotiators
neigh *verb*
  neighs
  neighing
  neighed
neigh *noun*
  neighs

neighbour *noun*
  neighbours
neighbouring
neighbourhood
  noun
  neighbourhoods
neighbourly
neither *adjective and
  conjunction*
neon
nephew *noun*
  nephews
nerve *noun*
  nerves
nerve-racking
nervous *adjective*
  nervously
nervousness

-ness
-ness makes nouns
from adjectives, e.g.
soft - softness. When
the adjective ends in
-y following a
consonant, you
change the y to i, e.g.
lively - liveliness.

nest *noun*
  nests
nest *verb*
  nests
  nesting
  nested
nestle *verb*
  nestles
  nestling
  nestled
nestling *noun*
  nestlings

net *noun*
  nets
net *adjective*
netball
nettle *noun*
  nettles
network *noun*
  networks
neuter *adjective*
neuter *verb*
  neuters
  neutering
  neutered
neutral *adjective*
  neutrally
neutrality
neutralize *verb*
  neutralizes
  neutralizing
  neutralized
neutron *noun*
  neutrons
never
nevertheless
  conjunction
☆ **new** *adjective*
  newer
  newest
  newly
newcomer *noun*
  newcomers
newness
news
newsagent *noun*
  newsagents
newsletter *noun*
  newsletters
newspaper *noun*
  newspapers

★ To **need** is to require something. ! **knead.**
☆ You use **new** in e.g *She has a new bike.* ! **knew.**

newt noun
newts

New Testament

newton noun
newtons

next adjective and adverb

next door

nib noun
nibs

nibble verb
nibbles
nibbling
nibbled

nice adjective
nicer
nicest
nicely

niceness

nicety noun
niceties

nick verb
nicks
nicking
nicked

nick noun
nicks

nickel noun
nickels

nickname noun
nicknames

nicotine

niece noun
nieces

★ **night** noun
nights

nightclub noun
nightclubs

nightdress noun
nightdresses

nightfall

nightingale noun
nightingales

nightly

nightmare noun
nightmares

nightmarish

nil

nimble adjective
nimbler
nimblest
nimbly

nine noun
nines

nineteen noun
nineteens

nineteenth

ninetieth

ninety noun
nineties

ninth adjective
ninthly

nip verb
nips
nipping
nipped

nip noun
nips

nipple noun
nipples

nippy adjective
nippier
nippiest

nit noun
nits

nitrate noun
nitrates

nitric acid

nitrogen

nitty-gritty

nitwit noun
nitwits

nobility

noble adjective
nobler
noblest
nobly

noble noun
nobles

nobleman noun
noblemen

noblewoman noun
noblewomen

nobody noun
nobodies

nocturnal adjective
nocturnally

nod verb
nods
nodding
nodded

noise noun
noises

noiseless adjective
noiselessly

noisiness

noisy adjective
noisier
noisiest
noisily

nomad noun
nomads

nomadic

no man's land

nominate verb
nominates
nominating
nominated

nomination noun
nominations

★ **Night** is the opposite of day. ! **knight.**

-nomy

-nomy makes words for subjects of study, e.g. **astronomy** (= the study of the stars). Most of these words end in **-onomy**.

★ **none**

non-

non- makes words meaning 'not', e.g. **non-existent, non-smoker.** You use a hyphen to make these words. When an un- word has a special meaning, e.g. **unprofessional,** you can use non- to make a word without the special meaning, e.g. **non-professional.**

non-existent

non-fiction

non-flammable

nonsense

nonsensical adjective
  nonsensically

non-stop

noodle

noon

no one

noose noun
  nooses

normal adjective
  normally

normality

north adjective and
  adverb

☆ **north** noun

north-east noun and
  adjective

northerly adjective
  and noun
  northerlies

northern

northerner noun
  northerners

northward adjective
  and adverb

northwards adverb

north-west

nose noun
  noses

nose verb
  noses
  nosing
  nosed

nosedive verb
  nosedives
  nosediving
  nosedived

nosedive noun
  nosedives

nosiness

nostalgia

nostalgic adjective
  nostalgically

nostril noun
  nostrils

nosy adjective
  nosier
  nosiest
  nosily

notable adjective
  notably

notch noun
  notches

note noun
  notes

note verb
  notes
  noting
  noted

notebook noun
  notebooks

notepaper

nothing

notice verb
  notices
  noticing
  noticed

notice noun
  notices

noticeable adjective
  noticeably

noticeboard noun
  noticeboards

notion noun
  notions

notoriety

notorious adjective
  notoriously

nougat

nought noun
  noughts

noun noun
  nouns

nourish verb
  nourishes
  nourishing
  nourished

nourishment

novel adjective

novel noun
  novels

novelist noun
  novelists

novelty noun
  novelties

★ You use **none** in e.g. none of us went. ! **nun.**

☆ You use a capital N in **the North,** when you mean a particular region.

November noun
Novembers

novice noun
novices

nowadays

nowhere

nozzle noun
nozzles

nuclear

nucleus noun
nuclei

nude adjective and
noun
nudes

nudge verb
nudges
nudging
nudged

nudist noun
nudists

nudity

nugget noun
nuggets

nuisance noun
nuisances

numb adjective
numbly

number noun
numbers

number verb
numbers
numbering
numbered

numbness

numeracy

numeral noun
numerals

numerate

numerator noun
numerators

numerical adjective
numerically

numerous

★ **nun** noun
nuns

nunnery noun
nunneries

nurse noun
nurses

nurse verb
nurses
nursing
nursed

nursery noun
nurseries

nurture verb
nurtures
nurturing
nurtured

nut noun
nuts

nutcrackers plural
noun

nutmeg noun
nutmegs

nutrient noun
nutrients

nutrition

nutritional adjective
nutritionally

nutritious

nutshell noun
nutshells

nutty adjective
nuttier
nuttiest

nuzzle verb
nuzzles
nuzzling
nuzzled

nylon adjective and
noun
nylons

nymph noun
nymphs

Oo

-o
Most nouns ending in
-o, e.g. **hero, potato,**
have plurals ending in
-oes, e.g. **heroes,
potatoes,** but a few
end in -os. The most
important are **kilos,
photos, pianos,
radios, ratios, solos,
videos, zeros.** Verbs
ending in -o usually
have the forms -oes
and -oed, e.g. **video -
videoes - videoed.**

oak noun
oaks

☆ **oar** noun
oars

oarsman noun
oarsmen

oarswoman noun
oarswomen

oasis noun
oases

oath noun
oaths

oatmeal

oats plural noun

. . . .

★ A **nun** is a member of a convent. ! **none.**
☆ An **oar** is used for rowing a boat. ! **or, ore.**

obedience
obedient *adjective*
  obediently
obey *verb*
  obeys
  obeying
  obeyed
obituary *noun*
  obituaries
object *noun*
  objects
object *verb*
  objects
  objecting
  objected
objection *noun*
  objections
objectionable
objective *adjective*
  objectively
objective *noun*
  objectives
objector *noun*
  objectors
obligation *noun*
  obligations
obligatory
oblige *verb*
  obliges
  obliging
  obliged
oblique *adjective*
  obliquely
oblong *adjective* and
  noun
  oblongs
oboe *noun*
  oboes
oboist *noun*
  oboists

obscene *adjective*
  obscenely
obscenity *noun*
  obscenities
obscure *adjective*
  obscurer
  obscurest
  obscurely
obscurity
observance *noun*
  observances
observant *adjective*
  observantly
observation *noun*
  observations
observatory *noun*
  observatories
observe *verb*
  observes
  observing
  observed
observer *noun*
  observers
obsessed
obsession *noun*
  obsessions
obsolete
obstacle *noun*
  obstacles
obstinacy
obstinate *adjective*
  obstinately
obstruct *verb*
  obstructs
  obstructing
  obstructed
obstruction *noun*
  obstructions
obstructive *adjective*
  obstructively

obtain *verb*
  obtains
  obtaining
  obtained
obtainable
obtuse *adjective*
  obtuser
  obtusest
  obtusely
obvious *adjective*
  obviously
occasion *noun*
  occasions
occasional *adjective*
  occasionally
occupant *noun*
  occupants
occupation *noun*
  occupations
occupy *verb*
  occupies
  occupying
  occupied
occur *verb*
  occurs
  occurring
  occurred
occurrence *noun*
  occurrences
ocean *noun*
  oceans
o'clock
octagon *noun*
  octagons
octagonal *adjective*
  octagonally
octave *noun*
  octaves
October *noun*
  Octobers

octopus noun
octopuses

odd adjective
odder
oddest
oddly

oddity noun
oddities

oddments plural noun

oddness

odds plural noun

odour noun
odours

odorous

oesophagus noun
oesophagi or
oesophaguses

★ **of**

☆ **off**

offence noun
offences

offend verb
offends
offending
offended

offender noun
offenders

offensive adjective
offensively

offer verb
offers
offering
offered

offer noun
offers

offhand

office noun
offices

officer noun
officers

official adjective
officially

official noun
officials

officious adjective
officiously

off-licence noun
off-licences

offset verb
offsets
offsetting
offset

offshore adjective
and adverb

offside

offspring noun
offspring

often

ogre noun
ogres

ohm noun
ohms

oil noun
oils

oil verb
oils
oiling
oiled

oilfield noun
oilfields

oilskin noun
oilskins

oil well noun
oil wells

oily adjective
oilier
oiliest

ointment noun
ointments

old adjective
older
oldest

Old Testament

olive noun
olives

Olympic Games
plural noun

Olympics plural
noun

ombudsman noun
ombudsmen

omelette noun
omelettes

omen noun
omens

ominous adjective
ominously

○ **omission** noun
omissions

omit verb
omits
omitting
omitted

omnivorous

once

✻ **one** adjective and
noun
ones

oneself

one-sided

one-way

ongoing

onion noun
onions

onlooker noun
onlookers

only

onshore adjective
and adverb

★ You use **of** in e.g. *a box of matches.* ! **off**.
☆ You use **off** in e.g. *turn off the light.* ! **of**.
○ An **omission** is something left out. ! **emission**.
✻ You use **one** in e.g. *one more time.* ! **won**.

onto preposition
onward adjective and adverb
onwards adverb
ooze verb
  oozes
  oozing
  oozed
opaque
open adjective
  openly
open verb
  opens
  opening
  opened
opener noun
  openers
opening noun
  openings
opera noun
  operas
operate verb
  operates
  operating
  operated
operatic
operation noun
  operations
operator noun
  operators
opinion noun
  opinions
opium
opponent noun
  opponents
opportunity noun
  opportunities
oppose verb
  opposes
  opposing
  opposed

opposite adjective
opposite noun
  opposites
opposition
oppress verb
  oppresses
  oppressing
  oppressed
oppression
oppressive adjective
  oppressively
oppressor noun
  oppressors
opt verb
  opts
  opting
  opted
optical adjective
  optically
optician noun
  opticians
optimism
optimist noun
  optimists
optimistic adjective
  optimistically
option noun
  options
optional adjective
  optionally
opulence
opulent adjective
  opulently
★ **or** conjunction
☆ **oral** adjective
  orally
orange adjective and noun
  oranges
orangeade noun
  orangeades

orang-utan noun
  orang-utans
oration noun
  orations
orator noun
  orators
oratorical
oratorio noun
  oratorios
oratory
orbit noun
  orbits
orbit verb
  orbits
  orbiting
  orbited
orbital
orchard noun
  orchards
orchestra noun
  orchestras
orchestral
orchid noun
  orchids
ordeal noun
  ordeals
order noun
  orders
order verb
  orders
  ordering
  ordered
orderliness
orderly
ordinal number noun
  ordinal numbers
ordinary adjective
  ordinarily
♢ **ore** noun
  ores

★ You use **or** in e.g. *Do you want a cake or a biscuit?* ! oar, ore.
☆ **Oral** means spoken aloud. ! aural.
♢ **Ore** is rock with metal in it. ! oar, or.

organ noun
  organs
organic adjective
  organically
organism noun
  organisms
organist noun
  organists
organization noun
  organizations
organize verb
  organizes
  organizing
  organized
organizer noun
  organizers
oriental
orienteering
origami
origin noun
  origins
original adjective
  originally
originality
originate verb
  originates
  originating
  originated
origination
originator noun
  originators
ornament noun
  ornaments
ornamental
  adjective
  ornamentally
ornamentation
ornithological
ornithologist
ornithology

orphan noun
  orphans
orphanage noun
  orphanages
orthodox
Orthodox Church
orthodoxy
oscillate verb
  oscillates
  oscillating
  oscillated
oscillation noun
  oscillations
ostrich noun
  ostriches
other adjective and
  noun
  others
otherwise
otter noun
  otters
ought
ounce noun
  ounces
ours
ourselves
outback
outboard motor
  noun
  outboard motors
outbreak noun
  outbreaks
outburst noun
  outbursts
outcast noun
  outcasts
outcome noun
  outcomes
outcry noun
  outcries

outdated
outdo verb
  outdoes
  outdoing
  outdid
  outdone
outdoor adjective
outdoors adverb
outer
outfit noun
  outfits
outgrow verb
  outgrows
  outgrowing
  outgrew
  outgrown
outhouse noun
  outhouses
outing noun
  outings
outlast verb
  outlasts
  outlasting
  outlasted
outlaw noun
  outlaws
outlaw verb
  outlaws
  outlawing
  outlawed
outlet noun
  outlets
outline noun
  outlines
outline verb
  outlines
  outlining
  outlined
outlook noun
  outlooks
outlying

outnumber verb
　outnumbers
　outnumbering
　outnumbered
outpatient noun
　outpatients
outpost noun
　outposts
output verb
　outputs
　outputting
　output
output noun
　outputs
outrage noun
　outrages
outrage verb
　outrages
　outraging
　outraged
outrageous adjective
　outrageously
outright
outset
outside adverb and
　preposition
outside noun
　outsides
outsider noun
　outsiders
outskirts plural noun
outspoken
outstanding
　adjective
　outstandingly
outward adjective
　outwardly
outwards adverb
outweigh verb
　outweighs
　outweighing
　outweighed

outwit verb
　outwits
　outwitting
　outwitted
oval adjective and
　noun
　ovals
ovary noun
　ovaries
oven noun
　ovens
over adverb and
　preposition
over noun
　overs

over-
over- makes words
meaning 'too' or 'too
much', e.g. **overactive**
and **overcook**. You do
not need a hyphen,
except in some words
beginning with e, e.g.
over-eager.

overall adjective
overalls plural noun
overarm adjective
overboard
overcast
overcoat noun
　overcoats
overcome verb
　overcomes
　overcoming
　overcame
　overcome
overdo verb
　overdoes
　overdoing
　overdid
　overdone

overdose noun
　overdoses
overdue
overflow verb
　overflows
　overflowing
　overflowed
overgrown
overhang verb
　overhangs
　overhanging
　overhung
overhaul verb
　overhauls
　overhauling
　overhauled
overhead adjective
overheads plural
　noun
overhear verb
　overhears
　overhearing
　overheard
overland adjective
overlap verb
　overlaps
　overlapping
　overlapped
overlook verb
　overlooks
　overlooking
　overlooked
overnight
overpower verb
　overpowers
　overpowering
　overpowered
overrun verb
　overruns
　overrunning
　overran
　overrun

ov - pa

170

overseas *adjective and adverb*

oversight *noun*
oversights

oversleep *verb*
oversleeps
oversleeping
overslept

overtake *verb*
overtakes
overtaking
overtook
overtaken

overthrow *verb*
overthrows
overthrowing
overthrew
overthrown

overthrow *noun*
overthrows

overtime

overture *noun*
overtures

overturn *verb*
overturns
overturning
overturned

overwhelm *verb*
overwhelms
overwhelming
overwhelmed

overwork *verb*
overworks
overworking
overworked

overwork *noun*

ovum *noun*
ova

owe *verb*
owes
owing
owed

owl *noun*
owls

own *adjective*

own *verb*
owns
owning
owned

owner *noun*
owners

ownership

ox *noun*
oxen

oxidation

oxide *noun*
oxides

oxidize *verb*
oxidizes
oxidizing
oxidized

oxygen

oyster *noun*
oysters

oz. *abbreviation*

ozone

Pp

pa *noun*
pas

pace *noun*
paces

pace *verb*
paces
pacing
paced

pacemaker *noun*
pacemakers

pacification

pacifism

pacifist *noun*
pacifists

pacify *verb*
pacifies
pacifying
pacified

pack *verb*
packs
packing
packed

pack *noun*
packs

package *noun*
packages

packet *noun*
packets

pad *noun*
pads

pad *verb*
pads
padding
padded

padding

paddle *verb*
paddles
paddling
paddled

paddle *noun*
paddles

paddock *noun*
paddocks

paddy *noun*
paddies

padlock *noun*
padlocks

pagan *adjective and noun*
pagans

page noun
pages

pageant noun
pageants

pageantry

pagoda noun
pagodas

paid see **pay**

★ **pail** noun
pails

☆ **pain** noun
pains

pain verb
pains
paining
pained

painful adjective
painfully

painkiller noun
painkillers

painless adjective
painlessly

painstaking

paint noun
paints

paint verb
paints
painting
painted

paintbox noun
paintboxes

paintbrush noun
paintbrushes

painter noun
painters

painting noun
paintings

○ **pair** noun
pairs

pair verb
pairs
pairing
paired

pal noun
pals

palace noun
palaces

palate noun
palates

✳ **pale** adjective
paler
palest

paleness

palette noun
palettes

paling noun
palings

palisade noun
palisades

pall verb
palls
palling
palled

pallid

pallor

palm noun
palms

palm verb
palms
palming
palmed

palmistry

Palm Sunday

paltry adjective
paltrier
paltriest

pampas plural noun

pamper verb
pampers
pampering
pampered

pamphlet noun
pamphlets

pan noun
pans

pancake noun
pancakes

panda noun
pandas

pandemonium

pander verb
panders
pandering
pandered

✳ **pane** noun
panes

panel noun
panels

pang noun
pangs

panic

panic verb
panics
panicking
panicked

panicky

pannier noun
panniers

panorama noun
panoramas

panoramic adjective
panoramically

pansy noun
pansies

pant verb
pants
panting
panted

★ A pail is a bucket. ! pale.
☆ A pain is an unpleasant feeling caused by injury or disease. ! pane.
○ A pair is a set of two. ! pear.
✳ Pale means 'almost white'. ! pail.
✳ A pane is a piece of glass in a window. ! pain.

panther *noun*
panthers

panties *plural noun*

pantomime *noun*
pantomimes

pantry *noun*
pantries

pants *plural noun*

paper *noun*
papers

paper *verb*
papers
papering
papered

paperback *noun*
paperbacks

papier mâché

papyrus *noun*
papyri

parable *noun*
parables

parachute *noun*
parachutes

parachutist

parade *noun*
parades

parade *verb*
parades
parading
paraded

paradise

paradox *noun*
paradoxes

paradoxical
adjective
paradoxically

paraffin

paragraph *noun*
paragraphs

parallel

parallelogram *noun*
parallelograms

paralyse *verb*
paralyses
paralysing
paralysed

paralysis *noun*
paralyses

paralytic *adjective*
paralytically

parapet *noun*
parapets

paraphernalia

paraphrase *verb*
paraphrases
paraphrasing
paraphrased

parasite *noun*
parasites

parasitic *adjective*
parasitically

parasol *noun*
parasols

paratrooper

paratroops *plural
noun*

parcel *noun*
parcels

parched

parchment

pardon *verb*
pardons
pardoning
pardoned

pardon *noun*
pardons

pardonable

parent *noun*
parents

parentage

parental

parenthood

parenthesis *noun*
parentheses

parish *noun*
parishes

parishioner *noun*
parishioners

park *noun*
parks

park *verb*
parks
parking
parked

parka *noun*
parkas

parliament *noun*
parliaments

parliamentary

parody *noun*
parodies

parole

parrot *noun*
parrots

parsley

parsnip *noun*
parsnips

parson *noun*
parsons

parsonage *noun*
parsonages

part *noun*
parts

part *verb*
parts
parting
parted

partial *adjective*
partially

partiality

participant noun
  participants
participate verb
  participates
  participating
  participated
participation
participle noun
  participles
particle noun
  particles
particular adjective
  particularly
particulars plural
  noun
parting noun
  partings
partition noun
  partitions
partly
partner noun
  partners
partnership
partridge noun
  partridges
part-time adjective
party noun
  parties
pass verb
  passes
  passing
  passed
pass noun
  passes
passable
passage noun
  passages
passageway noun
  passageways
★ **passed** see pass

passenger noun
  passengers
passer-by noun
  passers-by
passion noun
  passions
passionate adjective
  passionately
passive adjective
  passively
Passover
passport noun
  passports
password noun
  passwords
☆ **past** noun, adjective,
  and preposition
pasta noun
  pastas
paste noun
  pastes
paste verb
  pastes
  pasting
  pasted
pastel noun
  pastels
pasteurization
pasteurize verb
  pasteurizes
  pasteurizing
  pasteurized
pastille noun
  pastilles
pastime noun
  pastimes
pastoral
pastry noun
  pastries

pasture noun
  pastures
pasty noun
  pasties
pasty adjective
  pastier
  pastiest
pat verb
  pats
  patting
  patted
pat noun
  pats
patch noun
  patches
patch verb
  patches
  patching
  patched
patchwork
patchy adjective
  patchier
  patchiest
patent adjective
  patently
patent verb
  patents
  patenting
  patented
patent noun
  patents
paternal adjective
  paternally
path noun
  paths
pathetic adjective
  pathetically
patience
patient adjective
  patiently

. . . .

★ You use **passed** in e.g. We passed the house. **!** past.
☆ You use **past** in e.g. We went past the house. **!** passed.

patient *noun*
  patients

patio *noun*
  patios

patriot *noun*
  patriots

patriotic *adjective*
  patriotically

patriotism

patrol *verb*
  patrols
  patrolling
  patrolled

patrol *noun*
  patrols

patron *noun*
  patrons

patronage

patronize *verb*
  patronizes
  patronizing
  patronized

patter *verb*
  patters
  pattering
  pattered

patter *noun*
  patters

pattern *noun*
  patterns

pause *verb*
  pauses
  pausing
  paused

pause *noun*
  pauses

pave *verb*
  paves
  paving
  paved

pavement *noun*
  pavements

pavilion *noun*
  pavilions

paw *noun*
  paws

paw *verb*
  paws
  pawing
  pawed

pawn *noun*
  pawns

pawn *verb*
  pawns
  pawning
  pawned

pawnbroker *noun*
  pawnbrokers

pay *verb*
  pays
  paying
  paid

pay *noun*

payment *noun*
  payments

pea *noun*
  peas

★ **peace**

peaceful *adjective*
  peacefully

peach *noun*
  peaches

peacock *noun*
  peacocks

☆ **peak** *noun*
  peaks

○ **peak** *verb*
  peaks
  peaking
  peaked

peaked

✳ **peal** *verb*
  peals
  pealing
  pealed

✴ **peal** *noun*
  peals

peanut *noun*
  peanuts

✳ **pear** *noun*
  pears

pearl *noun*
  pearls

pearly *adjective*
  pearlier
  pearliest

peasant *noun*
  peasants

peasantry

peat

pebble *noun*
  pebbles

pebbly *adjective*
  pebblier
  pebbliest

peck *verb*
  pecks
  pecking
  pecked

peck *noun*
  pecks

peckish

peculiar *adjective*
  peculiarly

peculiarity *noun*
  peculiarities

pedal *noun*
  pedals

pedal *verb*
  pedals
  pedalling
  pedalled

. . . .

★ **Peace** is a time when there is no war. ! **piece.**
☆ A **peak** is the top of something. ! **peek.**
○ To **peak** is to reach the highest point. ! **peek.**
✳ To **peal** is to make a ringing sound of bells. ! **peel.**
✴ A **peal** is a ringing of bells. ! **peel.**
✳ A **pear** is a fruit. ! **pair.**

★ **peddle** verb
 peddles
 peddling
 peddled

pedestal noun
 pedestals

pedestrian noun
 pedestrians

pedestrian adjective

pedigree noun
 pedigrees

pedlar noun
 pedlars

☆ **peek** verb
 peeks
 peeking
 peeked

◐ **peel** noun
 peels

✳ **peel** verb
 peels
 peeling
 peeled

peep verb
 peeps
 peeping
 peeped

peep noun
 peeps

✱ **peer** verb
 peers
 peering
 peered

peer noun
 peers

peerless

peewit noun
 peewits

peg noun
 pegs

peg verb
 pegs
 pegging
 pegged

Pekinese noun
 Pekinese

pelican noun
 pelicans

pellet noun
 pellets

pelt verb
 pelts
 pelting
 pelted

pelt noun
 pelts

pen noun
 pens

penalize verb
 penalizes
 penalizing
 penalized

penalty noun
 penalties

pence see penny

pencil noun
 pencils

pencil verb
 pencils
 pencilling
 pencilled

pendant noun
 pendants

pendulum noun
 pendulums

penetrate verb
 penetrates
 penetrating
 penetrated

penetration

penfriend noun
 penfriends

penguin noun
 penguins

penicillin

peninsula noun
 peninsulas

peninsular

penis noun
 penises

penitence

penitent

penknife noun
 penknives

pennant noun
 pennants

penniless

penny noun
 pennies or pence

pension noun
 pensions

pensioner noun
 pensioners

pentagon noun
 pentagons

pentathlon noun
 pentathlons

peony noun
 peonies

people plural noun

people noun
 peoples

pepper noun
 peppers

peppermint noun
 peppermints

peppery

perceive verb
 perceives
 perceiving
 perceived

per cent

- -

★ To **peddle** is to sell things on the street. ! **pedal.**
☆ To **peek** is to look secretly at something. ! **peak.**
◐ **Peel** is the skin of fruit and vegetables. ! **peal.**
✳ To **peel** something is to take the skin off it. ! **peal.**
✱ To **peer** is to look closely at something. ! **pier.**

percentage *noun*
percentages

perceptible *adjective*
perceptibly

perception *noun*
perceptions

perceptive *adjective*
perceptively

perch *verb*
perches
perching
perched

perch *noun*
perch

percolator *noun*
percolators

percussion

percussive

perennial *adjective*
perennially

perennial *noun*
perennials

perfect *adjective*
perfectly

perfect *verb*
perfects
perfecting
perfected

perfection

perforate *verb*
perforates
perforating
perforated

perforation *noun*
perforations

perform *verb*
performs
performing
performed

performance *noun*
performances

performer *noun*
performers

perfume *noun*
perfumes

perhaps

peril *noun*
perils

perilous *adjective*
perilously

perimeter *noun*
perimeters

period *noun*
periods

periodic *adjective*
periodically

periodical *noun*
periodicals

periscope *noun*
periscopes

perish *verb*
perishes
perishing
perished

perishable

perm *noun*
perms

perm *verb*
perms
perming
permed

permanence

permanent *adjective*
permanently

permissible

permission

permissive *adjective*
permissively

permissiveness

permit *verb*
permits
permitting
permitted

permit *noun*
permits

perpendicular

perpetual *adjective*
perpetually

perpetuate *verb*
perpetuates
perpetuating
perpetuated

perplex *verb*
perplexes
perplexing
perplexed

perplexity

persecute *verb*
persecutes
persecuting
persecuted

persecution *noun*
persecutions

persecutor *noun*
persecutors

perseverance

persevere *verb*
perseveres
persevering
persevered

persist *verb*
persists
persisting
persisted

persistence

persistent *adjective*
persistently

★ **person** *noun*
persons *or* people

personal *adjective*
personally

personality *noun*
personalities

★ The normal plural is **people**: *three people came.* **Persons** is formal, e.g. in official reports.

personnel *plural noun*

perspective *noun*
perspectives

perspiration

perspire *verb*
perspires
perspiring
perspired

persuade *verb*
persuades
persuading
persuaded

persuasion

persuasive *adjective*
persuasively

perverse *adjective*
perversely

perversion *noun*
perversions

perversity

pervert *verb*
perverts
perverting
perverted

pervert *noun*
perverts

★ **Pesach**

pessimism

pessimist *noun*
pessimists

pessimistic *adjective*
pessimistically

pest *noun*
pests

pester *verb*
pesters
pestering
pestered

pesticide *noun*
pesticides

pestle *noun*
pestles

pet *noun*
pets

petal *noun*
petals

petition *noun*
petitions

petrify *verb*
petrifies
petrifying
petrified

petrochemical *noun*
petrochemicals

petrol

petroleum

petticoat *noun*
petticoats

pettiness

petty *adjective*
pettier
pettiest
pettily

pew *noun*
pews

pewter

pharmacy *noun*
pharmacies

phase *noun*
phases

phase *verb*
phases
phasing
phased

pheasant *noun*
pheasants

phenomenal *adjective*
phenomenally

phenomenon *noun*
phenomena

philatelist *noun*
philatelists

philately

philosopher *noun*
philosophers

philosophical *adjective*
philosophically

philosophy *noun*
philosophies

phobia *noun*
phobias

-phobia
-*phobia* makes words meaning 'a strong fear or dislike', e.g. **xenophobia** (= a dislike of strangers'). It comes from a Greek word and is only used with other Greek or Latin words.

phoenix *noun*
phoenixes

phone *noun*
phones

phone *verb*
phones
phoning
phoned

-phone
-*phone* makes words to do with sound, e.g. **telephone**, **saxophone**. You can sometimes make adjectives by using -*phonic*, e.g. **telephonic**, and nouns by using -*phony*, e.g. **telephony**.

★ The Hebrew name for Passover.

phonecard noun
phonecards

phone-in noun
phone-ins

phosphorescence

phosphorescent

phosphoric

phosphorus

photo noun
photos

photo-
photo- makes words
to do with light, e.g.
photograph,
photocopy. It is also
used in more
technical words such
as photochemistry (=
the chemistry of light)
and as a separate
word in photo (=
photograph) and
photo finish (= close
finish to a race).

photocopier noun
photocopiers

photocopy noun
photocopies

photocopy verb
photocopies
photocopying
photocopied

photoelectric

photograph noun
photographs

photograph verb
photographs
photographing
photographed

photographer noun
photographers

photographic
adjective
photographically

photography

phrase noun
phrases

phrase verb
phrases
phrasing
phrased

physical adjective
physically

physician noun
physicians

physicist noun
physicists

physics

physiological
adjective
physiologically

physiologist noun
physiologists

physiology

★ **pi**

pianist noun
pianists

piano noun
pianos

piccolo noun
piccolos

pick verb
picks
picking
picked

pick noun
picks

pickaxe noun
pickaxes

picket noun
pickets

picket verb
pickets
picketing
picketed

pickle noun
pickles

pickle verb
pickles
pickling
pickled

pickpocket noun
pickpockets

pick-up noun
pick-ups

picnic noun
picnics

picnic verb
picnics
picnicking
picnicked

picnicker noun
picnickers

pictogram noun
pictograms

pictorial adjective
pictorially

picture noun
pictures

picture verb
pictures
picturing
pictured

picturesque

☆ **pie** noun
pies

○ **piece** noun
pieces

piece verb
pieces
piecing
pieced

★ **Pi** is a Greek letter, used in mathematics. ! **pie**.
☆ A **pie** is a food with pastry. ! **pi**.
○ You use **piece** in e.g. *a piece of cake*. ! **peace**.

piecemeal
pie chart noun
  pie charts
★ **pier** noun
  piers
pierce verb
  pierces
  piercing
  pierced
pig noun
  pigs
pigeon noun
  pigeons
pigeon-hole noun
  pigeon-holes
piggy noun
  piggies
piggyback noun
  piggybacks
piglet noun
  piglets
pigment noun
  pigments
pigmy noun
  use **pygmy**
pigsty noun
  pigsties
pigtail noun
  pigtails
pike noun
  pikes
pilchard noun
  pilchards
pile noun
  piles
pile verb
  piles
  piling
  piled

pilfer verb
  pilfers
  pilfering
  pilfered
pilgrim noun
  pilgrims
pilgrimage noun
  pilgrimages
pill noun
  pills
pillage verb
  pillages
  pillaging
  pillaged
pillar noun
  pillars
pillion noun
  pillions
pillow noun
  pillows
pillowcase noun
  pillowcases
pilot noun
  pilots
pilot verb
  pilots
  piloting
  piloted
pimple noun
  pimples
pimply adjective
  pimplier
  pimpliest
pin noun
  pins
pin verb
  pins
  pinning
  pinned
pinafore noun
  pinafores

pincer noun
  pincers
pinch verb
  pinches
  pinching
  pinched
pinch noun
  pinches
pincushion noun
  pincushions
pine noun
  pines
pine verb
  pines
  pining
  pined
pineapple noun
  pineapples
ping-pong
pink adjective
  pinker
  pinkest
pink noun
  pinks
pint noun
  pints
pioneer noun
  pioneers
pious adjective
  piously
pip noun
  pips
pipe noun
  pipes
pipe verb
  pipes
  piping
  piped
pipeline noun
  pipelines

★ A **pier** is a long building on stilts going into the sea. **!** **peer**.

piper *noun*
pipers

piracy

pirate *noun*
pirates

★ pistil *noun*
pistils

★ pistol *noun*
pistols

piston *noun*
pistons

pit *noun*
pits

pit *verb*
pits
pitting
pitted

pitch *noun*
pitches

pitch *verb*
pitches
pitching
pitched

pitch-black

pitcher *noun*
pitchers

pitchfork *noun*
pitchforks

pitfall *noun*
pitfalls

pitiful *adjective*
pitifully

pitiless *adjective*
pitilessly

pity *verb*
pities
pitying
pitied

pity *noun*

pivot *noun*
pivots

pivot *verb*
pivots
pivoting
pivoted

pixie *noun*
pixies

pizza *noun*
pizzas

pizzicato

placard *noun*
placards

☆ place *noun*
places

place *verb*
places
placing
placed

placid *adjective*
placidly

plague *noun*
plagues

plague *verb*
plagues
plaguing
plagued

○ plaice *noun*
plaice

plaid *noun*
plaids

✳ plain *adjective*
plainer
plainest
plainly

plain *noun*
plains

plain clothes

plainness

plaintiff *noun*
plaintiffs

plaintive

plaintively

plait *noun*
plaits

plait *verb*
plaits
plaiting
plaited

plan *noun*
plans

plan *verb*
plans
planning
planned

✶ plane *noun*
planes

✶ plane *verb*
planes
planing
planed

planet *noun*
planets

planetary

plank *noun*
planks

plankton

planner *noun*
planners

plant *noun*
plants

plant *verb*
plants
planting
planted

plantation *noun*
plantations

planter *noun*
planters

★ A pistil is a part of a flower and a pistol is a gun.
☆ You use place in e.g. *a place in the country.* ! plaice.
○ A plaice is a fish. ! place.
✳ Plain means 'not pretty or decorated'. ! plane.
✶ A plane is an aeroplane, a level surface, a tool, or a tree. ! plain.
✶ To plane wood is to make it smooth with a tool. ! plain.

plaque noun
plaques

plasma

plaster noun
plasters

plaster verb
plasters
plastering
plastered

plasterer noun
plasterers

plaster of Paris

plastic adjective and
noun
plastics

Plasticine

plate noun
plates

plate verb
plates
plating
plated

plateau noun
plateaux

plateful noun
platefuls

platform noun
platforms

platinum

platoon noun
platoons

platypus noun
platypuses

play verb
plays
playing
played

play noun
plays

playback noun
playbacks

player noun
players

playful adjective
playfully

playfulness

playground noun
playgrounds

playgroup noun
playgroups

playmate noun
playmates

play-off noun
play-offs

playtime noun
playtimes

playwright noun
playwrights

plea noun
pleas

plead verb
pleads
pleading
pleaded

pleasant adjective
pleasanter
pleasantest
pleasantly

please verb
pleases
pleasing
pleased

pleasurable
adjective
pleasurably

pleasure noun
pleasures

pleat noun
pleats

pleated

pledge verb
pledges
pledging
pledged

pledge noun
pledges

plentiful adjective
plentifully

plenty

pliable

pliers plural noun

plight noun
plights

plod verb
plods
plodding
plodded

plodder noun
plodders

plop verb
plops
plopping
plopped

plop noun
plops

plot noun
plots

plot verb
plots
plotting
plotted

plotter noun
plotters

plough noun
ploughs

plough verb
ploughs
ploughing
ploughed

ploughman noun
ploughmen

plover noun
plovers

pluck verb
plucks
plucking
plucked

pluck noun

plucky adjective
pluckier
pluckiest
pluckily

plug noun
plugs

plug verb
plugs
plugging
plugged

★ **plum** noun
plums

plumage

☆ **plumb** verb
plumbs
plumbing
plumbed

plumber noun
plumbers

plumbing

plume noun
plumes

plumed

plump adjective
plumper
plumpest

plump verb
plumps
plumping
plumped

plunder verb
plunders
plundering
plundered

plunder noun

plunderer noun
plunderers

plunge verb
plunges
plunging
plunged

plunge noun
plunges

plural adjective and noun
plurals

plus preposition

plus noun
pluses

plutonium

plywood

pneumatic

pneumonia

poach verb
poaches
poaching
poached

poacher noun
poachers

pocket noun
pockets

pocket verb
pockets
pocketing
pocketed

pocketful noun
pocketfuls

pod noun
pods

podgy adjective
podgier
podgiest

poem noun
poems

poet noun
poets

poetic adjective
poetically

poetry

point noun
points

point verb
points
pointing
pointed

point-blank adjective

pointed adjective
pointedly

pointer noun
pointers

pointless adjective
pointlessly

poise noun

poise verb
poises
poising
poised

poison noun
poisons

poison verb
poisons
poisoning
poisoned

poisoner noun
poisoners

poisonous adjective
poisonously

poke verb
pokes
poking
poked

poke noun
pokes

poker noun
pokers

. . . .

★ A plum is a fruit. ! plumb.
☆ To plumb water is to see how deep it is. ! plum.

183 — po

polar
Polaroid
★ pole *noun*
  poles
police *plural noun*
policeman *noun*
  policemen
police officer *noun*
  police officers
policewoman *noun*
  policewomen
policy *noun*
  policies
polio
poliomyelitis
polish *verb*
  polishes
  polishing
  polished
polish *noun*
  polishes
polished
polite *adjective*
  politer
  politest
  politely
politeness
political *adjective*
  politically
politician *noun*
  politicians
politics
polka *noun*
  polkas
☆ poll *noun*
  polls
pollen
pollute *verb*
  pollutes
  polluting
  polluted

pollution
polo
polo neck *noun*
  polo necks
poltergeist *noun*
  poltergeists
polygon *noun*
  polygons
polystyrene
polythene
pomp
pomposity
pompous *adjective*
  pompously
pond *noun*
  ponds
ponder *verb*
  ponders
  pondering
  pondered
ponderous *adjective*
  ponderously
pony *noun*
  ponies
ponytail *noun*
  ponytails
pony-trekking
poodle *noun*
  poodles
pool *noun*
  pools
pool *verb*
  pools
  pooling
  pooled
poor *adjective*
  poorer
  poorest
  poorly

poorly *adjective and adverb*
pop *verb*
  pops
  popping
  popped
pop *noun*
  pops
popcorn
Pope *noun*
  Popes
poplar *noun*
  poplars
poppadom *noun*
  poppadoms
poppy *noun*
  poppies
popular *adjective*
  popularly
popularity
popularize *verb*
  popularizes
  popularizing
  popularized
populated
population *noun*
  populations
populous
porcelain
porch *noun*
  porches
porcupine *noun*
  porcupines
pore *noun*
  pores
○ pore *verb*
  pores
  poring
  pored
pork

★ A **pole** is a long thin stick. ! poll.
☆ A **poll** is a vote in an election. ! pole.
○ To **pore** over something is to study it closely. ! pour.

pornographic
pornography
porosity
porous
porpoise noun
  porpoises
porridge
port noun
  ports
portable
portcullis noun
  portcullises
porter noun
  porters
porthole noun
  portholes
portion noun
  portions
portliness
portly adjective
  portlier
  portliest
portrait noun
  portraits
portray verb
  portrays
  portraying
  portrayed
portrayal noun
  portrayals
pose verb
  poses
  posing
  posed
pose noun
  poses
poser noun
  posers
posh adjective
  posher
  poshest

position noun
  positions
positive adjective
  positively
positive noun
  positives
posse noun
  posses
possess verb
  possesses
  possessing
  possessed
possession noun
  possessions
possessive adjective
  possessively
possessor noun
  possessors
possibility noun
  possibilities
possible adjective
  possibly
post verb
  posts
  posting
  posted
post noun
  posts
postage
postal
postbox noun
  postboxes
postcard noun
  postcards
postcode noun
  postcodes
poster noun
  posters
postman noun
  postmen

postmark noun
  postmarks
post-mortem noun
  post-mortems
postpone verb
  postpones
  postponing
  postponed
postponement noun
  postponements
postscript noun
  postscripts
posture noun
  postures
posy noun
  posies
pot noun
  pots
pot verb
  pots
  potting
  potted
potassium
potato noun
  potatoes
potency
potent adjective
  potently
potential adjective
  potentially
potential noun
  potentials
pothole noun
  potholes
potholer noun
  potholer
potholing
potion noun
  potions
potter noun
  potters

potter *verb*
  potters
  pottering
  pottered
pottery *noun*
  potteries
potty *adjective*
  pottier
  pottiest
  pottily
potty *noun*
  potties
pouch *noun*
  pouches
poultry
pounce *verb*
  pounces
  pouncing
  pounced
pound *noun*
  pounds
pound *verb*
  pounds
  pounding
  pounded
★ **pour** *verb*
  pours
  pouring
  poured
pout *verb*
  pouts
  pouting
  pouted
poverty
powder *noun*
  powders
powder *verb*
  powders
  powdering
  powdered
powdery

power *noun*
  powers
powered
powerful *adjective*
  powerfully
powerhouse *noun*
  powerhouses
powerless
practicable
practical *adjective*
  practically
practice *noun*
  practices
practise *verb*
  practises
  practising
  practised
prairie *noun*
  prairies
praise *verb*
  praises
  praising
  praised
praise *noun*
  praises
pram *noun*
  prams
prance *verb*
  prances
  prancing
  pranced
prank *noun*
  pranks
prawn *noun*
  prawns
☆ **pray** *verb*
  prays
  praying
  prayed
prayer *noun*
  prayers

pre-
pre- makes words meaning 'before', e.g. **pre-date** (= to exist before something else), **prefabricated** (= made in advance). Many are spelt joined up, but not all.

preach *verb*
  preaches
  preaching
  preached
preacher *noun*
  preachers
precarious *adjective*
  precariously
precaution *noun*
  precautions
precede *verb*
  precedes
  preceding
  preceded
precedence
precedent *noun*
  precedents
precinct *noun*
  precincts
precious *adjective*
  preciously
precipice *noun*
  precipices
précis *noun*
  précis
precise *adjective*
  precisely
precision
predator *noun*
  predators
predatory

· ·
★ To **pour** a liquid is to tip it from a jug etc. ! **pore**.
☆ To **pray** is to say prayers. ! **prey**.

predecessor noun
predecessors

predict verb
predicts
predicting
predicted

predictable adjective
predictably

prediction noun
predictions

predominance

predominant
adjective
predominantly

predominate verb
predominates
predominating
predominated

preface noun
prefaces

prefect noun
prefects

prefer verb
prefers
preferring
preferred

preferable adjective
preferably

preference noun
preferences

prefix noun
prefixes

pregnancy noun
pregnancies

pregnant

prehistoric

prehistory

prejudice noun
prejudices

prejudiced

preliminary
adjective and noun
preliminaries

prelude noun
preludes

premier noun
premiers

première noun
premières

premises plural noun

premium noun
premiums

Premium Bond noun
Premium Bonds

preoccupation noun
preoccupations

preoccupied

prep

preparation noun
preparations

preparatory

prepare verb
prepares
preparing
prepared

preposition noun
prepositions

prescribe verb
prescribes
prescribing
prescribed

prescription noun
prescriptions

presence

present adjective
presently

present noun
presents

present verb
presents
presenting
presented

presentation noun
presentations

presenter noun
presenters

preservation

preservative noun
preservatives

preserve verb
preserves
preserving
preserved

preside verb
presides
presiding
presided

presidency noun
presidencies

president noun
presidents

presidential
adjective
presidentially

press verb
presses
pressing
pressed

press noun
presses

press-up noun
press-ups

pressure noun
pressures

pressurize verb
pressurizes
pressurizing
pressurized

prestige

prestigious adjective
prestigiously

presumably

presume *verb*
presumes
presuming
presumed

presumption *noun*
presumptions

presumptuous
adjective
presumptuously

pretence *noun*
pretences

pretend *verb*
pretends
pretending
pretended

pretender *noun*
pretenders

prettiness

pretty *adjective* and
adverb
prettier
prettiest
prettily

prevail *verb*
prevails
prevailing
prevailed

prevalent

prevent *verb*
prevents
preventing
prevented

prevention

preventive

preview *noun*
previews

previous *adjective*
previously

★ **prey** *verb*
preys
preying
preyed

prey *noun*

price *noun*
prices

price *verb*
prices
pricing
priced

priceless

prick *verb*
pricks
pricking
pricked

prick *noun*
pricks

prickle *noun*
prickles

prickly *adjective*
pricklier
prickliest

pride *noun*
prides

priest *noun*
priests

priestess *noun*
priestesses

priesthood

prig *noun*
prigs

priggish *adjective*
priggishly

prim *adjective*
primmer
primmest
primly

primness

primary *adjective*
primarily

primate *noun*
primates

prime *adjective*

prime *verb*
primes
priming
primed

prime *noun*
primes

prime minister
noun
prime ministers

primer *noun*
primers

primeval

primitive *adjective*
primitively

primrose *noun*
primroses

prince *noun*
princes

princely

princess *noun*
princesses

☆ **principal** *adjective*
principally

◐ **principal** *noun*
principals

✳ **principle** *noun*
principles

print *verb*
prints
printing
printed

print *noun*
prints

printer *noun*
printers

printout *noun*
printouts

priority *noun*
priorities

- -

★ To prey on animals is to hunt and kill them. ! **pray**.
☆ Principal means 'chief' or 'main'. ! **principle**.
◐ A principal is a head of a college. ! **principle**.
✳ A principle is a rule or belief. ! **principal**.

★ **prise** verb
prises
prising
prised

prism noun
prisms

prison noun
prisons

prisoner noun
prisoners

privacy

private adjective
privately

private noun
privates

privatization

privatize verb
privatizes
privatizing
privatized

privet

privilege noun
privileges

privileged

prize noun
prizes

☆ **prize** verb
prizes
prizing
prized

pro noun
pros

pro-
pro- makes words
meaning 'in favour
of', e.g. **pro-choice**. In
this type of word you
use a hyphen.

probability noun
probabilities

probable adjective
probably

probation

probationary

probe verb
probes
probing
probed

probe noun
probes

problem noun
problems

procedure noun
procedures

proceed verb
proceeds
proceeding
proceeded

proceedings plural
noun

proceeds plural noun

process noun
processes

process verb
processes
processing
processed

procession noun
processions

proclaim verb
proclaims
proclaiming
proclaimed

proclamation noun
proclamations

prod verb
prods
prodding
prodded

prodigal adjective
prodigally

produce verb
produces
producing
produced

produce noun

producer noun
producers

product noun
products

production noun
productions

productive adjective
productively

productivity

profession noun
professions

professional
adjective
professionally

professional noun
professionals

professor noun
professors

proficiency

proficient adjective
proficiently

profile noun
profiles

○ **profit** noun
profits

profit verb
profits
profiting
profited

profitable adjective
profitably

profound adjective
profoundly

profundity

profuse adjective
profusely

★ To **prise** something is to open it. ! **prize**.
☆ To **prize** something is to value it highly. ! **prise**.
○ A **profit** is extra money made by selling something. ! **prophet**.

profusion
★ **program** noun
 programs
program verb
 programs
 programming
 programmed
★ **programme** noun
 programmes
progress noun
progress verb
 progresses
 progressing
 progressed
progression
progressive adjective
 progressively
prohibit verb
 prohibits
 prohibiting
 prohibited
prohibition noun
 prohibitions
project noun
 projects
project verb
 projects
 projecting
 projected
projection noun
 projections
projectionist noun
 projectionists
projector noun
 projectors
prologue noun
 prologues
prolong verb
 prolongs
 prolonging
 prolonged

promenade noun
 promenades
prominence
prominent adjective
 prominently
promise verb
 promises
 promising
 promised
promise noun
 promises
promontory noun
 promontories
promote verb
 promotes
 promoting
 promoted
promoter noun
 promoter
promotion noun
 promotions
prompt adjective
 prompter
 promptest
 promptly
prompt verb
 prompts
 prompting
 prompted
prompter noun
 prompters
promptness
prone
prong noun
 prongs
pronoun noun
 pronouns
pronounce verb
 pronounces
 pronouncing
 pronounced

pronouncement noun
 pronouncements
pronunciation noun
 pronunciations
proof adjective and noun
 proofs
prop verb
 props
 propping
 propped
prop noun
 props
propaganda
propel verb
 propels
 propelling
 propelled
propellant noun
 propellants
propeller noun
 propellers
proper adjective
 properly
property noun
 properties
prophecy noun
 prophecies
prophesy verb
 prophesies
 prophesying
 prophesied
☆ **prophet** noun
 prophets
prophetic adjective
 prophetically
proportion noun
 proportions

★ You use **program** when you are talking about computers. In other meanings you use **programme**.
☆ A **prophet** is someone who makes predictions about the future. ! **profit**.

proportional adjective
proportionally
proportionate adjective
proportionately
propose verb
proposes
proposing
proposed
proposal noun
proposals
proprietor noun
proprietors
propulsion
prose
prosecute verb
prosecutes
prosecuting
prosecuted
prosecution noun
prosecutions
prosecutor noun
prosecutors
prospect noun
prospects
prospect verb
prospects
prospecting
prospected
prospector noun
prospectors
prosper verb
prospers
prospering
prospered
prosperity
prosperous adjective
prosperously
prostitute noun
prostitutes

protect verb
protects
protecting
protected
protection
protective adjective
protectively
protector noun
protectors
protein noun
proteins
protest verb
protests
protesting
protested
protest noun
protests
protester noun
protesters
Protestant noun
Protestants
proton noun
protons
protoplasm
prototype noun
prototypes
protractor noun
protractors
protrude verb
protrudes
protruding
protruded
protrusion noun
protrusions
proud adjective
prouder
proudest
proudly
prove verb
proves
proving
proved

proverb noun
proverbs
proverbial adjective
proverbially
provide verb
provides
providing
provided
province noun
provinces
provincial
provision noun
provisions
provisional adjective
provisionally
provocative adjective
provocatively
provoke verb
provokes
provoking
provoked
provocation noun
provocations
prow noun
prows
prowl verb
prowls
prowling
prowled
prowler noun
prowlers
prudence
prudent adjective
prudently
prune noun
prunes
prune verb
prunes
pruning
pruned

pry *verb*
pries
prying
pried

psalm *noun*
psalms

pseudonym *noun*
pseudonyms

psychiatric

psychiatrist *noun*
psychiatrists

psychiatry

psychic

psychological
adjective
psychologically

psychologist *noun*
psychologists

psychology

pub *noun*
pubs

puberty

public *adjective* and
noun
publicly

publication *noun*
publications

publicity

publicize *verb*
publicizes
publicizing
publicized

publish *verb*
publishes
publishing
published

publisher *noun*
publishers

puck *noun*
pucks

pucker *verb*
puckers
puckering
puckered

pudding *noun*
puddings

puddle *noun*
puddles

puff *verb*
puffs
puffing
puffed

puff *noun*
puffs

puffin *noun*
puffins

pull *verb*
pulls
pulling
pulled

pull *noun*
pulls

pulley *noun*
pulleys

pullover *noun*
pullovers

pulp *noun*
pulps

pulp *verb*
pulps
pulping
pulped

pulpit *noun*
pulpits

pulse *noun*
pulses

pulverize *verb*
pulverizes
pulverizing
pulverized

puma *noun*
pumas

pumice

pump *verb*
pumps
pumping
pumped

pump *noun*
pumps

pumpkin *noun*
pumpkins

pun *noun*
puns

pun *verb*
puns
punning
punned

punch *verb*
punches
punching
punched

punch *noun*
punches

punch *noun*
punches

punchline *noun*
punchlines

punch-up *noun*
punch-ups

punctual *adjective*
punctually

punctuality

punctuate *verb*
punctuates
punctuating
punctuated

punctuation

puncture *noun*
punctures

punish *verb*
punishes
punishing
punished

punishment noun
punishments
punk noun
punks
punt noun
punts
punt verb
punts
punting
punted
puny adjective
punier
puniest
pup noun
pups
pupa noun
pupae
pupil noun
pupils
puppet noun
puppets
puppy noun
puppies
purchase verb
purchases
purchasing
purchased
purchase noun
purchases
purchaser noun
purchasers
purdah
pure adjective
purer
purest
purely
purge verb
purges
purging
purged
purge noun
purges

purification
purifier noun
purifiers
purify verb
purifies
purifying
purified
★ **Puritan** noun
Puritans
puritan noun
puritans
puritanical adjective
puritanically
purity
purple noun
purpose noun
purposes
purposely
purr verb
purrs
purring
purred
purse noun
purses
pursue verb
pursues
pursuing
pursued
pursuer noun
pursuers
pursuit noun
pursuits
☆ **pus** noun
push verb
pushes
pushing
pushed
push noun
pushes
pushchair noun
pushchairs

○ **puss** or **pussy** noun
pusses or pussies
✳ **put** verb
puts
putting
put
✳ **putt** verb
putts
putting
putted
putter noun
putters
putty
puzzle verb
puzzles
puzzling
puzzled
puzzle noun
puzzles
pygmy noun
pygmies
pyjamas
pylon noun
pylons
pyramid noun
pyramids
pyramidal
python noun
pythons

Qq

quack verb
quacks
quacking
quacked
quack noun
quacks

. . . .

★ You use a capital P when you are talking about people in history, and a small p when you mean anyone who is morally strict.
☆ **Pus** is yellow stuff produced in sore places on the body. ! **puss**.
○ **Puss** is a word for a cat. ! **pus**.
✳ To **put** something somewhere is to place it there. ! **putt**.
✳ To **putt** a ball is to tap it gently. ! **put**.

quad noun
　quads
quadrangle noun
　quadrangles
quadrant noun
　quadrants
quadrilateral noun
　quadrilaterals
quadruple adjective
　and noun
quadruple verb
　quadruples
　quadrupling
　quadrupled
quadruplet noun
　quadruplets
quail verb
　quails
　quailing
　quailed
quail noun
　quail or quails
quaint adjective
　quainter
　quaintest
　quaintly
quaintness noun
quake verb
　quakes
　quaking
　quaked
Quaker noun
　Quakers
qualification noun
　qualifications
qualify verb
　qualifies
　qualifying
　qualified
quality noun
　qualities

quantity noun
　quantities
quarantine
quarrel noun
　quarrels
quarrel verb
　quarrels
　quarrelling
　quarrelled
quarrelsome
quarry noun
　quarries
quart noun
　quarts
quarter noun
　quarters
quartet noun
　quartets
quartz
quaver verb
　quavers
　quavering
　quavered
quaver noun
　quavers
★ **quay** noun
　quays
queasy adjective
　queasier
　queasiest
queen noun
　queens
queer adjective
　queerer
　queerest
quench verb
　quenches
　quenching
　quenched

query verb
　queries
　querying
　queried
query noun
　queries
quest noun
　quests
question noun
　questions
question verb
　questions
　questioning
　questioned
questionable
　adjective
　questionably
questioner noun
　questioner
questionnaire noun
　questionnaires
☆ **queue** noun
　queues
queue verb
　queues
　queueing
　queued
quibble verb
　quibbles
　quibbling
　quibbled
quibble noun
　quibbles
quiche noun
　quiches
quick adjective
　quicker
　quickest
　quickly
quicken verb
　quickens
　quickening
　quickened

. . . .

★ A **quay** is a place where ships tie up. **! key.**
☆ A **queue** is a line of people waiting for something. **! cue.**

quicksand noun
quicksands

quid noun
quid

quiet adjective
quieter
quietest
quietly

quieten verb
quietens
quietening
quietened

quill noun
quills

quilt noun
quilts

quintet noun
quintets

quit verb
quits
quitting
quitted
quit

quitter noun
quitters

quite

quiver verb
quivers
quivering
quivered

quiver noun
quivers

quiz noun
quizzes

quiz verb
quizzes
quizzing
quizzed

quoit noun
quoits

quota noun
quotas

quotation noun
quotations

quote verb
quotes
quoting
quoted

quotient noun
quotients

Rr

rabbi noun
rabbis

rabbit noun
rabbits

rabid

rabies

raccoon noun
raccoons

race noun
races

race verb
races
racing
raced

race noun
races

racecourse noun
racecourses

racer noun
racers

racial adjective
racially

racism

racist noun
racists

rack noun
racks

rack verb
racks
racking
racked

racket noun
rackets

radar

radial adjective
radially

radiance

radiant adjective
radiantly

radiate verb
radiates
radiating
radiated

radiation

radiator noun
radiators

radical adjective
radically

radical noun
radicals

radii see **radius**

radio noun
radios

radioactive

radioactivity

radish noun
radishes

radium

radius noun
radii

raffle noun
raffles

raffle verb
raffles
raffling
raffled

raft noun
 rafts
rafter noun
 rafters
rag noun
 rags
rage noun
 rages
rage verb
 rages
 raging
 raged
ragged
ragtime
raid noun
 raids
raid verb
 raids
 raiding
 raided
raider noun
 raiders
rail noun
 rails
railings plural noun
railway noun
 railways
rain verb
 rains
 raining
 rained
rain noun
 rains
rainbow noun
 rainbows
raincoat noun
 raincoats
raindrop noun
 raindrops
rainfall

rainforest noun
 rainforests
raise verb
 raises
 raising
 raised
raisin noun
 raisins
rake verb
 rakes
 raking
 raked
rake noun
 rakes
rally verb
 rallies
 rallying
 rallied
rally noun
 rallies
ram verb
 rams
 ramming
 rammed
ram noun
 rams
Ramadan
ramble noun
 rambles
ramble verb
 rambles
 rambling
 rambled
rambler noun
 ramblers
ramp noun
 ramps
rampage verb
 rampages
 rampaging
 rampaged

rampage noun
ran see run
ranch noun
 ranches
random
rang see ring
range noun
 ranges
range verb
 ranges
 ranging
 ranged
★ **ranger** noun
 rangers
rank noun
 ranks
rank verb
 ranks
 ranking
 ranked
ransack verb
 ransacks
 ransacking
 ransacked
ransom verb
 ransoms
 ransoming
 ransomed
ransom noun
 ransoms
☆ **rap** verb
 raps
 rapping
 rapped
rap noun
 raps
rapid adjective
 rapidly
rapidity
rapids plural noun

. . . .
★ You use a capital R when you mean a senior Guide.
☆ To **rap** is to knock loudly. ! **wrap**.

rare adjective
rarer
rarest
rarely

rarity noun
rarities

rascal noun
rascals

rash adjective
rasher
rashest
rashly

rash noun
rashes

rasher noun
rashers

raspberry noun
raspberries

Rastafarian noun
Rastafarians

rat noun
rats

rate noun
rates

rate verb
rates
rating
rated

rather

ratio noun
ratios

ration noun
rations

ration verb
rations
rationing
rationed

rational adjective
rationally

rationalize verb
rationalizes
rationalizing
rationalized

rattle verb
rattles
rattling
rattled

rattle noun
rattles

rattlesnake noun
rattlesnakes

rave verb
raves
raving
raved

rave noun
raves

raven noun
ravens

ravenous adjective
ravenously

ravine noun
ravines

raw adjective
rawer
rawest

ray noun
rays

razor noun
razors

re-
re- makes words
meaning 'again', e.g.
reproduce. These
words are normally
spelt joined up, but a
few need a hyphen so
you don't confuse
them with other
words, e.g. **re-cover**
(= to put a new cover
on); **recover** has
another meaning. You
also need a hyphen in
words beginning with
e, e.g. **re-enter**.

reach verb
reaches
reaching
reached

reach noun
reaches

react verb
reacts
reacting
reacted

reaction noun
reactions

reactor noun
reactors

★ **read** verb
reads
reading
read

readable

reader noun
readers

readily

readiness

reading noun
readings

ready adjective
readier
readiest

☆ **real** adjective

realism

realist noun
realists

realistic adjective
realistically

reality noun
realities

realization

realize verb
realizes
realizing
realized

★ To **read** is to look at something written or printed. ! **reed**.
☆ **Real** means 'true' or 'existing'. ! **reel**.

really

realm noun
realms

reap verb
reaps
reaping
reaped

reaper noun
reapers

reappear verb
reappears
reappearing
reappeared

reappearance noun
reappearances

rear adjective and
noun
rears

rear verb
rears
rearing
reared

rearrange verb
rearranges
rearranging
rearranged

rearrangement noun
rearrangements

reason noun
reasons

reason verb
reasons
reasoning
reasoned

reasonable adjective
reasonably

reassurance noun
reassurances

reassure verb
reassures
reassuring
reassured

rebel verb
rebels
rebelling
rebelled

rebel noun
rebels

rebellion noun
rebellions

rebellious adjective
rebelliously

rebound verb
rebounds
rebounding
rebounded

rebuild verb
rebuilds
rebuilding
rebuilt

recall verb
recalls
recalling
recalled

recap verb
recaps
recapping
recapped

recapture verb
recaptures
recapturing
recaptured

recede verb
recedes
receding
receded

receipt noun
receipts

receive verb
receives
receiving
received

receiver noun
receivers

recent adjective
recently

receptacle noun
receptacles

reception noun
receptions

receptionist noun
receptionists

recess noun
recesses

recession noun
recessions

recipe noun
recipes

reciprocal adjective
reciprocally

reciprocal noun
reciprocals

recital noun
recitals

recitation noun
recitations

recite verb
recites
reciting
recited

reckless adjective
recklessly

recklessness

reckon verb
reckons
reckoning
reckoned

reclaim verb
reclaims
reclaiming
reclaimed

reclamation noun
  reclamations
recline verb
  reclines
  reclining
  reclined
recognition
recognizable adjective
  recognizably
recognize verb
  recognizes
  recognizing
  recognized
recoil verb
  recoils
  recoiling
  recoiled
recollect verb
  recollects
  recollecting
  recollected
recollection noun
  recollections
recommend verb
  recommends
  recommending
  recommended
recommendation noun
  recommendations
reconcile verb
  reconciles
  reconciling
  reconciled
reconciliation noun
  reconciliations
reconstruction noun
  reconstructions
record noun
  records

record verb
  records
  recording
  recorded
recorder noun
  recorders
recover verb
  recovers
  recovering
  recovered
recovery noun
  recoveries
recreation noun
  recreations
recreational adjective
  recreationally
recruit noun
  recruits
recruit verb
  recruits
  recruiting
  recruited
rectangle noun
  rectangles
rectangular
recur verb
  recurs
  recurring
  recurred
recurrence noun
  recurrences
recycle verb
  recycles
  recycling
  recycled
red adjective
  redder
  reddest
red noun
  reds

redden verb
  reddens
  reddening
  reddened
reddish
redeem verb
  redeems
  redeeming
  redeemed
redeemer noun
  redeemers
redemption noun
  redemptions
redhead noun
  redheads
reduce verb
  reduces
  reducing
  reduced
reduction noun
  reductions
redundancy noun
  redundancies
redundant adjective
  redundantly
★ **reed** noun
  reeds
reedy
reef noun
  reefs
reef knot noun
  reef knots
reek verb
  reeks
  reeking
  reeked
☆ **reel** noun
  reels
reel verb
  reels
  reeling
  reeled

★ A reed is a plant or a thin strip. ! read.
☆ A reel is a cylinder on which something is wound. ! real.

refer verb
refers
referring
referred
referee noun
referees
referee verb
referees
refereeing
refereed
reference noun
references
referendum noun
referendums
refill verb
refills
refilling
refilled
refill noun
refills
refine verb
refines
refining
refined
refinement noun
refinements
refinery noun
refineries
reflect verb
reflects
reflecting
reflected
reflective adjective
reflectively
reflex noun
reflexes
reflexive adjective
reflexively
reform verb
reforms
reforming
reformed

reform noun
reforms
reformation noun
reformations
★ **Reformation**
reformer noun
reformers
refract verb
refracts
refracting
refracted
refraction
refrain verb
refrains
refraining
refrained
refrain noun
refrains
refresh verb
refreshes
refreshing
refreshed
refreshment noun
refreshments
refrigerate verb
refrigerates
refrigerating
refrigerated
refrigeration
refrigerator noun
refrigerators
refuel verb
refuels
refuelling
refuelled
refuge noun
refuges
refugee noun
refugees
refund verb
refunds
refunding
refunded

refund noun
refunds
refusal
refuse verb
refuses
refusing
refused
refuse
regain verb
regains
regaining
regained
regard verb
regards
regarding
regarded
regard noun
regards
regarding preposition
regardless
regatta noun
regattas
reggae
regiment noun
regiments
regimental
region noun
regions
regional adjective
regionally
register noun
registers
register verb
registers
registering
registered
registration noun
registrations

★ You use a capital R when you mean the historical religious movement.

regret noun
regrets

regret verb
regrets
regretting
regretted

regretful adjective
regretfully

regrettable adjective
regrettably

regular adjective
regularly

regularity

regulate verb
regulates
regulating
regulated

regulation noun
regulations

regulator noun
regulators

rehearsal noun
rehearsals

rehearse verb
rehearses
rehearsing
rehearsed

★ **reign** verb
reigns
reigning
reigned

reign noun
reigns

☆ **rein** noun
reins

reindeer noun
reindeer

reinforce verb
reinforces
reinforcing
reinforced

reinforcement noun
reinforcements

reject verb
rejects
rejecting
rejected

reject noun
rejects

rejection noun
rejections

rejoice verb
rejoices
rejoicing
rejoiced

relate verb
relates
relating
related

relation noun
relations

relationship noun
relationships

relative adjective
relatively

relative noun
relatives

relax verb
relaxes
relaxing
relaxed

relaxation

relay verb
relays
relaying
relayed

relay noun
relays

release verb
releases
releasing
released

release noun
releases

relegate verb
relegates
relegating
relegated

relegation

relent verb
relents
relenting
relented

relentless adjective
relentlessly

relevance

relevant adjective
relevantly

reliability

reliable adjective
reliably

reliance

reliant

relic noun
relics

relief noun
reliefs

relieve verb
relieves
relieving
relieved

religion noun
religions

religious adjective
religiously

reluctance

reluctant adjective
reluctantly

rely verb
relies
relying
relied

. . . .

★ To **reign** is to rule as a king or queen. ! **rein**.
☆ A **rein** is a strap used to guide a horse. ! **reign**.

remain verb
　remains
　remaining
　remained
remainder noun
　remainders
remains
remark verb
　remarks
　remarking
　remarked
remark noun
　remarks
remarkable adjective
　remarkably
remedial adjective
　remedially
remedy noun
　remedies
remember verb
　remembers
　remembering
　remembered
remembrance
remind verb
　reminds
　reminding
　reminded
reminder noun
　reminders
reminisce verb
　reminisces
　reminiscing
　reminisced
reminiscence noun
　reminiscences
reminiscent
remnant noun
　remnants
remorse

remorseful adjective
　remorsefully
remorseless adjective
　remorselessly
remote adjective
　remoter
　remotest
　remotely
remoteness
removal noun
　removals
remove verb
　removes
　removing
　removed
★ **Renaissance**
render verb
　renders
　rendering
　rendered
rendezvous noun
　rendezvous
renew verb
　renews
　renewing
　renewed
renewable
renewal noun
　renewals
renown
renowned
rent noun
　rents
rent verb
　rents
　renting
　rented
repair verb
　repairs
　repairing
　repaired

repair noun
　repairs
repay verb
　repays
　repaying
　repaid
repayment noun
　repayments
repeat verb
　repeats
　repeating
　repeated
repeat noun
　repeats
repeatedly
repel verb
　repels
　repelling
　repelled
repellent
repent verb
　repents
　repenting
　repented
repentance
repentant
repetition noun
　repetitions
repetitive adjective
　repetitively
replace verb
　replaces
　replacing
　replaced
replacement noun
　replacements
replay noun
　replays
replica noun
　replicas

★ You use a capital R when you mean the historical period.

reply verb
replies
replying
replied

reply noun
replies

report verb
reports
reporting
reported

report noun
reports

reporter noun
reporters

repossess verb
repossesses
repossessing
repossessed

represent verb
represents
representing
represented

representation noun
representations

representative adjective and noun
representatives

repress verb
represses
repressing
repressed

repression noun
repressions

repressive adjective
repressively

reprieve verb
reprieves
reprieving
reprieved

reprieve noun
reprieves

reprimand verb
reprimands
reprimanding
reprimanded

reprisal noun
reprisals

reproach verb
reproaches
reproaching
reproached

reproduce verb
reproduces
reproducing
reproduced

reproduction noun
reproduction

reproductive adjective
reproductively

reptile noun
reptiles

republic noun
republics

republican adjective and noun
republicans

★ **Republican** adjective and noun
Republicans

repulsion

repulsive adjective
repulsively

reputation noun
reputations

request verb
requests
requesting
requested

request noun
requests

require verb
requires
requiring
required

requirement noun
requirements

reread verb
rereads
rereading
reread

rescue verb
rescues
rescuing
rescued

rescue noun
rescues

rescuer noun
rescuers

research noun
researches

researcher noun
researchers

resemblance noun
resemblances

resemble verb
resembles
resembling
resembled

resent verb
resents
resenting
resented

resentful adjective
resentfully

resentment

reservation noun
reservations

reserve verb
reserves
reserving
reserved

★ You use a capital R when you mean the political party in the USA.

reserve noun
reserves

reservoir noun
reservoirs

reshuffle noun
reshuffles

reside verb
resides
residing
resided

residence noun
residences

resident noun
residents

resign verb
resigns
resigning
resigned

resignation noun
resignations

resin noun
resins

resinous

resist verb
resists
resisting
resisted

resistance noun
resistances

resistant

resolute adjective
resolutely

resolution noun
resolutions

resolve verb
resolves
resolving
resolved

resort noun
resorts

resort verb
resorts
resorting
resorted

resound verb
resounds
resounding
resounded

resource noun
resources

respect verb
respects
respecting
respected

respect noun
respects

respectability

respectable
adjective
respectably

respectful adjective
respectfully

respective adjective
respectively

respiration

respirator noun
respirators

respiratory

respond verb
responds
responding
responded

response noun
responses

responsibility noun
responsibilities

responsible adjective
responsibly

rest verb
rests
resting
rested

rest noun
rests

restaurant noun
restaurants

restful adjective
restfully

restless adjective
restlessly

restlessness

restoration noun
restorations

restore verb
restores
restoring
restored

restrain verb
restrains
restraining
restrained

restraint noun
restraints

restrict verb
restricts
restricting
restricted

restriction noun
restrictions

restrictive adjective
restrictively

result verb
results
resulting
resulted

result noun
results

resume verb
resumes
resuming
resumed

resumption noun
resumptions

re

re Try also words beginning with **rh-** or **wr-** 204

resuscitate verb
resuscitates
resuscitating
resuscitated

retail verb
retails
retailing
retailed

retail noun

retain verb
retains
retaining
retained

retina noun
retinas

retire verb
retires
retiring
retired

retirement

retort verb
retorts
retorting
retorted

retort noun
retorts

retrace verb
retraces
retracing
retraced

retreat verb
retreats
retreating
retreated

retrievable adjective
retrievably

retrieval noun
retrievals

retrieve verb
retrieves
retrieving
retrieved

retriever noun
retrievers

return verb
returns
returning
returned

return noun
returns

reunion noun
reunions

rev verb
revs
revving
revved

rev noun
revs

reveal verb
reveals
revealing
revealed

revelation noun
revelations

revenge

revenue noun
revenues

revere verb
reveres
revering
revered

reverence

★ **Reverend**

★ **reverent** adjective
reverently

reversal noun
reversals

reverse verb
reverses
reversing
reversed

reverse noun
reverses

reversible adjective
reversibly

review verb
reviews
reviewing
reviewed

☆ **review** noun
reviews

reviewer noun
reviewers

revise verb
revises
revising
revised

revision noun
revisions

revival noun
revivals

revive verb
revives
reviving
revived

revolt verb
revolts
revolting
revolted

revolt noun
revolts

revolution noun
revolutions

revolutionary
adjective and noun
revolutionaries

revolutionize verb
revolutionizes
revolutionizing
revolutionized

★ You use **Reverend** as a title of a member of the clergy, and **reverent** as an ordinary word meaning 'showing respect'.
☆ A **review** is a piece of writing about a film, play, etc. ! **revue**.

revolve verb
revolves
revolving
revolved

revolver noun
revolvers

★ **revue** noun
revues

reward verb
rewards
rewarding
rewarded

reward noun
rewards

rewind verb
rewinds
rewinding
rewound

rewrite verb
rewrites
rewriting
rewrote
rewritten

rheumatic

rheumatism

rhinoceros noun
rhinoceroses or
rhinoceros

rhododendron noun
rhododendrons

rhombus noun
rhombuses

rhubarb

rhyme verb
rhymes
rhyming
rhymed

rhyme noun
rhymes

rhythm noun
rhythms

rhythmic or
rhythmical adjective
rhythmically

rib noun
ribs

ribbon noun
ribbons

rice

rich adjective
richer
richest
richly

riches plural noun

richness

rick noun
ricks

rickety

rickshaw noun
rickshaws

ricochet verb
ricochets
ricocheting
ricocheted

rid verb
rids
ridding
rid

riddance

riddle noun
riddles

ride verb
rides
riding
rode
ridden

ride noun
rides

rider noun
riders

ridge noun
ridges

ridicule verb
ridicules
ridiculing
ridiculed

ridiculous adjective
ridiculously

rifle noun
rifles

rift noun
rifts

rig verb
rigs
rigging
rigged

rigging

right adjective
rightly

☆ **right** noun
rights

○ **right** verb
rights
righting
righted

righteous adjective
righteously

righteousness

rightful adjective
rightfully

right-handed

rightness

rigid adjective
rigidly

rigidity

rim noun
rims

rind noun
rinds

ring noun
rings

★ A **revue** is an entertainment of short sketches. ! **review**.
☆ A **right** is something you are entitled to. ! **rite, write**.
○ To **right** something is to make it right. ! **rite, write**.

★ **ring** verb
  rings
  ringing
  rang
  rung

☆ **ring** verb
  rings
  ringing
  ringed

ring noun
  rings

ringleader noun
  ringleaders

ringlet noun
  ringlets

ringmaster noun
  ringmasters

rink noun
  rinks

rinse verb
  rinses
  rinsing
  rinsed

rinse noun
  rinses

riot verb
  riots
  rioting
  rioted

riot noun
  riots

riotous adjective
  riotously

rip verb
  rips
  ripping
  ripped

rip noun
  rips

ripe adjective
  riper
  ripest

ripen verb
  ripens
  ripening
  ripened

ripeness

rip-off noun
  rip-offs

ripple noun
  ripples

ripple verb
  ripples
  rippling
  rippled

rise verb
  rises
  rising
  rose
  risen

rise noun
  rises

risk verb
  risks
  risking
  risked

risk noun
  risks

risky adjective
  riskier
  riskiest
  riskily

risotto noun
  risottos

rissole noun
  rissoles

○ **rite** noun
  rites

ritual noun
  rituals

rival noun
  rivals

rival verb
  rivals
  rivalling
  rivalled

rivalry noun
  rivalries

river noun
  rivers

rivet noun
  rivets

rivet verb
  rivets
  riveting
  riveted

✳ **road** noun
  roads

roadroller noun
  roadrollers

roadside noun
  roadsides

roadway noun
  roadways

roam verb
  roams
  roaming
  roamed

roar verb
  roars
  roaring
  roared

roar noun
  roars

roast verb
  roasts
  roasting
  roasted

rob verb
  robs
  robbing
  robbed

- -

★ The past tense is **rang** and the past participle is **rung** when you mean 'to make a sound like a bell'. ! **wring**.

☆ The past tense and past participle is **ringed** when you mean 'to put a ring round something'. ! **wring**.

○ A **rite** is a ceremony or ritual. ! **right, write**.

✳ A **road** is a hard surface for traffic to use. ! **rode**.

robber noun
  robbers

robbery noun
  robberies

robe noun
  robes

robin noun
  robins

robot noun
  robots

robust adjective
  robustly

rock verb
  rocks
  rocking
  rocked

rock noun
  rocks

rocker noun
  rockers

rockery noun
  rockeries

rocket noun
  rockets

rocky adjective
  rockier
  rockiest
  rockily

rod noun
  rods

★ **rode** see ride

rodent noun
  rodents

rodeo noun
  rodeos

rogue noun
  rogues

roguish adjective
  roguishly

☆ **role** noun
  roles

roll verb
  rolls
  rolling
  rolled

○ **roll** noun
  rolls

roller noun
  rollers

Roman adjective and noun
  Romans

Roman Catholic noun
  Roman Catholics

romance noun
  romances

Roman numeral

romantic adjective
  romantically

Romany

romp verb
  romps
  romping
  romped

romp noun
  romps

rompers plural noun

roof noun
  roofs

rook noun
  rooks

room noun
  rooms

roomful adjective
  roomfuls

roomy adjective
  roomier
  roomiest
  roomily

roost noun
  roosts

✳ **root** noun
  roots

root verb
  roots
  rooting
  rooted

rope noun
  ropes

rose noun
  roses

rose see rise

rosette noun
  rosettes

rosy adjective
  rosier
  rosiest
  rosily

rot verb
  rots
  rotting
  rotted

rot noun

rota noun
  rotas

rotary

rotate verb
  rotates
  rotating
  rotated

rotation noun
  rotations

rotor noun
  rotors

rotten

rottenness

rottweiler noun
  rottweilers

. . . .

★ **Rode** is the past tense of **ride**. ! road.
☆ A **role** is a part in a play or film. ! roll.
○ A **roll** is a small loaf of bread or an act of rolling. ! role.
✳ A **root** is the part of a plant that grows underground. ! route.

rough adjective
rougher
roughest
roughly

roughness

roughage

roughen verb
roughens
roughening
roughened

round adjective,
adverb, and
preposition
rounder
roundest
roundly

round noun
rounds

round verb
rounds
rounding
rounded

roundabout
adjective and noun
roundabouts

rounders noun

Roundhead noun
Roundheads

rouse verb
rouses
rousing
roused

rout verb
routs
routing
routed

rout noun
routs

★ **route** noun
routes

routine noun
routines

routine adjective
routinely

rove verb
roves
roving
roved

rover noun
rovers

☆ **row** noun
rows

◉ **row** verb
rows
rowing
rowed

rowdiness

rowdy adjective
rowdier
rowdiest
rowdily

rower noun
rowers

rowlock noun
rowlocks

royal adjective
royally

royalty

rub verb
rubs
rubbing
rubbed

rub noun
rubs

rubber noun
rubbers

rubbery

rubbish

rubble

ruby noun
rubies

rucksack noun
rucksacks

rudder noun
rudders

ruddy adjective
ruddier
ruddiest

rude adjective
ruder
rudest
rudely

rudeness

ruffian noun
ruffians

ruffle verb
ruffles
ruffling
ruffled

rug noun
rugs

✷ **rugby**

rugged adjective
ruggedly

rugger

ruin verb
ruins
ruining
ruined

ruin noun
ruins

ruinous adjective
ruinously

rule noun
rules

rule verb
rules
ruling
ruled

ruler noun
rulers

ruling noun
rulings

★ A **route** is the way you go to get to a place. ! **root**.
☆ A **row** is a line of people or things and rhymes with 'go'. A **row** is also a noise or argument and rhymes with 'cow'.
◉ To **row** means to use oars to make a boat move and rhymes with 'go'.
✷ You can use a small r when you mean the game.

rum noun
rums

rumble verb
rumbles
rumbling
rumbled

rumble noun
rumbles

rummage verb
rummages
rummaging
rummaged

rummy

rumour noun
rumours

rump noun
rumps

run verb
runs
running
ran
run

run noun
runs

runaway noun
runaways

rung noun
rungs

rung see ring

runner noun
runners

runner-up noun
runners-up

runny adjective
runnier
runniest
runnily

runway noun
runways

rural

rush verb
rushes
rushing
rushed

rush noun
rushes

rusk noun
rusks

rust noun

rust verb
rusts
rusting
rusted

rustic

rustle verb
rustles
rustling
rustled

rustler noun
rustlers

rusty adjective
rustier
rustiest
rustily

rut noun
ruts

ruthless adjective
ruthlessly

ruthlessness

rutted

★ **rye** noun

Ss

sabbath noun
sabbaths

sabotage noun

sabotage verb
sabotages
sabotaging
sabotaged

saboteur noun
saboteurs

☆ **sac** noun
sacs

saccharin

sachet noun
sachets

✪ **sack** noun
sacks

sack verb
sacks
sacking
sacked

sacred

sacrifice noun
sacrifices

sacrificial adjective
sacrificially

sacrifice verb
sacrifices
sacrificing
sacrificed

sad adjective
sadder
saddest
sadly

sadness

sadden verb
saddens
saddening
saddened

saddle noun
saddles

saddle verb
saddles
saddling
saddled

. . . .

★ **Rye** is a type of cereal or bread. ! wry.
☆ A **sac** is a bag-like part of an animal or plant. ! sack.
✪ A **sack** is a large bag. ! sac.

sadist noun
sadists

sadism

sadistic adjective
sadistically

safari noun
safaris

safe adjective
safer
safest
safely

safe noun
safes

safeguard noun
safeguards

safety

sag verb
sags
sagging
sagged

saga noun
sagas

sago

said see say

sail verb
sails
sailing
sailed

★ **sail** noun
sails

sailboard noun
sailboards

sailor noun
sailors

saint noun
saints

saintly adjective
saintlier
saintliest

sake

salaam interjection

salad noun
salads

salami noun
salamis

salary noun
salaries

☆ **sale** noun
sales

salesman noun
salesmen

salesperson noun
salespersons

saleswoman noun
saleswomen

saline

saliva

sally verb
sallies
sallying
sallied

salmon noun
salmon

salon noun
salons

saloon noun
saloons

salt noun

salt verb
salts
salting
salted

salty adjective
saltier
saltiest

salute verb
salutes
saluting
saluted

salute noun
salutes

salvage verb
salvages
salvaging
salvaged

salvation

same

samosa noun
samosas

sample noun
samples

sample verb
samples
sampling
sampled

sanctuary noun
sanctuaries

sand noun
sands

sand verb
sands
sanding
sanded

sander noun
sanders

sandal noun
sandals

sandbag noun
sandbags

sandpaper

sands plural noun

sandstone

sandwich noun
sandwiches

sandy adjective
sandier
sandiest

sane adjective
saner
sanest
sanely

- -

★ A **sail** is a sheet that catches the wind to make a boat go. ! sale.
☆ You use **sale** in e.g. *The house is for sale*. ! sail.

sang see sing
sanitary
sanitation
sanity
sank see sink
Sanskrit
sap noun
sap verb
 saps
 sapping
 sapped
sapling noun
 saplings
sapphire noun
 sapphires
sarcasm
sarcastic adjective
 sarcastically
sardine noun
 sardines
sari noun
 saris
sash noun
 sashes
sat see sit
satchel noun
 satchels
satellite noun
 satellites
satin
satire noun
 satires
satirical adjective
 satirically
satirist noun
 satirists
satisfaction
satisfactory
 adjective
 satisfactorily

satisfy verb
 satisfies
 satisfying
 satisfied
saturate verb
 saturates
 saturating
 saturated
saturation
Saturday noun
 Saturdays
★ **sauce** noun
 sauces
saucepan noun
 saucepans
saucer noun
 saucers
saucy adjective
 saucier
 sauciest
 saucily
sauna noun
 saunas
saunter verb
 saunters
 sauntering
 sauntered
sausage noun
 sausages
savage adjective
 savagely
savage noun
 savages
savage verb
 savages
 savaging
 savaged
savagery
savannah noun
 savannahs

save verb
 saves
 saving
 saved
saver noun
 savers
savings plural noun
saviour noun
 saviours
savoury
saw noun
 saws
saw verb
 saws
 sawing
 sawed
 sawn
saw see see
sawdust
saxophone noun
 saxophones
say verb
 says
 saying
 said
say noun
saying noun
 sayings
scab noun
 scabs
scabbard noun
 scabbards
scaffold noun
 scaffolds
scaffolding
scald verb
 scalds
 scalding
 scalded

★ A sauce is a liquid you put on food. ! **source**.

scale *noun*
scales

scale *verb*
scales
scaling
scaled

scales *plural noun*

scaly *adjective*
scalier
scaliest

scalp *noun*
scalps

scalp *verb*
scalps
scalping
scalped

scamper *verb*
scampers
scampering
scampered

scampi *plural noun*

scan *verb*
scans
scanning
scanned

scan *noun*
scans

scandal *noun*
scandals

scandalous *adjective*
scandalous

scanner *noun*
scanners

scanty *adjective*
scantier
scantiest
scantily

scapegoat *noun*
scapegoats

scar *noun*
scars

scar *verb*
scars
scarring
scarred

scarce *adjective*
scarcer
scarcest
scarcely

scarcity *noun*
scarcities

scare *verb*
scares
scaring
scared

scare *noun*
scares

scarecrow *noun*
scarecrows

scarf *noun*
scarves

scarlet

scary *adjective*
scarier
scariest
scarily

scatter *verb*
scatters
scattering
scattered

★ **scene** *noun*
scenes

scenery

☆ **scent** *noun*
scents

scent *verb*
scents
scenting
scented

sceptic *noun*
sceptics

sceptical *adjective*
sceptically

scepticism

schedule *noun*
schedules

scheme *noun*
schemes

scheme *verb*
schemes
scheming
schemed

schemer *noun*
schemers

scholar *noun*
scholars

scholarly

scholarship *noun*
scholarships

school *noun*
schools

schoolboy *noun*
schoolboys

schoolchild *noun*
schoolchildren

schoolgirl *noun*
schoolgirls

schoolteacher *noun*
schoolteachers

schooner *noun*
schooners

science

scientific *adjective*
scientifically

scientist *noun*
scientists

scissors *plural noun*

scoff *verb*
scoffs
scoffing
scoffed

· ·

★ A scene is a place or part of a play. **!** seen.
☆ A scent is a smell or perfume. **!** cent, sent.

scold verb
scolds
scolding
scolded

scone noun
scones

scoop noun
scoops

scoop verb
scoops
scooping
scooped

scooter noun
scooters

scope

scorch verb
scorches
scorching
scorched

score noun
scores

score verb
scores
scoring
scored

scorer noun
scorers

scorn noun

scorn verb
scorns
scorning
scorned

scorpion noun
scorpions

Scot noun
Scots

scoundrel noun
scoundrels

scour verb
scours
scouring
scoured

★ **Scout** noun
Scouts

scout noun
scouts

scowl verb
scowls
scowling
scowled

scramble verb
scrambles
scrambling
scrambled

scramble noun
scrambles

scrap verb
scraps
scrapping
scrapped

scrap noun
scraps

scrape verb
scrapes
scraping
scraped

scrape noun
scrapes

scraper noun
scrapers

scrappy adjective
scrappier
scrappiest
scrappily

scratch verb
scratches
scratching
scratched

scratch noun
scratches

scrawl verb
scrawls
scrawling
scrawled

scrawl noun
scrawls

scream verb
screams
screaming
screamed

scream noun
screams

screech verb
screeches
screeching
screeched

screech noun
screeches

screen noun
screens

screen verb
screens
screening
screened

screw noun
screws

screw verb
screws
screwing
screwed

screwdriver noun
screwdrivers

scribble verb
scribbles
scribbling
scribbled

scribble noun
scribbles

scribbler noun
scribblers

script noun
scripts

scripture noun
scriptures

★ You use a capital S when you mean a member of the Scout Association.

scroll noun
scrolls

scrotum noun
scrotums or scrota

scrounge verb
scrounges
scrounging
scrounged

scrounger noun
scroungers

scrub verb
scrubs
scrubbing
scrubbed

scrub noun

scruffy adjective
scruffier
scruffiest
scruffily

scrum noun
scrums

scrummage noun
scrummages

scrutinize verb
scrutinizes
scrutinizing
scrutinized

scrutiny noun
scrutinies

scuba diving

scuffle noun
scuffles

scuffle verb
scuffles
scuffling
scuffled

scullery noun
sculleries

sculptor noun
sculptors

sculpture noun
sculptures

scum

scurry verb
scurries
scurrying
scurried

scurvy

scuttle verb
scuttles
scuttling
scuttled

scuttle noun
scuttles

scythe noun
scythes

★ **sea** noun
seas

seabed

seafarer noun
seafarers

seafaring

seafood

seagull noun
seagulls

sea horse noun
sea horses

seal verb
seals
sealing
sealed

seal noun
seals

sea lion noun
sea lions

☆ **seam** noun
seams

seaman noun
seamen

seamanship

seaplane noun
seaplanes

seaport noun
seaports

search verb
searches
searching
searched

search noun
searches

searcher noun
searchers

searchlight noun
searchlights

seashore noun
seashores

seasick

seasickness

seaside

season noun
seasons

season verb
seasons
seasoning
seasoned

seasonal adjective
seasonally

seasoning noun
seasonings

seat noun
seats

seat verb
seats
seating
seated

seat belt noun
seat belts

seaward adjective
and adverb

. . . .

★ A **sea** is an area of salt water. ! **see**.
☆ A **seam** is a line of stitching in cloth. ! **seem**.

seawards adverb
seaweed noun
  seaweeds
secateurs plural
  noun
secluded
seclusion
second adjective
  secondly
second noun
  seconds
second verb
  seconds
  seconding
  seconded
secondary
second-hand
  adjective
secrecy
secret adjective
  secretly
secret noun
  secrets
secretary noun
  secretaries
secrete verb
  secretes
  secreting
  secreted
secretion noun
  secretions
secretive adjective
  secretively
secretiveness
sect noun
  sects
section noun
  sections
sectional
sector noun
  sectors

secure adjective
  securer
  securest
  securely
secure verb
  secures
  securing
  secured
security
sedate adjective
  sedately
sedation
sedative noun
  sedatives
sediment
sedimentary
★ **see** verb
  sees
  seeing
  saw
  seen
seed noun
  seeds
seedling noun
  seedlings
seek verb
  seeks
  seeking
  sought
☆ **seem** verb
  seems
  seeming
  seemed
seemingly
✆ **seen** see see
seep verb
  seeps
  seeping
  seeped
seepage

see-saw noun
  see-saws
seethe verb
  seethes
  seething
  seethed
segment noun
  segments
segmented
segregate verb
  segregates
  segregating
  segregated
segregation
seismograph noun
  seismographs
seize verb
  seizes
  seizing
  seized
seizure noun
  seizures
seldom
select verb
  selects
  selecting
  selected
select adjective
self noun
  selves
self-confidence
self-confident
  adjective
  self-confidently
self-conscious
  adjective
  self-consciously
self-contained
selfish adjective
  selfishly

. . . .

★ You use see in e.g. *I can't see anything.* ! **sea**.
☆ You use seem in e.g. *they seem tired.* ! **seam**.
✆ **Seen** is the past participle of **see**. ! **scene**.

selfishness
selfless adjective
  selflessly
self-service
★ **sell** verb
  sells
  selling
  sold
semaphore
semen

> **semi-**
> semi- makes words
> meaning 'half', e.g.
> **semi-automatic,**
> **semi-skimmed.**
> A few words are spelt
> joined up, e.g.
> **semicircle,**
> **semicolon,** but most
> of them have hyphens.

semibreve noun
  semibreves
semicircle noun
  semicircles
semicircular
semicolon noun
  semicolons
semi-detached
semi-final noun
  semi-finals
semi-finalist noun
  semi-finalists
semitone noun
  semitones
semolina
senate
senator noun
  senators

send verb
  sends
  sending
  sent
senior adjective and
  noun
  seniors
seniority
sensation noun
  sensations
sensational adjective
  sensationally
sense noun
  senses
sense verb
  senses
  sensing
  sensed
senseless adjective
  senselessly
sensible adjective
  sensibly
sensitive adjective
  sensitively
sensitivity noun
  sensitivities
sensitize verb
  sensitizes
  sensitizing
  sensitized
sensor noun
  sensors
☆ **sent** see **send**
sentence noun
  sentences
sentence verb
  sentences
  sentencing
  sentenced
sentiment noun
  sentiments

sentimental
  adjective
  sentimentally
sentimentality
sentinel noun
  sentinels
sentry noun
  sentries
separable
separate adjective
  separately
separate verb
  separates
  separating
  separated
separation noun
  separations
September noun
  Septembers
septic
sequel noun
  sequels
sequence noun
  sequences
sequin noun
  sequins
serene adjective
  serenely
serenity
sergeant noun
  sergeants
sergeant major
  noun
  sergeant majors
○ **serial** noun
  serials
series noun
  series
serious adjective
  seriously

- -

★ To **sell** something means 'to exchange it for money'. ! **cell**.
☆ You use **sent** in e.g. *he was sent home*. ! **cent, scent**.
○ A **serial** is a story or programme in separate parts. ! **cereal**.

seriousness

sermon noun
sermons

serpent noun
serpents

servant noun
servants

serve verb
serves
serving
served

server noun
servers

serve noun
serves

service noun
services

service verb
services
servicing
serviced

serviette noun
serviettes

session noun
sessions

set verb
sets
setting
set

set noun
sets

set square noun
set squares

★ **sett** noun
setts

settee noun
settees

setting noun
settings

settle verb
settles
settling
settled

settlement noun
settlements

settler noun
settlers

set-up noun
set-ups

seven

seventeen

seventeenth

seventh adjective and
noun
seventhly

seventieth

seventy adjective and
noun
seventies

sever verb
severs
severing
severed

several adjective
severally

severe adjective
severer
severest
severely

severity

☆ **sew** verb
sews
sewing
sewed
sewn

sewage

sewer noun
sewers

sex noun
sexes

sexism

sexist adjective and
noun
sexists

sextet noun
sextets

sexual adjective
sexually

sexuality

sexy adjective
sexier
sexiest
sexily

shabbiness

shabby adjective
shabbier
shabbiest
shabbily

shack noun
shacks

shade noun
shades

shade verb
shades
shading
shaded

shadow noun
shadows

shadow verb
shadows
shadowing
shadowed

shadowy

shady adjective
shadier
shadiest

shaft noun
shafts

shaggy adjective
shaggier
shaggiest
shaggily

★ A **sett** is a badger's burrow.
☆ To **sew** is to work with a needle and thread. ! sow.

shake *verb*
shakes
shaking
shook
shaken

★ **shake** *noun*
shakes

shaky *adjective*
shakier
shakiest
shakily

shall *verb*
should

shallow *adjective*
shallower
shallowest
shallowly

sham *noun*
shams

shamble *verb*
shambles
shambling
shambled

shambles *noun*

shame *verb*
shames
shaming
shamed

shame *noun*

shameful *adjective*
shamefully

shameless *adjective*
shamelessly

shampoo *noun*
shampoos

shampoo *verb*
shampoos
shampooing
shampooed

shamrock

shandy *noun*
shandies

shan't *verb*

shanty *noun*
shanties

shape *noun*
shapes

shape *verb*
shapes
shaping
shaped

shapeless *adjective*
shapelessly

shapely *adjective*
shapelier
shapeliest

share *noun*
shares

share *verb*
shares
sharing
shared

shark *noun*
sharks

sharp *adjective*
sharper
sharpest
sharply

sharp *noun*
sharps

sharpen *verb*
sharpens
sharpening
sharpened

sharpener *noun*
sharpeners

sharpness

shatter *verb*
shatters
shattering
shattered

shave *verb*
shaves
shaving
shaved

shave *noun*
shaves

shaver *noun*
shavers

shavings *plural noun*

shawl *noun*
shawls

she

sheaf *noun*
sheaves

☆ **shear** *verb*
shears
shearing
sheared
shorn

shearer *noun*
shearers

shears *plural noun*

sheath *noun*
sheaths

sheathe *verb*
sheathes
sheathing
sheathed

shed *noun*
sheds

shed *verb*
sheds
shedding
shed

she'd *verb*

sheen

sheep *noun*
sheep

sheepdog *noun*
sheepdogs

. . . .

★ To **shake** is to tremble or quiver. ! **sheikh**.
☆ To **shear** is to cut wool from a sheep. ! **sheer**.

sheepish adjective
sheepishly

★ **sheer** adjective
sheerer
sheerest

sheet noun
sheets

sheikh noun
sheikhs

shelf noun
shelves

shell noun
shells

shell verb
shells
shelling
shelled

she'll verb

shellfish noun
shellfish

shelter noun
shelters

shelter verb
shelters
sheltering
sheltered

shelve verb
shelves
shelving
shelved

shepherd noun
shepherds

sherbet noun
sherbets

sheriff noun
sheriffs

sherry noun
sherries

she's verb

shield noun
shields

shield verb
shields
shielding
shielded

shift noun
shifts

shift verb
shifts
shifting
shifted

shilling noun
shillings

shimmer verb
shimmers
shimmering
shimmered

shin noun
shins

shine verb
shines
shining
shone
shined

shine noun

shingle

shiny adjective
shinier
shiniest

-ship
-ship makes nouns,
e.g. friendship. Other
noun suffixes are
-dom, -hood, -ment,
and -ness.

ship noun
ships

ship verb
ships
shipping
shipped

shipping

shipwreck noun
shipwrecks

shipwrecked

shipyard noun
shipyards

shire noun
shires

shirk verb
shirks
shirking
shirked

shirt noun
shirts

shiver verb
shivers
shivering
shivered

shiver noun
shivers

shivery

shoal noun
shoals

shock verb
shocks
shocking
shocked

shock noun
shocks

shoddy adjective
shoddier
shoddiest
shoddily

shoe noun
shoes

shoelace noun
shoelaces

shoestring noun
shoestrings

shone see shine

shook see shake

★ You use **sheer** in e.g. *sheer joy*. ! **shear**.

shoot verb
shoots
shooting
shot

★ **shoot** noun
shoots

shop noun
shops

shop verb
shops
shopping
shopped

shopkeeper noun
shopkeepers

shoplifter noun
shoplifters

shopper noun
shoppers

shopping

shore noun
shores

shorn see shear

short adjective
shorter
shortest
shortly

shortness

shortage noun
shortages

shortbread

shortcake noun
shortcakes

shortcoming noun
shortcomings

shorten verb
shortens
shortening
shortened

shorthand

short-handed

shortly

shorts plural noun

short-sighted

shot noun
shots

shot see shoot

shotgun noun
shotguns

should

shoulder noun
shoulders

shoulder verb
shoulders
shouldering
shouldered

shout verb
shouts
shouting
shouted

shout noun
shouts

shove verb
shoves
shoving
shoved

shovel noun
shovels

shovel verb
shovels
shovelling
shovelled

show verb
shows
showing
showed
shown

show noun
shows

shower noun
showers

shower verb
showers
showering
showered

showery

showjumper noun
showjumpers

showjumping

showman noun
showmen

showmanship

showroom noun
showrooms

showiness

showy adjective
showier
showiest
showily

shrank see shrink

shrapnel

shred noun
shreds

shred verb
shreds
shredding
shredded

shrew noun
shrews

shrewd adjective
shrewder
shrewdest
shrewdly

shrewdness

shriek verb
shrieks
shrieking
shrieked

shriek noun
shrieks

- -

★ To **shoot** is to fire at someone with a gun. ! chute.

shrill adjective
shriller
shrillest
shrilly

shrillness

shrimp noun
shrimps

shrine noun
shrines

shrink verb
shrinks
shrinking
shrank
shrunk

shrinkage

shrivel verb
shrivels
shrivelling
shrivelled

shroud noun
shrouds

shroud verb
shrouds
shrouding
shrouded

Shrove Tuesday

shrub noun
shrubs

shrubbery noun
shrubberies

shrug verb
shrugs
shrugging
shrugged

shrug noun
shrugs

shrunk see shrink

shrunken adjective

shudder verb
shudders
shuddering
shuddered

shudder noun
shudders

shuffle verb
shuffles
shuffling
shuffled

shuffle noun
shuffles

shunt verb
shunts
shunting
shunted

shunter noun
shunters

shut verb
shuts
shutting
shut

shutter noun
shutters

shuttle noun
shuttles

shuttlecock noun
shuttlecocks

shy adjective
shyer
shyest
shyly

Siamese

sick adjective
sicker
sickest

sicken verb
sickens
sickening
sickened

sickly adjective
sicklier
sickliest

sickness noun
sicknesses

side noun
sides

side verb
sides
siding
sided

sideboard noun
sideboards

sidecar noun
sidecars

sideline noun
sidelines

sideshow noun
sideshows

sideways

siding noun
sidings

siege noun
sieges

sieve noun
sieves

sift verb
sifts
sifting
sifted

sigh verb
sighs
sighing
sighed

sigh noun
sighs

★ **sight** noun
sights

sight verb
sights
sighting
sighted

sightseer noun
sightseers

sightseeing

. . . .

★ A **sight** is something you see. ! site.

sign verb
signs
signing
signed

sign noun
signs

signal noun
signals

signal verb
signals
signalling
signalled

signaller noun
signallers

signalman noun
signalmen

signature noun
signatures

★ **signet** noun
signets

significance

significant adjective
significantly

signify verb
signifies
signifying
signified

signing

signpost noun
signposts

Sikh noun
Sikhs

silence noun
silences

silence verb
silences
silencing
silenced

silencer noun
silencers

silent adjective
silently

silhouette noun
silhouettes

silicon

silk

silken

silkworm noun
silkworms

silky adjective
silkier
silkiest
silkily

sill noun
sills

silliness

silly adjective
sillier
silliest
sillily

silver

silvery

similar adjective
similarly

similarity

simile noun
similes

simmer verb
simmers
simmering
simmered

simple adjective
simpler
simplest

simplicity

simplification

simplify verb
simplifies
simplifying
simplified

simply

simulate verb
simulates
simulating
simulated

simulation noun
simulations

simulator noun
simulators

simultaneous
adjective
simultaneously

sin noun
sins

sin verb
sins
sinning
sinned

since preposition,
adverb, and
conjunction

sincere adjective
sincerer
sincerest
sincerely

sincerity

sinew noun
sinews

sinful adjective
sinfully

sinfulness

sing verb
sings
singing
sang
sung

singer noun
singers

singe verb
singes
singeing
singed

★ A **signet** is a seal worn in a ring. ! **cygnet**.

single adjective
singly
single noun
singles
single verb
singles
singling
singled
single-handed
singular adjective
singularly
singular noun
singulars
sinister adjective
sinisterly
sink verb
sinks
sinking
sank or sunk
sunk
sink noun
sinks
sinner noun
sinners
sinus noun
sinuses
sip verb
sips
sipping
sipped
siphon noun
siphons
siphon verb
siphons
siphoning
siphoned
sir
siren noun
sirens
sister noun
sisters

sisterly
sister-in-law noun
sisters-in-law
sit verb
sits
sitting
sat
sitter noun
sitters
★ **site** noun
sites
site verb
sites
siting
sited
sit-in noun
sit-ins
situated
situation noun
situations
six noun
sixes
sixpence noun
sixpences
sixteen noun
sixteens
sixteenth
sixth
sixthly
sixtieth
sixty noun
sixties
size noun
sizes
size verb
sizes
sizing
sized
sizeable

sizzle verb
sizzles
sizzling
sizzled
skate verb
skates
skating
skated
☆ **skate** noun
skates or skate
skateboard noun
skateboards
skater noun
skaters
skeletal adjective
skeletally
skeleton noun
skeletons
sketch noun
sketches
sketch verb
sketches
sketching
sketched
sketchy adjective
sketchier
sketchiest
sketchily
skewer noun
skewers
ski verb
skis
skiing
skied
ski'd
ski noun
skis

★ A **site** is a place where something will be built. ! **sight**.
☆ The plural is **skate** when you mean the fish.

skid verb
skids
skidding
skidded

skid noun
skids

skier noun
skiers

skilful adjective
skilfully

skill noun
skills

skilled

skim verb
skims
skimming
skimmed

skimp verb
skimps
skimping
skimped

skimpy adjective
skimpier
skimpiest
skimpily

skin noun
skins

skin verb
skins
skinning
skinned

skinny adjective
skinnier
skinniest

skint

skip verb
skips
skipping
skipped

skip noun
skips

skipper noun
skippers

skirt noun
skirts

skirt verb
skirts
skirting
skirted

skirting noun
skirtings

skit noun
skits

skittish adjective
skittishly

skittle noun
skittles

skull noun
skulls

skunk noun
skunks

sky noun
skies

skylark noun
skylarks

skylight noun
skylights

skyscraper noun
skyscrapers

slab noun
slabs

slack adjective
slacker
slackest
slackly

slacken verb
slackens
slackening
slackened

slackness

slacks plural noun

slag heap noun
slag heaps

slain see slay

slam verb
slams
slamming
slammed

slang

slant verb
slants
slanting
slanted

slant noun
slants

slap verb
slaps
slapping
slapped

slap noun
slaps

slapstick

slash verb
slashes
slashing
slashed

slash noun
slashes

slat noun
slats

slate noun
slates

slaty adjective
slatier
slatiest

slaughter verb
slaughters
slaughtering
slaughtered

slaughter noun

slaughterhouse
noun
slaughterhouses

slave noun
slaves

slave verb
slaves
slaving
slaved

slavery

★ **slay** verb
slays
slaying
slew
slain

sled noun
sleds

sledge noun
sledges

sledgehammer
noun
sledgehammers

sleek adjective
sleeker
sleekest
sleekly

sleep verb
sleeps
sleeping
slept

sleep noun

sleeper noun
sleepers

sleepiness

sleepless

sleepwalker noun
sleepwalkers

sleepwalking

sleepy adjective
sleepier
sleepiest
sleepily

sleet

sleeve noun
sleeves

sleeveless

☆ **sleigh** noun
sleighs

slender adjective
slenderer
slenderest

slept see sleep

slew see slay

slice noun
slices

slice verb
slices
slicing
sliced

slick adjective
slicker
slickest
slickly

slick noun
slicks

slide verb
slides
sliding
slid

slide noun
slides

slight adjective
slighter
slightest
slightly

slim adjective
slimmer
slimmest
slimly

slim verb
slims
slimming
slimmed

slime

slimmer noun
slimmers

slimy adjective
slimier
slimiest

sling verb
slings
slinging
slung

sling noun
slings

slink verb
slinks
slinking
slunk

slip verb
slips
slipping
slipped

slip noun
slips

slipper noun
slippers

slippery

slipshod

slit noun
slits

slit verb
slits
slitting
slit

slither verb
slithers
slithering
slithered

sliver noun
slivers

slog verb
slogs
slogging
slogged

· ·

★ To **slay** people is to kill them. ! **sleigh**.
☆ A **sleigh** is a vehicle for sliding on snow. ! **slay**.

slog *noun*
slogs

slogan *noun*
slogans

slop *verb*
slops
slopping
slopped

slope *verb*
slopes
sloping
sloped

slope *noun*
slopes

sloppiness

sloppy *adjective*
sloppier
sloppiest
sloppily

slops *plural noun*

slosh *verb*
sloshes
sloshing
sloshed

slot *noun*
slots

sloth *noun*
sloths

slouch *verb*
slouches
slouching
slouched

slovenly

slow *adjective*
slower
slowest
slowly

slow *verb*
slows
slowing
slowed

slowcoach *noun*
slowcoaches

slowness

sludge

slug *noun*
slugs

slum *noun*
slums

slumber

slumber *verb*
slumbers
slumbering
slumbered

slump *verb*
slumps
slumping
slumped

slump *noun*
slumps

slung see **sling**

slunk see **slink**

slur *noun*
slurs

slush

slushy *adjective*
slushier
slushiest
slushily

sly *adjective*
slyer
slyest
slyly

slyness

smack *verb*
smacks
smacking
smacked

smack *noun*
smacks

small *adjective*
smaller
smallest

smallpox

smart *adjective*
smarter
smartest
smartly

smart *verb*
smarts
smarting
smarted

smarten *verb*
smartens
smartening
smartened

smartness

smash *verb*
smashes
smashing
smashed

smash *noun*
smashes

smashing

smear *verb*
smears
smearing
smeared

smear *noun*
smears

smell *verb*
smells
smelling
smelt *or* smelled

smell *noun*
smells

smelly *adjective*
smellier
smelliest

smelt *verb*
smelts
smelting
smelted

smile noun
smiles

smile verb
smiles
smiling
smiled

smith noun
smiths

smithereens plural
noun

smock noun
smocks

smog

smoke noun

smoke verb
smokes
smoking
smoked

smokeless

smoker noun
smokers

smoky adjective
smokier
smokiest

smooth adjective
smoother
smoothest
smoothly

smooth verb
smooths
smoothing
smoothed

smoothness

smother verb
smothers
smothering
smothered

smoulder verb
smoulders
smouldering
smouldered

smudge verb
smudges
smudging
smudged

smudge noun
smudges

smuggle verb
smuggles
smuggling
smuggled

smuggler noun
smugglers

smut noun
smuts

smutty adjective
smuttier
smuttiest
smuttily

snack noun
snacks

snag noun
snags

snail noun
snails

snake noun
snakes

snaky adjective
snakier
snakiest

snap verb
snaps
snapping
snapped

snap noun
snaps

snappy adjective
snappier
snappiest
snappily

snapshot noun
snapshots

snare noun
snares

snare verb
snares
snaring
snared

snarl verb
snarls
snarling
snarled

snarl noun
snarls

snatch verb
snatches
snatching
snatched

snatch noun
snatches

sneak verb
sneaks
sneaking
sneaked

sneak noun
sneaks

sneaky adjective
sneakier
sneakiest
sneakily

sneer verb
sneers
sneering
sneered

sneeze verb
sneezes
sneezing
sneezed

sneeze noun
sneezes

sniff verb
sniffs
sniffing
sniffed

sniff noun
sniffs

snigger verb
sniggers
sniggering
sniggered

snigger noun
sniggers

snip verb
snips
snipping
snipped

snip noun
snips

snipe verb
snipes
sniping
sniped

sniper noun
snipers

snippet noun
snippets

snivel verb
snivels
snivelling
snivelled

snob noun
snobs

snobbery

snobbish adjective
snobbishly

snooker

snoop verb
snoops
snooping
snooped

snooper noun
snoopers

snore verb
snores
snoring
snored

snorkel noun
snorkels

snort verb
snorts
snorting
snorted

snort noun
snorts

snout noun
snouts

snow noun

snow verb
snows
snowing
snowed

snowball noun
snowballs

snowdrop noun
snowdrops

snowflake noun
snowflakes

snowman noun
snowmen

snowplough noun
snowploughs

snowshoe noun
snowshoes

snowstorm noun
snowstorms

snowy adjective
snowier
snowiest

snub verb
snubs
snubbing
snubbed

snuff

snug adjective
snugger
snuggest
snugly

snuggle verb
snuggles
snuggling
snuggled

soak verb
soaks
soaking
soaked

so-and-so noun
so-and-so's

soap noun
soaps

soapiness noun

soapy adjective
soapier
soapiest
soapily

★ **soar** verb
soars
soaring
soared

sob verb
sobs
sobbing
sobbed

sob noun
sobs

sober adjective
soberly

sobriety

so-called

soccer

sociability

sociable adjective
sociably

social adjective
socially

socialism

socialist noun
socialists

. . . .

★ To **soar** is to rise or fly high. ! **sore**.

society noun
societies

sociological adjective
sociologically

sociologist noun
sociologists

sociology

sock noun
socks

sock verb
socks
socking
socked

socket noun
sockets

soda

sodium

sofa noun
sofas

soft adjective
softer
softest
softly

soften verb
softens
softening
softened

softness

software

soggy adjective
soggier
soggiest
soggily

soil noun

soil verb
soils
soiling
soiled

solar

sold see sell

solder noun

solder verb
solders
soldering
soldered

soldier noun
soldiers

★ **sole** noun
soles

sole adjective
solely

solemn adjective
solemnly

solemnity

solicitor noun
solicitors

solid adjective
solidly

solid noun
solids

solidify verb
solidifies
solidifying
solidified

solidity

soliloquy noun
soliloquies

solitary

solitude

solo noun
solos

soloist noun
soloists

solstice noun
solstices

solubility

soluble adjective
solubly

solution noun
solutions

solve verb
solves
solving
solved

solvent adjective and noun
solvents

sombre adjective
sombrely

☆ **some** adjective and pronoun

somebody

somehow

someone

somersault noun
somersaults

something

sometime

sometimes

somewhat

somewhere

○ **son** noun
sons

sonar noun
sonars

song noun
songs

songbird noun
songbirds

sonic adjective
sonically

sonnet noun
sonnets

. . . .

★ A **sole** is a fish or a part of a shoe. ! soul.

☆ You use **some** in e.g. *Have some cake*. ! sum.

○ A **son** is a male child. ! sun.

soon adverb
sooner
soonest

soot

soothe verb
soothes
soothing
soothed

sooty adjective
sootier
sootiest

sophisticated

sophistication

sopping

soppy adjective
soppier
soppiest
soppily

soprano noun
sopranos

sorcerer noun
sorcerers

sorceress noun
sorceresses

sorcery

★ **sore** adjective
sorer
sorest
sorely

sore noun
sores

soreness

sorrow noun
sorrows

sorrowful adjective
sorrowfully

sorry adjective
sorrier
sorriest

sort noun
sorts

sort verb
sorts
sorting
sorted

sought see seek

☆ **soul** noun
souls

sound noun
sounds

sound verb
sounds
sounding
sounded

sound adjective
sounder
soundest
soundly

soundness

soundtrack noun
soundtracks

soup noun
soups

sour adjective
sourer
sourest
sourly

❍ **source** noun
sources

sourness

south adjective and
adverb

✳ **south** noun

south-east noun and
adjective

southerly adjective
and noun
southerlies

southern adjective

southerner noun
southerners

southward adjective
and adverb

southwards adverb

south-west noun and
adjective

souvenir noun
souvenirs

sovereign noun
sovereigns

✱ **sow** verb
sows
sowing
sowed
sown

sow noun
sows

sower noun
sowers

soya bean noun
soya beans

space noun
spaces

space verb
spaces
spacing
spaced

spacecraft noun
spacecraft

spaceman noun
spacemen

spaceship noun
spaceships

spacewoman noun
spacewomen

spacious adjective
spaciously

. . . .

★ You use **sore** in e.g. *I've got a sore tooth*. ! **soar**.
☆ A **soul** is a person's spirit. ! **sole**.
❍ The **source** is where something comes from. ! **sauce**.
✳ You use a capital S in **the South**, when you mean a particular region.
✱ To **sow** is to put seed in the ground. ! **sew**.

spaciousness

spade *noun*
spades

spaghetti

span *verb*
spans
spanning
spanned

span *noun*
spans

spaniel *noun*
spaniels

spank *verb*
spanks
spanking
spanked

spanner *noun*
spanners

spar *noun*
spars

spar *verb*
spars
sparring
sparred

spare *verb*
spares
sparing
spared

spare *adjective and noun*
spares

sparing *adjective*
sparingly

spark *noun*
sparks

spark *verb*
sparks
sparking
sparked

sparkle *verb*
sparkles
sparkling
sparkled

sparkler *noun*
sparklers

sparrow *noun*
sparrows

sparse *adjective*
sparser
sparsest
sparsely

sparseness

spastic *noun*
spastics

spat see **spit**

spatter *verb*
spatters
spattering
spattered

spawn *noun*

spawn *verb*
spawns
spawning
spawned

speak *verb*
speaks
speaking
spoke
spoken

speaker *noun*
speakers

spear *noun*
spears

spear *verb*
spears
spearing
speared

special *adjective*
specially

specialist *noun*
specialists

speciality *noun*
specialities

specialization

specialize *verb*
specializes
specializing
specialized

species *noun*
species

specific *adjective*
specifically

specification *noun*
specifications

specify *verb*
specifies
specifying
specified

specimen *noun*
specimens

speck *noun*
specks

speckled

spectacle *noun*
spectacles

spectacular *adjective*
spectacularly

spectator *noun*
spectators

spectre *noun*
spectres

spectrum *noun*
spectra

speech *noun*
speeches

speechless

speed *noun*
speeds

★ **speed** *verb*
speeds
speeding
sped *or* speeded

speedboat *noun*
speedboats

speedometer *noun*
speedometers

speedway *noun*
speedways

speedy *adjective*
speedier
speediest
speedily

spell *verb*
spells
spelling
spelt
spelled

spell *noun*
spells

spelling *noun*
spellings

spend *verb*
spends
spending
spent

sperm *noun*
sperms *or* sperm

sphere *noun*
spheres

spherical *adjective*
spherically

spice *noun*
spices

spicy *adjective*
spicier
spiciest

spider *noun*
spiders

spied see **spy**

spike *noun*
spikes

spiky *adjective*
spikier
spikiest

☆ **spill** *verb*
spills
spilling
spilt *or* spilled

spill *noun*
spills

spin *verb*
spins
spinning
spun

spin *noun*
spins

spinach

spindle *noun*
spindles

spin-drier *noun*
spin-driers

spine *noun*
spines

spinal

spin-off *noun*
spin-offs

spinster *noun*
spinsters

spiny *adjective*
spiniest
spiniest

spiral *adjective*
spirally

spire *noun*
spires

spirit *noun*
spirits

spiritual *adjective*
spiritually

spiritual *noun*
spirituals

spiritualism

spiritualist *noun*
spiritualists

spit *verb*
spits
spitting
spat

spit *noun*
spits

spite

spiteful *adjective*
spitefully

spittle

splash *verb*
splashes
splashing
splashed

splash *noun*
splashes

splashdown *noun*
splashdowns

splendid *adjective*
splendidly

splendour

splint *noun*
splints

splinter *noun*
splinters

splinter *verb*
splinters
splintering
splintered

split *verb*
splits
splitting
split

split *noun*
splits

- -

★ You use **sped** in e.g. *Cars sped past* and **speeded** in e.g. *They speeded up the process.*

☆ You use **spilled** in e.g. *I spilled the milk.* You use **spilt** in e.g. *I can see spilt milk.* You use **spilled** or **spilt** in e.g. *I have spilled/spilt the milk.*

splutter verb
splutters
spluttering
spluttered

★ **spoil** verb
spoils
spoiling
spoilt or spoiled

spoils plural noun

spoilsport noun
spoilsports

spoke noun
spokes

spoke see speak

spoken see speak

spokesperson noun
spokespersons

sponge noun
sponges

sponge verb
sponges
sponging
sponged

sponger noun
spongers

sponginess noun

spongy adjective
spongier
spongiest
spongily

sponsor noun
sponsors

sponsorship noun
sponsorships

spontaneity

spontaneous
adjective
spontaneously

spooky adjective
spookier
spookiest
spookily

spool noun
spools

spoon noun
spoons

spoon verb
spoons
spooning
spooned

spoonful noun
spoonfuls

sport noun
sports

sporting

sportsman noun
sportsmen

sportsmanship

sportswoman noun
sportswomen

spot noun
spots

spot verb
spots
spotting
spotted

spotless adjective
spotlessly

spotlight noun
spotlights

spotter noun
spotters

spotty adjective
spottier
spottiest
spottily

spout noun
spouts

spout verb
spouts
spouting
spouted

sprain verb
sprains
spraining
sprained

sprain noun
sprains

sprang see spring

sprawl verb
sprawls
sprawling
sprawled

spray verb
sprays
spraying
sprayed

spray noun
sprays

spread verb
spreads
spreading
spread

spread noun
spreads

spreadsheet noun
spreadsheets

sprightliness

sprightly adjective
sprightlier
sprightliest

spring verb
springs
springing
sprang
sprung

spring noun
springs

springboard noun
springboards

- -

★ You use **spoiled** in e.g. *They spoiled the party*. You use **spoilt** in e.g. *a spoilt child*. You use **spoiled** or **spoilt** in e.g. *They have spoiled/spoilt the party*.

spring-clean verb
spring-cleans
spring-cleaning
spring-cleaned

springtime

springy adjective
springier
springiest

sprinkle verb
sprinkles
sprinkling
sprinkled

sprinkler noun
sprinklers

sprint verb
sprints
sprinting
sprinted

sprinter noun
sprinters

sprout verb
sprouts
sprouting
sprouted

sprout noun
sprouts

spruce noun
spruces

spruce adjective
sprucer
sprucest

sprung see **spring**

spud noun
spuds

spun see **spin**

spur noun
spurs

spur verb
spurs
spurring
spurred

spurt verb
spurts
spurting
spurted

spurt noun
spurts

spy noun
spies

spy verb
spies
spying
spied

squabble verb
squabbles
squabbling
squabbled

squabble noun
squabbles

squad noun
squads

squadron noun
squadrons

squalid adjective
squalidly

squall noun
squalls

squally adjective
squallier
squalliest

squalor

squander verb
squanders
squandering
squandered

square adjective
squarely

square noun
squares

square verb
squares
squaring
squared

squareness

squash verb
squashes
squashing
squashed

squash noun
squashes

squat verb
squats
squatting
squatted

squat adjective
squatter
squattest
squatly

squatter noun
squatters

squaw noun
squaws

squawk verb
squawks
squawking
squawked

squawk noun
squawks

squeak verb
squeaks
squeaking
squeaked

squeak noun
squeaks

squeaky adjective
squeakier
squeakiest
squeakily

squeal verb
squeals
squealing
squealed

squeal noun
squeals

squeeze verb
squeezes
squeezing
squeezed

squeeze noun
squeezes

squeezer noun
squeezers

squelch verb
squelches
squelching
squelched

squelch noun
squelches

squid noun
squid or squids

squint verb
squints
squinting
squinted

squint noun
squints

squire noun
squires

squirm verb
squirms
squirming
squirmed

squirrel noun
squirrels

squirt verb
squirts
squirting
squirted

stab verb
stabs
stabbing
stabbed

stab noun
stabs

stability

stabilize verb
stabilizes
stabilizing
stabilized

stabilizer noun
stabilizers

stable adjective
stabler
stablest
stably

stable noun
stables

stack verb
stacks
stacking
stacked

stack noun
stacks

stadium noun
stadiums or stadia

staff noun
staffs

stag noun
stags

stage noun
stages

stage verb
stages
staging
staged

stagecoach noun
stagecoaches

stagger verb
staggers
staggering
staggered

stagnant adjective
stagnantly

stain noun
stains

stain verb
stains
staining
stained

stainless

★ **stair** noun
stairs

staircase noun
staircases

☆ **stake** noun
stakes

stake verb
stakes
staking
staked

stalactite noun
stalactites

stalagmite noun
stalagmites

stale adjective
staler
stalest

stalk noun
stalks

stalk verb
stalks
stalking
stalked

stall noun
stalls

stall verb
stalls
stalling
stalled

stallion noun
stallions

stalls plural noun

stamen noun
stamens

stamina

★ A stair is one of a set of steps. ! stare.
☆ A stake is a pointed stick or post. ! steak.

stammer *verb*
stammers
stammering
stammered

stammer *noun*
stammers

stamp *noun*
stamps

stamp *verb*
stamps
stamping
stamped

stampede *noun*
stampedes

stand *verb*
stands
standing
stood

stand *noun*
stands

standard *adjective*
and noun
standards

standardize *verb*
standardizes
standardizing
standardized

standby *noun*
standbys

standstill *noun*
standstills

stank see **stink**

stanza *noun*
stanzas

staple *noun*
staples

staple *adjective*

stapler *noun*
staplers

star *noun*
stars

starry *adjective*
starrier
starriest
starrily

star *verb*
stars
starring
starred

starboard

starch *noun*
starches

starchy *adjective*
starchier
starchiest

★ **stare** *verb*
stares
staring
stared

starfish *noun*
starfish *or* starfishes

starling *noun*
starlings

start *verb*
starts
starting
started

start *noun*
starts

starter *noun*
starters

startle *verb*
startles
startling
startled

starvation

starve *verb*
starves
starving
starved

state *noun*
states

state *verb*
states
stating
stated

stateliness

stately *adjective*
statelier
stateliest

statement *noun*
statements

statesman *noun*
statesmen

statesmanship

stateswoman *noun*
stateswomen

static *adjective*
statically

station *noun*
stations

station *verb*
stations
stationing
stationed

☆ **stationary** *adjective*

◐ **stationery** *noun*

stationmaster *noun*
stationmasters

statistic *noun*
statistics

statistical *adjective*
statistically

statistician *noun*
statisticians

statistics

statue *noun*
statues

status *noun*
statuses

- -

★ To **stare** is to look at something without moving your eyes. ! **stair**.
☆ **Stationary** means 'not moving'. ! **stationery**.
◐ **Stationery** means 'paper and envelopes'. ! **stationary**.

staunch adjective
stauncher
staunchest
staunchly

stave noun
staves

stave verb
staves
staving
staved
stove

stay verb
stays
staying
stayed

stay noun
stays

steadiness

steady adjective
steadier
steadiest
steadily

steady verb
steadies
steadying
steadied

★ **steak** noun
steaks

☆ **steal** verb
steals
stealing
stole
stolen

stealth

stealthy adjective
stealthier
stealthiest
stealthily

steam noun

steam verb
steams
steaming
steamed

steamy adjective
steamier
steamiest
steamily

steamer noun
steamers

steamroller noun
steamrollers

steamship noun
steamships

steed noun
steeds

steel noun

○ **steel** verb
steels
steeling
steeled

steely adjective
steelier
steeliest

steep adjective
steeper
steepest
steeply

steepness

steeple noun
steeples

steeplechase noun
steeplechases

steeplejack noun
steeplejacks

steer verb
steers
steering
steered

steer noun
steers

stem noun
stems

stem verb
stems
stemming
stemmed

stench noun
stenches

stencil noun
stencils

✳ **step** noun
steps

step verb
steps
stepping
stepped

stepchild noun
stepchildren

stepfather noun
stepfathers

stepladder noun
stepladders

stepmother noun
stepmothers

✱ **steppe** noun
steppes

stereo adjective and noun
stereos

stereophonic adjective
stereophonically

sterile

sterility

sterilization

sterilize verb
sterilizes
sterilizing
sterilized

sterling

. . . .

★ A **steak** is a thick slice of meat. ! **stake**.
☆ To **steal** is to take something that is not yours. ! **steel**.
○ To **steel** yourself is to find courage to do something hard. ! **steal**.
✳ A **step** is a movement of the feet or part of a stair. ! **steppe**.
✱ A **steppe** is a grassy plain. ! **step**.

stern noun
  sterns

stern adjective
  sterner
  sternest
  sternly

sternness

stethoscope noun
  stethoscopes

stew verb
  stews
  stewing
  stewed

stew noun
  stews

steward noun
  stewards

stewardess noun
  stewardesses

stick verb
  sticks
  sticking
  stuck

stick noun
  sticks

sticker noun
  stickers

stickiness

stickleback noun
  sticklebacks

sticky adjective
  stickier
  stickiest
  stickily

stiff adjective
  stiffer
  stiffest
  stiffly

stiffen verb
  stiffens
  stiffening
  stiffened

stiffness

stifle verb
  stifles
  stifling
  stifled

stile noun
  stiles

still adjective
  stiller
  stillest

still adverb

still verb
  stills
  stilling
  stilled

stillness

stilts

stimulant noun
  stimulants

stimulate verb
  stimulates
  stimulating
  stimulated

stimulation

stimulus noun
  stimuli

sting noun
  stings

sting verb
  stings
  stinging
  stung

stingy adjective
  stingier
  stingiest
  stingily

stink noun
  stinks

stink verb
  stinks
  stinking
  stank
  stunk

stir verb
  stirs
  stirring
  stirred

stir noun
  stirs

stirrup noun
  stirrups

stitch noun
  stitches

stoat noun
  stoats

stock noun
  stocks

stock verb
  stocks
  stocking
  stocked

stockade noun
  stockades

stockbroker noun
  stockbrokers

stocking noun
  stockings

stockpile noun
  stockpiles

stocks plural noun

stocky adjective
  stockier
  stockiest
  stockily

stodgy adjective
  stodgier
  stodgiest
  stodgily

stoke verb
  stokes
  stoking
  stoked

stole noun
stoles

stole see **steal**

stolen see **steal**

stomach noun
stomachs

stomach verb
stomachs
stomaching
stomached

stone noun
stones or stone

stone verb
stones
stoning
stoned

stony adjective
stonier
stoniest

stood see **stand**

stool noun
stools

stoop verb
stoops
stooping
stooped

stop verb
stops
stopping
stopped

stop noun
stops

stoppage noun
stoppages

stopper noun
stoppers

stopwatch noun
stopwatches

storage

store verb
stores
storing
stored

store noun
stores

★ **storey** noun
storeys

stork noun
storks

storm noun
storms

storm verb
storms
storming
stormed

stormy adjective
stormier
stormiest
stormily

☆ **story** noun
stories

stout adjective
stouter
stoutest
stoutly

stoutness

stove noun
stoves

stove see **stave**

stow verb
stows
stowing
stowed

stowaway noun
stowaways

straddle verb
straddles
straddling
straddled

straggle verb
straggles
straggling
straggled

straggler noun
stragglers

straggly adjective
stragglier
straggliest

✪ **straight** adjective
straighter
straightest

straighten verb
straightens
straightening
straightened

straightforward
adjective
straightforwardly

strain verb
strains
straining
strained

strain noun
strains

strainer noun
strainers

✳ **strait** noun
straits

✱ **straits** plural noun

strand noun
strands

stranded

strange adjective
stranger
strangest
strangely

strangeness

stranger noun
strangers

• •

★ A **storey** is a floor of a building. **!** **story**.
☆ You use **story** in e.g. *read me a story*. **!** **storey**.
✪ **Straight** means 'not curving or bending'. **!** **strait**.
✳ A **strait** is a narrow stretch of water. **!** **straight**.
✱ You use **straits** in the phrase *in dire straits*.

st

strangle *verb*
strangles
strangling
strangled

strangler *noun*
stranglers

strangulation

strap *noun*
straps

strap *verb*
straps
strapping
strapped

strategic *adjective*
strategically

strategist *noun*
strategists

strategy *noun*
strategies

stratum *noun*
strata

straw *noun*
straws

strawberry *noun*
strawberries

stray *verb*
strays
straying
strayed

stray *adjective*
streak *noun*
streaks

streak *verb*
streaks
streaking
streaked

streaky *adjective*
streakier
streakiest
streakily

stream *noun*
streams

stream *verb*
streams
streaming
streamed

streamer *noun*
streamers

streamline *verb*
streamlines
streamlining
streamlined

street *noun*
streets

strength *noun*
strengths

strengthen *verb*
strengthens
strengthening
strengthened

strenuous *adjective*
strenuously

stress *noun*
stresses

stress *verb*
stresses
stressing
stressed

stretch *verb*
stretches
stretching
stretched

stretch *noun*
stretches

stretcher *noun*
stretchers

strew *verb*
strews
strewing
strewed
strewn

stricken

strict *adjective*
stricter
strictest
strictly

strictness

stride *verb*
strides
striding
strode
stridden

stride *noun*
strides

strife

strike *verb*
strikes
striking
struck

strike *noun*
strikes

striker *noun*
strikers

striking *adjective*
strikingly

string *noun*
strings

string *verb*
strings
stringing
strung

stringiness

stringy *adjective*
stringier
stringiest
stringily

strip *verb*
strips
stripping
stripped

strip *noun*
strips

stripe noun
stripes
striped
stripy adjective
stripier
stripiest
strive verb
strives
striving
strove
striven
strobe noun
strobes
strode see stride
stroke noun
strokes
stroke verb
strokes
stroking
stroked
stroll verb
strolls
strolling
strolled
stroll noun
strolls
strong adjective
stronger
strongest
strongly
stronghold noun
strongholds
strove see strive
struck see strike
structural adjective
structurally
structure noun
structures
struggle verb
struggles
struggling
struggled

struggle noun
struggles
strum verb
strums
strumming
strummed
strung see string
strut verb
struts
strutting
strutted
strut noun
struts
stub verb
stubs
stubbing
stubbed
stub noun
stubs
stubble
stubborn adjective
stubbornly
stubbornness
stuck see stick
stuck-up
stud noun
studs
student noun
students
studio noun
studios
studious adjective
studiously
study verb
studies
studying
studied
study noun
studies
stuff noun

stuff verb
stuffs
stuffing
stuffed
stuffiness
stuffing noun
stuffings
stuffy adjective
stuffier
stuffiest
stuffily
stumble verb
stumbles
stumbling
stumbled
stump noun
stumps
stump verb
stumps
stumping
stumped
stun verb
stuns
stunning
stunned
stung see sting
stunk see stink
stunt noun
stunts
stupendous adjective
stupendously
stupid adjective
stupider
stupidest
stupidly
stupidity
sturdiness
sturdy adjective
sturdier
sturdiest
sturdily

stutter verb
stutters
stuttering
stuttered

stutter noun
stutters

★ **sty** noun
sties

style noun
styles

style verb
styles
styling
styled

stylish adjective
stylishly

stylus noun
styluses

subcontinent noun
subcontinents

subdivide verb
subdivides
subdividing
subdivided

subdivision noun
subdivisions

subdue verb
subdues
subduing
subdued

subject adjective and noun
subjects

subject verb
subjects
subjecting
subjected

subjective adjective
subjectively

submarine noun
submarines

submerge verb
submerges
submerging
submerged

submersion

submission noun
submissions

submissive adjective
submissively

submit verb
submits
submitting
submitted

subordinate adjective and noun
subordinates

subordinate verb
subordinates
subordinating
subordinated

subordination

subscribe verb
subscribes
subscribing
subscribed

subscriber noun
subscribers

subscription noun
subscriptions

subsequent adjective
subsequently

subside verb
subsides
subsiding
subsided

subsidence

subsidize verb
subsidizes
subsidizing
subsidized

subsidy noun
subsidies

substance noun
substances

substantial adjective
substantially

substitute verb
substitutes
substituting
substituted

substitute noun
substitutes

substitution noun
substitutions

subtle adjective
subtler
subtlest
subtly

subtlety noun
subtleties

subtract verb
subtracts
subtracting
subtracted

subtraction noun
subtractions

suburb noun
suburbs

suburban

suburbia

subway noun
subways

succeed verb
succeeds
succeeding
succeeded

success noun
successes

successful adjective
successfully

- -

★ A **sty** is a place for pigs or a swelling on the eye. In the second meaning you can also use *stye*, plural *styes*.

succession noun
  successions
successive adjective
  successively
successor noun
  successors
such
suck verb
  sucks
  sucking
  sucked
suck noun
  sucks
suction
sudden adjective
  suddenly
suddenness
suds plural noun
sue verb
  sues
  suing
  sued
suede
suet
suffer verb
  suffers
  suffering
  suffered
sufficiency
sufficient adjective
  sufficiently
suffix noun
  suffixes
suffocate verb
  suffocates
  suffocating
  suffocated
suffocation
sugar
sugary

suggest verb
  suggests
  suggesting
  suggested
suggestion noun
  suggestions
suicidal adjective
  suicidally
suicide noun
  suicides
★ **suit** noun
  suits
suit verb
  suits
  suiting
  suited
suitability
suitable adjective
  suitably
suitcase noun
  suitcases
☆ **suite** noun
  suites
suitor noun
  suitors
sulk verb
  sulks
  sulking
  sulked
sulkiness
sulky adjective
  sulkier
  sulkiest
  sulkily
sullen adjective
  sullenly
sullenness
sulphur
sulphuric acid
sultan noun
  sultans

sultana noun
  sultanas
◉ **sum** noun
  sums
sum verb
  sums
  summing
  summed
summarize verb
  summarizes
  summarizing
  summarized
summary noun
  summaries
summer noun
  summers
summertime
summit noun
  summits
summon verb
  summons
  summoning
  summoned
summons noun
  summonses
✳ **sun** noun
  suns
sun verb
  suns
  sunning
  sunned
sunbathe verb
  sunbathes
  sunbathing
  sunbathed
sunburn
sunburned or
sunburnt
✱ **sundae** noun
  sundaes

- -
★ A **suit** is a set of matching clothes. ! **suite**.
☆ A **suite** is a set of furniture or a group of rooms. ! **suit**.
◉ A **sum** is an amount or total. ! **some**.
✳ A **sun** is a large star. ! **son**.
✱ A **sundae** is a cocktail of fruit and ice cream. ! **Sunday**.

★ **Sunday** noun
Sundays

sundial noun
sundials

sunflower noun
sunflowers

sung see **sing**
sunglasses
sunk see **sink**
sunlight
sunlit
sunny adjective
sunnier
sunniest
sunnily

sunrise noun
sunrises

sunset noun
sunsets

sunshade noun
sunshades

sunshine
sunspot noun
sunspots

sunstroke
suntan noun
suntans

suntanned
super

> **super-**
> super- makes words
> meaning 'very good'
> or 'extra', e.g.
> **supermarket,**
> **supermodel.** They
> are normally spelt
> joined up.

superb adjective
superbly

superficial adjective
superficially

superfluous adjective
superfluously

superintend verb
superintends
superintending
superintended

superintendent
noun
superintendents

superior adjective
and noun
superiors

superiority
superlative adjective
superlatively

superlative noun
superlatives

supermarket noun
supermarkets

supernatural
adjective
supernaturally

supersonic adjective
supersonically

superstition noun
superstitions

superstitious
adjective
superstitiously

supervise verb
supervises
supervising
supervised

supervision
supervisor
supper noun
suppers

supple adjective
suppler
supplest
supplely

supplement noun
supplements

supplementary
suppleness
supply verb
supplies
supplying
supplied

supplier noun
suppliers

supply noun
supplies

support verb
supports
supporting
supported

support noun
supports

supporter noun
supporters

suppose verb
supposes
supposing
supposed

supposedly
supposition noun
suppositions

suppress verb
suppresses
suppressing
suppressed

suppression
supremacy
supreme adjective
supremely

sure adjective
surer
surest
surely

surf noun

. . . .

★ Sunday is a day of the week. ! **sundae**.

surf *verb*
surfs
surfing
surfed

surface *noun*
surfaces

surface *verb*
surfaces
surfacing
surfaced

surfboard *noun*
surfboards

surfer *noun*
surfers

surge *verb*
surges
surging
surged

surge *noun*
surges

surgeon *noun*
surgeons

surgery *noun*
surgeries

surgical *adjective*
surgically

surname *noun*
surnames

surpass *verb*
surpasses
surpassing
surpassed

surplus *noun*
surpluses

surprise *verb*
surprises
surprising
surprised

surprise *noun*
surprises

surrender *verb*
surrenders
surrendering
surrendered

surrender *noun*
surrenders

surround *verb*
surrounds
surrounding
surrounded

surroundings *plural noun*

survey *noun*
surveys

survey *verb*
surveys
surveying
surveyed

surveyor *noun*
surveyors

survival

survive *verb*
survives
surviving
survived

survivor *noun*
survivors

suspect *verb*
suspects
suspecting
suspected

suspect *noun*
suspects

suspend *verb*
suspends
suspending
suspended

suspense

suspension *noun*
suspensions

suspicion *noun*
suspicions

suspicious *adjective*
suspiciously

sustain *verb*
sustains
sustaining
sustained

swagger *verb*
swaggers
swaggering
swaggered

swallow *verb*
swallows
swallowing
swallowed

swallow *noun*
swallows

swam see **swim**

swamp *verb*
swamps
swamping
swamped

swamp *noun*
swamps

swampy *adjective*
swampier
swampiest

swan *noun*
swans

swank *verb*
swanks
swanking
swanked

swap *verb*
swaps
swapping
swapped

swap *noun*
swaps

swarm *noun*
swarms

swarm *verb*
swarms
swarming
swarmed

swastika *noun*
swastikas

★ **swat** *verb*
swats
swatting
swatted

swatter *noun*
swatters

sway *verb*
sways
swaying
swayed

swear *verb*
swears
swearing
swore
sworn

sweat *verb*
sweats
sweating
sweated

sweat *noun*

sweater *noun*
sweaters

sweatshirt *noun*
sweatshirts

sweaty *adjective*
sweatier
sweatiest
sweatily

swede *noun*
swedes

sweep *verb*
sweeps
sweeping
swept

sweep *noun*
sweeps

sweeper *noun*
sweepers

sweet *adjective*
sweeter
sweetest
sweetly

sweet *noun*
sweets

sweetcorn

sweeten *verb*
sweetens
sweetening
sweetened

sweetener *noun*
sweeteners

sweetheart *noun*
sweethearts

sweetness

swell *verb*
swells
swelling
swelled
swollen

swell *noun*
swells

swelling *noun*
swellings

swelter *verb*
swelters
sweltering
sweltered

swept see **sweep**

swerve *verb*
swerves
swerving
swerved

swerve *noun*
swerves

swift *adjective*
swifter
swiftest
swiftly

swift *noun*
swifts

swiftness

swill *verb*
swills
swilling
swilled

swill *noun*

swim *verb*
swims
swimming
swam
swum

swim *noun*
swims

swimmer *noun*
swimmers

swimsuit *noun*
swimsuits

swindle *verb*
swindles
swindling
swindled

swindler *noun*
swindlers

swindle *noun*
swindles

swine *noun*
swine or swines

swing *verb*
swings
swinging
swung

swing *noun*
swings

swipe *verb*
swipes
swiping
swiped

. . . .

★ To **swat** an insect is to hit it. ! **swot**.

swipe noun
swipes
swirl verb
swirls
swirling
swirled
swirl noun
swirls
swish verb
swishes
swishing
swished
swish noun
swishes
Swiss roll noun
Swiss rolls
switch verb
switches
switching
switched
switch noun
switches
switchboard noun
switchboards
swivel verb
swivels
swivelling
swivelled
swollen see **swell**
swoon verb
swoons
swooning
swooned
swoop verb
swoops
swooping
swooped
swoop noun
swoops

swop verb
swops
swopping
swopped
sword noun
swords
swore see **swear**
sworn see **swear**
★ **swot** verb
swots
swotting
swotted
swot noun
swots
swum see **swim**
swung see **swing**
sycamore noun
sycamores
syllabic adjective
syllabically
syllable noun
syllables
syllabus noun
syllabuses
symbol noun
symbols
symbolic adjective
symbolically
symbolism
symbolize verb
symbolizes
symbolizing
symbolized
symmetrical
adjective
symmetrically
symmetry
sympathetic
adjective
sympathetically

sympathize verb
sympathizes
sympathizing
sympathized
sympathy noun
sympathies
symphonic adjective
symphonically
symphony noun
symphonies
symptom noun
symptoms
symptomatic
adjective
symptomatically
synagogue noun
synagogues
synchronization
synchronize verb
synchronizes
synchronizing
synchronized
syncopated
synonym noun
synonyms
synonymous
adjective
synonymously
synthesis noun
syntheses
synthesize verb
synthesizes
synthesizing
synthesized
synthesizer noun
synthesizers
synthetic adjective
synthetically
syringe noun
syringes

. . . .

★ To **swot** is to study hard. ! **swat.**

syrup noun
syrups

syrupy

system noun
systems

systematic adjective
systematically

Tt

-t
See the note at -ed.

tab noun
tabs

tabby noun
tabbies

table noun
tables

tablecloth noun
tablecloths

tablespoon noun
tablespoons

tablespoonful noun
tablespoonfuls

tablet noun
tablets

tack noun
tacks

tack verb
tacks
tacking
tacked

tackle verb
tackles
tackling
tackled

tackle noun
tackles

tacky adjective
tackier
tackiest
tackily

tact

tactful adjective
tactfully

tactical adjective
tactically

tactics plural noun

tactless adjective
tactlessly

tadpole noun
tadpoles

tag noun
tags

tag verb
tags
tagging
tagged

★ **tail** noun
tails

tail verb
tails
tailing
tailed

tailback noun
tailbacks

tailless

tailor noun
tailors

take verb
takes
taking
took
taken

takeaway noun
takeaways

takings plural noun

talc

talcum powder

☆ **tale** noun
tales

talent noun
talents

talented

talk verb
talks
talking
talked

talk noun
talks

talkative adjective
talkatively

talker noun
talkers

tall adjective
taller
tallest

tally verb
tallies
tallying
tallied

Talmud

talon noun
talons

tambourine noun
tambourines

tame adjective
tamer
tamest
tamely

tame verb
tames
taming
tamed

tameness

tamer noun
tamers

- -

★ A **tail** is a part at the back of an animal. ! tale.
☆ A **tale** is a story. ! tail.

tamper verb
tampers
tampering
tampered

tampon noun
tampons

tan noun
tans

tan verb
tans
tanning
tanned

tandem noun
tandems

tang noun
tangs

tangent noun
tangents

tangerine noun
tangerines

tangle verb
tangles
tangling
tangled

tangle noun
tangles

tank noun
tanks

tankard noun
tankards

tanker noun
tankers

tanner noun
tanners

tantalize verb
tantalizes
tantalizing
tantalized

tantrum noun
tantrums

tap noun
taps

tap verb
taps
tapping
tapped

tap dance noun
tap dances

tap dancer noun
tap dancers

tap dancing

tape noun
tapes

tape verb
tapes
taping
taped

tape-measure noun
tape-measures

taper verb
tapers
tapering
tapered

taper noun
tapers

tape recorder noun
tape recorders

tapestry noun
tapestries

tapeworm noun
tapeworms

tapioca

tar noun

tar verb
tars
tarring
tarred

tarantula noun
tarantulas

target noun
targets

target verb
targets
targeting
targeted

tarmac

tarmacadam

tarnish verb
tarnishes
tarnishing
tarnished

tarpaulin noun
tarpaulins

tarry adjective
tarrier
tarriest

tart noun
tarts

tart adjective
tarter
tartest
tartly

tartan noun
tartans

task noun
tasks

tassel noun
tassels

taste verb
tastes
tasting
tasted

taste noun
tastes

tasteful adjective
tastefully

tasteless adjective
tastelessly

tasty adjective
tastier
tastiest
tastily

tattered

tatters plural noun

tattoo noun
tattoos

tattoo verb
tattoos
tattooing
tattooed

tatty adjective
tattier
tattiest
tattily

taught see **teach**

taunt verb
taunts
taunting
taunted

taunt noun
taunts

taut adjective
tauter
tautest
tautly

tautness

tavern noun
taverns

tawny adjective
tawnier
tawniest

tax noun
taxes

tax verb
taxes
taxing
taxed

taxable

taxation

taxi noun
taxis

taxi verb
taxis
taxiing
taxied

taxpayer noun
taxpayers

★ **tea** noun
teas

teabag noun
teabags

teacake noun
teacakes

teach verb
teaches
teaching
taught

teacher noun
teachers

tea cloth or
tea towel noun
tea cloths or
tea towels

teacup noun
teacups

teak

☆ **team** noun
teams

teapot noun
teapots

tear verb
tears
tearing
tore
torn

○ **tear** noun
tears

tearful adjective
tearfully

tear gas

tease verb
teases
teasing
teased

teaspoon noun
teaspoons

teaspoonful noun
teaspoonfuls

teat noun
teats

tech noun
techs

technical adjective
technically

technicality noun
technicalities

technician noun
technicians

technique noun
techniques

technological
adjective
technologically

technology noun
technologies

teddy bear noun
teddy bears

tedious adjective
tediously

tediousness

tedium

✲ **tee** noun
tees

✱ **teem** verb
teems
teeming
teemed

teenage

teenager noun
teenagers

teens

teeth see **tooth**

teetotal

teetotaller noun
teetotallers

. . . .

★ **Tea** is a hot drink. ! **tee.**

☆ You use **team** in e.g. *a football team*. ! **teem.**

○ A **tear** is a drop of water from an eye and rhymes with 'here', or a split in
something and rhymes with 'hair'.

✲ A **tee** is part of a golf course. ! **tea.**

✱ You use **teem** in e.g. *a place teeming with people*. ! **team.**

telecommunications
  plural noun
telegram noun
  telegrams
telegraph noun
  telegraphs
telegraphic adjective
  telegraphically
telegraphy
telepathic adjective
  telepathically
telepathy
telephone noun
  telephones
telephone verb
  telephones
  telephoning
  telephoned
telephonist noun
  telephonists
telescope noun
  telescopes
telescopic adjective
  telescopically
teletext
televise verb
  televises
  televising
  televised
television noun
  televisions
tell verb
  tells
  telling
  told
tell-tale adjective
  and noun
  tell-tales
telly noun
  tellies
temper noun
  tempers

temperate
temperature noun
  temperatures
tempest noun
  tempests
tempestuous
  adjective
  tempestuously
temple noun
  temples
tempo noun
  tempos
temporary adjective
  temporarily
tempt verb
  tempts
  tempting
  tempted
temptation noun
  temptations
tempter noun
  tempters
temptress noun
  temptresses
ten noun
  tens
tenancy noun
  tenancies
tenant noun
  tenants
tend verb
  tends
  tending
  tended
tendency noun
  tendencies
tender adjective
  tenderer
  tenderest
  tenderly
tender noun
  tenders

tender verb
  tenders
  tendering
  tendered
tenderness
tendon noun
  tendons
tendril noun
  tendrils
tennis
tenor noun
  tenors
tenpin bowling
tense adjective
  tenser
  tensest
  tensely
tense noun
  tenses
tension noun
  tensions
tent noun
  tents
tentacle noun
  tentacles
tenth
tenthly
tepid
term noun
  terms
term verb
  terms
  terming
  termed
terminal noun
  terminals
terminate verb
  terminates
  terminating
  terminated

te - th

termination noun
terminations
terminus noun
termini
terrace noun
terraces
terrapin noun
terrapins
terrible adjective
terribly
terrier noun
terriers
terrific adjective
terrifically
terrify verb
terrifies
terrifying
terrified
territorial adjective
territorially
territory noun
territories
terror noun
terrors
terrorism
terrorist adjective
and noun
terrorists
terrorize verb
terrorizes
terrorizing
terrorized
tessellation noun
tessellations
test noun
tests
test verb
tests
testing
tested
testament noun
testaments

testicle noun
testicles
testify verb
testifies
testifying
testified
testimonial noun
testimonials
testimony noun
testimonies
testy adjective
testier
testiest
tether verb
tethers
tethering
tethered
tether noun
tethers
text noun
texts
textbook noun
textbooks
textile noun
textiles
texture noun
textures
than
thank verb
thanks
thanking
thanked
thankful adjective
thankfully
thankless adjective
thanklessly
thanks plural noun
that adjective,
pronoun, and
conjunction

thatch noun
thatch verb
thatches
thatching
thatched
thatcher noun
thatchers
thaw verb
thaws
thawing
thawed
theatre noun
theatres
theatrical adjective
theatrically
thee
theft noun
thefts
★ **their**
☆ **theirs**
them
theme noun
themes
theme park noun
theme parks
themselves
then
theologian noun
theologians
theological adjective
theologically
theology
theorem noun
theorems
theoretical adjective
theoretically
theory noun
theories
therapist noun
therapists

. . . .

★ You use **their** in e.g. *this is their house*. **!** there, they're.
☆ You use **theirs** in e.g. *the house is theirs*. Note that there is no apostrophe in
this word.

therapy noun
therapies

★ **there** adverb

thereabouts

therefore

thermal adjective
thermally

thermometer noun
thermometers

Thermos noun
Thermoses

thermostat noun
thermostats

thermostatic
adjective
thermostatically

thesaurus noun
thesauri or
thesauruses

these

they

they'd verb

they'll verb

☆ **they're** verb

they've verb

thick adjective
thicker
thickest
thickly

thicken verb
thickens
thickening
thickened

thicket noun
thickets

thickness noun
thicknesses

thief noun
thieves

thigh noun
thighs

thimble noun
thimbles

thin adjective
thinner
thinnest
thinly

thin verb
thins
thinning
thinned

thine

thing noun
things

think verb
thinks
thinking
thought

thinker noun
thinkers

thinness

third

thirdly

Third World

thirst

thirsty adjective
thirstier
thirstiest
thirstily

thirteen

thirteenth

thirtieth

thirty noun
thirties

this

thistle noun
thistles

thorn noun
thorns

thorny adjective
thornier
thorniest

thorough adjective
thoroughly

thoroughness

those

thou

though

thought noun
thoughts

thought see **think**

thoughtful adjective
thoughtfully

thoughtfulness

thoughtless adjective
thoughtlessly

thoughtlessness

thousand noun
thousands

thousandth

○ **thrash** verb
thrashes
thrashing
thrashed

thread noun
threads

thread verb
threads
threading
threaded

threadbare

threat noun
threats

threaten verb
threatens
threatening
threatened

three noun
threes

★ You use there in e.g. *Look over there.* ! their, they're.
☆ They're is short for *they are.* ! their, there.
○ To thrash someone is to beat them. ! thresh.

three-dimensional *adjective*
three-dimensionally

★ **thresh** *verb*
threshes
threshing
threshed

threshold *noun*
thresholds

threw see **throw**

thrift

thrifty *adjective*
thriftier
thriftiest
thriftily

thrill *noun*
thrills

thrill *verb*
thrills
thrilling
thrilled

thriller *noun*
thrillers

thrive *verb*
thrives
thriving
thrived *or* throve *or* thriven

throat *noun*
throats

throb *verb*
throbs
throbbing
throbbed

throb *noun*
throbs

throne *noun*
thrones

throng *noun*
throngs

throttle *verb*
throttles
throttling
throttled

throttle *noun*
throttles

through

throughout

throve see **thrive**

throw *verb*
throws
throwing
threw
thrown

throw *noun*
throws

thrush *noun*
thrushes

thrust *verb*
thrusts
thrusting
thrust

thud *noun*
thuds

thud *verb*
thuds
thudding
thudded

thumb *noun*
thumbs

thump *verb*
thumps
thumping
thumped

thump *noun*
thumps

thunder *noun*

thunder *verb*
thunders
thundering
thundered

thunderous *adjective*
thunderously

thunderstorm *noun*
thunderstorms

Thursday *noun*
Thursdays

thus

thy

tick *verb*
ticks
ticking
ticked

tick *noun*
ticks

ticket *noun*
tickets

tickle *verb*
tickles
tickling
tickled

ticklish *adjective*
ticklishly

tidal

tiddler *noun*
tiddlers

tiddlywink *noun*
tiddlywinks

tide *noun*
tides

tide *verb*
tides
tiding
tided

tidiness

tidy *adjective*
tidier
tidiest
tidily

tie *verb*
ties
tying
tied

. . . .

★ To **thresh** corn is to beat it to separate the grain. ! **thrash**.

tie noun
ties

tie-break noun
tie-breaks

tiger noun
tigers

tight adjective
tighter
tightest
tightly

tighten verb
tightens
tightening
tightened

tightness

tightrope noun
tightropes

tights plural noun

tigress noun
tigresses

tile noun
tiles

tiled

till preposition and
conjunction

till noun
tills

till verb
tills
tilling
tilled

tiller noun
tillers

tilt verb
tilts
tilting
tilted

tilt noun
tilts

timber noun
timbers

time noun
times

time verb
times
timing
timed

timer noun
timers

times

timetable noun
timetables

timid adjective
timidly

timidity

timing

timpani plural noun

tin noun
tins

tin verb
tins
tinning
tinned

tingle verb
tingles
tingling
tingled

tingle noun
tingles

tinker verb
tinkers
tinkering
tinkered

tinker noun
tinkers

tinkle verb
tinkles
tinkling
tinkled

tinkle noun
tinkles

tinny adjective
tinnier
tinniest
tinnily

tinsel

tint noun
tints

tint verb
tints
tinting
tinted

tiny adjective
tinier
tiniest

tip verb
tips
tipping
tipped

tip noun
tips

tiptoe verb
tiptoes
tiptoeing
tiptoed

tiptoe noun

★ **tire** verb
tires
tiring
tired

tired

tireless adjective
tirelessly

tiresome adjective
tiresomely

tissue noun
tissues

tit noun
tits

titbit noun
titbits

• •

★ To **tire** is to become tired. ! **tyre.**

title *noun*
titles

titter *verb*
titters
tittering
tittered

★ **to** *preposition*

toad *noun*
toads

toadstool *noun*
toadstools

toast *verb*
toasts
toasting
toasted

toast *noun*
toasts

toaster *noun*
toasters

tobacco *noun*
tobaccos

tobacconist *noun*
tobacconists

toboggan *noun*
toboggans

tobogganing

today

toddler *noun*
toddlers

☆ **toe** *noun*
toes

toffee *noun*
toffees

toga *noun*
togas

together

toil *verb*
toils
toiling
toiled

toilet *noun*
toilets

token *noun*
tokens

told see tell

tolerable *adjective*
tolerably

tolerance

tolerant *adjective*
tolerantly

tolerate *verb*
tolerates
tolerating
tolerated

toll *noun*
tolls

toll *verb*
tolls
tolling
tolled

tomahawk *noun*
tomahawks

tomato *noun*
tomatoes

tomb *noun*
tombs

tomboy *noun*
tomboys

tombstone *noun*
tombstones

tomcat *noun*
tomcats

tommy-gun *noun*
tommy-guns

tomorrow

tom-tom *noun*
tom-toms

○ **ton** *noun*
tons

tonal *adjective*
tonally

tone *noun*
tones

tone *verb*
tones
toning
toned

tone-deaf

tongs *plural noun*

tongue *noun*
tongues

tonic *noun*
tonics

tonight

✵ **tonne** *noun*
tonnes

tonsillitis

tonsils *plural noun*

✳ **too** *adverb*

took see take

tool *noun*
tools

tooth *noun*
teeth

toothache

toothbrush *noun*
toothbrushes

toothed

toothpaste *noun*
toothpastes

top *noun*
tops

top *verb*
tops
topping
topped

topic *noun*
topics

topical *adjective*
topically

topicality

- -

★ You use to in e.g. *go to bed* or *I want to stay.* ! too, two.
☆ A toe is a part of a foot. ! tow.
○ A ton is a non-metric unit of weight. ! tonne.
✵ A tonne is a metric unit of weight. ! ton.
✳ You use too in e.g. *it's too late* or *I want to come too.* ! to, two.

topless

topmost

topping noun
toppings

topple verb
topples
toppling
toppled

topsy-turvy

torch noun
torches

tore see **tear**

toreador noun
toreadors

torment verb
torments
tormenting
tormented

torment noun
torments

tormentor noun
tormentors

torn see **tear**

tornado noun
tornadoes

torpedo noun
torpedoes

torpedo verb
torpedoes
torpedoing
torpedoed

torrent noun
torrents

torrential adjective
torrentially

torso noun
torsos

tortoise noun
tortoises

torture verb
tortures
torturing
tortured

torture noun
tortures

torturer noun
torturers

Tory noun
Tories

toss verb
tosses
tossing
tossed

toss noun
tosses

total noun
totals

total adjective
totally

total verb
totals
totalling
totalled

totalitarian

totem pole noun
totem poles

totter verb
totters
tottering
tottered

touch verb
touches
touching
touched

touch noun
touches

touchy adjective
touchier
touchiest
touchily

tough adjective
tougher
toughest
toughly

toughen verb
toughens
toughening
toughened

toughness

tour noun
tours

tourism

tourist noun
tourists

tournament noun
tournaments

★ **tow** verb
tows
towing
towed

tow noun

toward or **towards**

towel noun
towels

towelling

tower noun
towers

tower verb
towers
towering
towered

town noun
towns

towpath noun
towpaths

toxic adjective
toxically

toy noun
toys

• •

★ To **tow** something is to pull it along. ! **toe**.

to - tr

toy verb
toys
toying
toyed

toyshop noun
toyshops

trace noun
traces

trace verb
traces
tracing
traced

traceable

track noun
tracks

track verb
tracks
tracking
tracked

tracker noun
trackers

tracksuit noun
tracksuits

tract noun
tracts

traction

tractor noun
tractors

trade noun
trades

trade verb
trades
trading
traded

trademark noun
trademarks

trader noun
traders

tradesman noun
tradesmen

trade union noun
trade unions

tradition noun
traditions

traditional adjective
traditionally

traffic noun

traffic verb
traffics
trafficking
trafficked

tragedy noun
tragedies

tragic adjective
tragically

trail noun
trails

trail verb
trails
trailing
trailed

trailer noun
trailers

train noun
trains

train verb
trains
training
trained

trainer noun
trainers

traitor noun
traitors

tram noun
trams

tramp noun
tramps

tramp verb
tramps
tramping
tramped

trample verb
tramples
trampling
trampled

trampoline noun
trampolines

trance noun
trances

tranquil adjective
tranquilly

★ **tranquillity**

tranquillizer noun
tranquillizers

transact verb
transacts
transacting
transacted

transaction noun
transactions

transatlantic

transfer verb
transfers
transferring
transferred

transfer noun
transfers

transferable

transference

transform verb
transforms
transforming
transformed

transformation noun
transformations

transformer noun
transformers

transfusion noun
transfusions

transistor noun
transistors

★ Note that there are two ls in this word.

transition *noun*
transitions

transitional *adjective*
transitionally

transitive *adjective*
transitively

translate *verb*
translates
translating
translated

translation *noun*
translations

translator *noun*
translators

translucent

transmission *noun*
transmissions

transmit *verb*
transmits
transmitting
transmitted

transmitter *noun*
transmitters

transparency *noun*
transparencies

transparent
adjective
transparently

transpire *verb*
transpires
transpiring
transpired

transplant *verb*
transplants
transplanting
transplanted

transplant *noun*
transplants

transplantation
noun
transplantations

transport *verb*
transports
transporting
transported

transportation

transport

transporter *noun*
transporters

trap *verb*
traps
trapping
trapped

trap *noun*
traps

trapdoor *noun*
trapdoors

trapeze *noun*
trapezes

trapezium *noun*
trapeziums

trapezoid *noun*
trapezoids

trapper *noun*
trappers

trash

trashy *adjective*
trashier
trashiest
trashily

travel *verb*
travels
travelling
travelled

travel *noun*

traveller *noun*
travellers

traveller's cheque
noun
traveller's cheques

trawler *noun*
trawlers

tray *noun*
trays

treacherous
adjective
treacherously

treachery

treacle

tread *verb*
treads
treading
trod
trodden

tread *noun*
treads

treason

treasure *noun*
treasures

treasure *verb*
treasures
treasuring
treasured

treasurer *noun*
treasurers

treasury *noun*
treasuries

treat *verb*
treats
treating
treated

treat *noun*
treats

treatment *noun*
treatments

treaty *noun*
treaties

tr

treble adjective and
noun
trebles

treble verb
trebles
trebling
trebled

tree noun
trees

trek verb
treks
trekking
trekked

trek noun
treks

trellis noun
trellises

tremble verb
trembles
trembling
trembled

tremble noun
trembles

tremendous
adjective
tremendously

tremor noun
tremors

trench noun
trenches

trend noun
trends

trendiness

trendy adjective
trendier
trendiest
trendily

trespass verb
trespasses
trespassing
trespassed

trespasser noun
trespassers

trestle noun
trestles

trial noun
trials

triangle noun
triangles

triangular

tribal adjective
tribally

tribe noun
tribes

tribesman noun
tribesmen

tributary noun
tributaries

tribute noun
tributes

trick noun
tricks

trick verb
tricks
tricking
tricked

trickery

trickster noun
tricksters

trickle verb
trickles
trickling
trickled

trickle noun
trickles

tricky adjective
trickier
trickiest
trickily

tricycle noun
tricycles

tried see **try**

trifle noun
trifles

trifle verb
trifles
trifling
trifled

trifling

trigger noun
triggers

trigger verb
triggers
triggering
triggered

trillion noun
trillions

trim adjective
trimmer
trimmest
trimly

trim verb
trims
trimming
trimmed

trim noun
trims

★ **Trinity**

trio noun
trios

trip verb
trips
tripping
tripped

trip noun
trips

tripe

triple adjective
triply

triple noun
triples

★ You use a capital T when you mean the three persons of God in Christianity.

triple *verb*
triples
tripling
tripled

triplet *noun*
triplets

tripod *noun*
tripods

triumph *noun*
triumphs

triumphant *adjective*
triumphantly

trivial *adjective*
trivially

triviality *noun*
trivialities

trod see tread
trodden see tread
troll *noun*
trolls

trolley *noun*
trolleys

trombone *noun*
trombones

troop *noun*
troops

troop *verb*
troops
trooping
trooped

troops *plural noun*
trophy *noun*
trophies

tropic *noun*
tropics

tropical *adjective*
trot *verb*
trots
trotting
trotted

trot *noun*
trots

trouble *noun*
troubles

trouble *verb*
troubles
troubling
troubled

troublesome
trough *noun*
troughs

trousers *plural noun*
trout *noun*
trout

trowel *noun*
trowels

truancy *noun*
truancies

truant *noun*
truants

truce *noun*
truces

truck *noun*
trucks

trudge *verb*
trudges
trudging
trudged

true *adjective*
truer
truest
truly

trump *noun*
trumps

trump *verb*
trumps
trumping
trumped

trumpet *noun*
trumpets

trumpet *verb*
trumpets
trumpeting
trumpeted

trumpeter *noun*
trumpeters

truncheon *noun*
truncheons

trundle *verb*
trundles
trundling
trundled

trunk *noun*
trunks

trunks *plural noun*
trust *verb*
trusts
trusting
trusted

trust
trustful *adjective*
trustfully

trustworthy
adjective
trustworthily

trusty *adjective*
trustier
trustiest
trustily

truth *noun*
truths

truthful *adjective*
truthfully

truthfulness
try *verb*
tries
trying
tried

try *noun*
tries

T-shirt *noun*
T-shirts

tub *noun*
tubs

tuba *noun*
tubas

tube *noun*
tubes

tuber *noun*
tubers

tubing

tubular

tuck *verb*
tucks
tucking
tucked

tuck *noun*
tucks

Tuesday *noun*
Tuesdays

tuft *noun*
tufts

tug *noun*
tugs

tug *verb*
tugs
tugging
tugged

tulip *noun*
tulips

tumble *verb*
tumbles
tumbling
tumbled

tumble *noun*
tumbles

tumble-drier *noun*
tumble-driers

tumbler *noun*
tumblers

tummy *noun*
tummies

tumour *noun*
tumours

tumult

tumultuous *adjective*
tumultuously

tuna *noun*
tuna *or* tunas

tundra

tune *noun*
tunes

tune *verb*
tunes
tuning
tuned

tuneful *adjective*
tunefully

tunic *noun*
tunics

tunnel *noun*
tunnels

tunnel *verb*
tunnels
tunnelling
tunnelled

turban *noun*
turbans

turbine *noun*
turbines

turbulence

turbulent *adjective*
turbulently

turf *noun*
turfs *or* turves

turkey *noun*
turkeys

Turkish bath *noun*
Turkish baths

Turkish delight

turmoil

turn *verb*
turns
turning
turned

turn *noun*
turns

turncoat *noun*
turncoats

turnip *noun*
turnips

turnover *noun*
turnovers

turnstile *noun*
turnstiles

turntable *noun*
turntables

turpentine

turquoise

turret *noun*
turrets

turtle *noun*
turtles

tusk *noun*
tusks

tussle *verb*
tussles
tussling
tussled

tussle *noun*
tussles

tutor *noun*
tutors

tweak *verb*
tweaks
tweaking
tweaked

tweak *noun*
tweaks

tweed

tweezers *plural noun*

twelve noun
  twelves
twelfth
twentieth
twenty noun
  twenties
twice
twiddle verb
  twiddles
  twiddling
  twiddled
twiddle noun
  twiddles
twig noun
  twigs
twig verb
  twigs
  twigging
  twigged
twilight
twin noun
  twins
twin verb
  twins
  twinning
  twinned
twine
twinkle verb
  twinkles
  twinkling
  twinkled
twinkle noun
  twinkles
twirl verb
  twirls
  twirling
  twirled
twirl noun
  twirls
twist verb
  twists
  twisting
  twisted

twist noun
  twists
twister noun
  twisters
twitch verb
  twitches
  twitching
  twitched
twitch noun
  twitches
twitter verb
  twitters
  twittering
  twittered
★ two adjective and
  noun
  twos
tying see tie
type noun
  types
type verb
  types
  typing
  typed
typewriter noun
  typewriters
typewritten
typhoon noun
  typhoons
typical adjective
  typically
typist noun
  typists
tyranny noun
  tyrannies
tyrannical adjective
  tyrannically
tyrant noun
  tyrants
☆ tyre noun
  tyres

Uu

udder noun
  udders
ugliness
ugly adjective
  uglier
  ugliest
ulcer noun
  ulcers
ultimate adjective
  ultimately
ultraviolet
umbilical cord noun
  umbilical cords
umbrella noun
  umbrellas
umpire noun
  umpires

un-
un- makes words
meaning 'not', e.g.
unable, unhappiness.
Some of these words
have special
meanings, e.g.
unprofessional. See
the note at non-.

unable
unaided
unanimity
unanimous adjective
  unanimously
unavoidable
  adjective
  unavoidably
unaware

★ You use two in e.g. two people or there are two of them. ! to, too.
☆ A tyre is a rubber cover for a wheel. ! tire.

unawares

unbearable adjective
unbearably

unbelievable
adjective
unbelievably

unblock verb
unblocks
unblocking
unblocked

unborn

uncalled for

uncanny adjective
uncannier
uncanniest

uncertain adjective
uncertainly

uncertainty

uncle noun
uncles

uncomfortable
adjective
uncomfortably

uncommon
adjective
uncommonly

unconscious
adjective
unconsciously

unconsciousness

uncontrollable
adjective
uncontrollably

uncountable

uncouth

uncover verb
uncovers
uncovering
uncovered

undecided

undeniable adjective
undeniably

under

underarm adjective

underclothes plural
noun

underdeveloped

underdone

underfoot

undergo verb
undergoes
undergoing
underwent
undergone

undergraduate
noun
undergraduates

underground
adjective and noun
undergrounds

undergrowth

underhand

underlie verb
underlies
underlying
underlay
underlain

underline verb
underlines
underlining
underlined

undermine verb
undermines
undermining
undermined

underneath
preposition

underpants plural
noun

underpass noun
underpasses

underprivileged

understand verb
understands
understanding
understood

understandable
adjective
understandably

understanding

undertake verb
undertakes
undertaking
undertook
undertaken

undertaker noun
undertakers

undertaking noun
undertakings

underwater

underwear

underworld

undesirable
adjective
undesirably

undeveloped

undo verb
undoes
undoing
undid
undone

undoubted adjective
undoubtedly

undress verb
undresses
undressing
undressed

unearth verb
unearths
unearthing
unearthed

unearthly

unease
uneasiness
uneasy adjective
  uneasier
  uneasiest
  uneasily
uneatable
unemployed
unemployment
uneven adjective
  unevenly
unevenness
unexpected adjective
  unexpectedly
unfair adjective
  unfairly
unfairness
unfaithful adjective
  unfaithfully
unfamiliar
unfamiliarity
unfasten verb
  unfastens
  unfastening
  unfastened
unfavourable
  adjective
  unfavourably
unfinished
unfit
unfold verb
  unfolds
  unfolding
  unfolded
unforgettable
  adjective
  unforgettably
unforgivable
  adjective
  unforgivably

unfortunate
  adjective
  unfortunately
unfreeze verb
  unfreezes
  unfreezing
  unfroze
  unfrozen
unfriendliness
unfriendly
ungrateful adjective
  ungratefully
unhappiness
unhappy adjective
  unhappier
  unhappiest
  unhappily
unhealthy adjective
  unhealthier
  unhealthiest
  unhealthily
unheard-of
unicorn noun
  unicorns
unification
uniform noun
  uniforms
uniform adjective
  uniformly
uniformed
uniformity
unify verb
  unifies
  unifying
  unified
unimportance
unimportant
uninhabited

unintentional
  adjective
  unintentionally
uninterested
uninteresting
union noun
  unions
unique adjective
  uniquely
uniqueness
unisex
unison
unit noun
  units
unite verb
  unites
  uniting
  united
unity noun
  unities
universal adjective
  universally
universe
university noun
  universities
unjust adjective
  unjustly
unkind adjective
  unkinder
  unkindest
  unkindly
unkindness
unknown
unleaded
unless
unlike
unlikely adjective
  unlikelier
  unlikeliest

unload *verb*
  unloads
  unloading
  unloaded
unlock *verb*
  unlocks
  unlocking
  unlocked
unlucky *adjective*
  unluckier
  unluckiest
  unluckily
unmistakable
  adjective
  unmistakably
unnatural *adjective*
  unnaturally
unnecessary
  adjective
  unnecessarily
unoccupied
unpack *verb*
  unpacks
  unpacking
  unpacked
unpleasant *adjective*
  unpleasantly
unpleasantness
unplug *verb*
  unplugs
  unplugging
  unplugged
unpopular *adjective*
  unpopularly
unpopularity
unravel *verb*
  unravels
  unravelling
  unravelled
unreal

unreasonable
  adjective
  unreasonably
unrest
unroll *verb*
  unrolls
  unrolling
  unrolled
unruliness
unruly *adjective*
  unrulier
  unruliest
unscrew *verb*
  unscrews
  unscrewing
  unscrewed
unseemly
unseen
unselfish *adjective*
  unselfishly
unselfishness
unsightly
unskilled
unsound *adjective*
  unsoundly
unsteadiness
unsteady *adjective*
  unsteadier
  unsteadiest
  unsteadily
unsuccessful
  adjective
  unsuccessfully
unsuitable *adjective*
  unsuitably
unthinkable
  adjective
  unthinkably
untidiness

untidy *adjective*
  untidier
  untidiest
  untidily
untie *verb*
  unties
  untying
  untied
until
untimely
unto
untold
untoward
untrue *adjective*
  untruly
untruthful *adjective*
  untruthfully
unused
unusual *adjective*
  unusually
unwanted
unwell
unwilling *adjective*
  unwillingly
unwillingness
unwind *verb*
  unwinds
  unwinding
  unwound
unwrap *verb*
  unwraps
  unwrapping
  unwrapped
unzip *verb*
  unzips
  unzipping
  unzipped
update *verb*
  updates
  updating
  updated

upgrade verb
upgrades
upgrading
upgraded

upheaval noun
upheavals

uphill

uphold verb
upholds
upholding
upheld

upholstery

upkeep

uplands plural noun

upon

upper

upright adjective
uprightly

upright noun
uprights

uprising noun
uprisings

uproar noun
uproars

upset verb
upsets
upsetting
upset

upset noun
upsets

upshot

upside down

upstairs

upstart noun
upstarts

upstream adjective

uptake

uptight

upward adjective and
adverb

upwards adverb

uranium

urban

urbanization

urbanize verb
urbanizes
urbanizing
urbanized

urchin noun
urchins

Urdu

urge verb
urges
urging
urged

urge noun
urges

urgency

urgent adjective
urgently

urinary

urinate verb
urinates
urinating
urinated

urination

urine

urn noun
urns

-us
Most nouns ending in
-us come from Latin
words, e.g. **bonus** and
terminus. They
normally have plurals
ending in -uses, e.g.
bonuses and
terminuses. Some
more technical words
have plurals ending in
-i, e.g. **nucleus -
nuclei**.

usable

usage noun
usages

use verb
uses
using
used

use noun
uses

useful adjective
usefully

usefulness

useless adjective
uselessly

uselessness

user noun
users

user-friendly
adjective
user-friendlier
user-friendliest

usher noun
ushers

usher verb
ushers
ushering
ushered

usherette noun
usherettes

usual adjective
usually

usurp verb
usurps
usurping
usurped

usurper noun
usurpers

utensil noun
utensils

uterus noun
uteri

utilization
utilize *verb*
  utilizes
  utilizing
  utilized
utmost
utter *adjective*
utter *verb*
  utters
  uttering
  uttered
utterance *noun*
  utterances
utterly *adverb*
U-turn *noun*
  U-turns

Vv

vacancy *noun*
  vacancies
vacant *adjective*
  vacantly
vacate *verb*
  vacates
  vacating
  vacated
vacation *noun*
  vacations
vaccinate *verb*
  vaccinates
  vaccinating
  vaccinated
vaccination *noun*
  vaccinations
vaccine *noun*
  vaccines
vacuum *noun*
  vacuums

vagina *noun*
  vaginas
vague *adjective*
  vaguer
  vaguest
  vaguely
vagueness
★ **vain** *adjective*
  vainer
  vainest
  vainly
☆ **vale** *noun*
  vales
valentine *noun*
  valentines
valiant *adjective*
  valiantly
valid *adjective*
  validly
validity
valley *noun*
  valleys
valour
valuable *adjective*
  valuably
valuables *plural noun*
valuation *noun*
  valuations
value *noun*
  values
value *verb*
  values
  valuing
  valued
valueless
valuer *noun*
  valuers
valve *noun*
  valves

vampire *noun*
  vampires
van *noun*
  vans
vandal *noun*
  vandals
vandalism
◐ **vane** *noun*
  vanes
vanilla
vanish *verb*
  vanishes
  vanishing
  vanished
vanity
vanquish *verb*
  vanquishes
  vanquishing
  vanquished
vaporize *verb*
  vaporizes
  vaporizing
  vaporized
vapour *noun*
  vapours
variable *adjective*
  variably
variable *noun*
  variables
variation *noun*
  variations
varied
variety *noun*
  varieties
various *adjective*
  variously
varnish *noun*
  varnishes

★ **Vain** means 'conceited' or 'proud'. ! **vane**, **vein**.
☆ A **vale** is a valley. ! **veil**.
◐ A **vane** is a pointer that shows which way the wind is blowing. ! **vain**, **vein**.

varnish verb
varnishes
varnishing
varnished
vary verb
varies
varying
varied
vase noun
vases
vast adjective
vastly
vastness
vat noun
vats
vault verb
vaults
vaulting
vaulted
vault noun
vaults
veal
vector noun
vectors
Veda
veer verb
veers
veering
veered
vegan noun
vegans
vegetable noun
vegetables
vegetarian noun
vegetarians
vegetate verb
vegetates
vegetating
vegetated
vegetation
vehicle noun
vehicles

★ **veil** noun
veils
veil verb
veils
veiling
veiled
☆ **vein** noun
veins
velocity noun
velocities
velvet
velvety
vendetta noun
vendettas
vendor noun
vendors
venerable adjective
venerably
venereal disease
noun
venereal diseases
venetian blind noun
venetian blinds
vengeance
venison
Venn diagram noun
Venn diagrams
venom
venomous adjective
venomously
vent noun
vents
ventilate verb
ventilates
ventilating
ventilated
ventilation
ventilator noun
ventilators
ventriloquism

ventriloquist noun
ventriloquists
venture verb
ventures
venturing
ventured
venture noun
ventures
veranda noun
verandas
verb noun
verbs
verdict noun
verdicts
verge verb
verges
verging
verged
verge noun
verges
verification
verify verb
verifies
verifying
verified
vermin
verruca noun
verrucas
versatile
versatility
verse noun
verses
version noun
versions
versus
vertebra noun
vertebrae
vertebrate noun
vertebrates
vertex noun
vertices

• •

★ A **veil** is a covering for the face. ! **vale.**
☆ A **vein** carries blood to the heart. ! **vain, vane.**

vertical *adjective*
vertically

very

Vesak

vessel *noun*
vessels

vest *noun*
vests

vested *adjective*
vested

vestment *noun*
vestments

vestry *noun*
vestries

vet *noun*
vets

veteran *noun*
veterans

veterinary

veto *verb*
vetoes
vetoing
vetoed

veto *noun*
vetoes

vex *verb*
vexes
vexing
vexed

vexation

via

viaduct *noun*
viaducts

vibrate *verb*
vibrates
vibrating
vibrated

vibration *noun*
vibrations

vicar *noun*
vicars

vicarage *noun*
vicarages

vice *noun*
vices

vice-president *noun*
vice-presidents

vice versa

vicinity *noun*
vicinities

vicious *adjective*
viciously

viciousness

victim *noun*
victims

victimize *verb*
victimizes
victimizing
victimized

victor *noun*
victors

Victorian *adjective
and noun*
Victorians

victorious *adjective*
victoriously

victory *noun*
victories

video *noun*
videos

video *verb*
videoes
videoing
videoed

videotape *noun*
videotapes

view *noun*
views

view *verb*
views
viewing
viewed

viewer *noun*
viewers

vigilance

vigilant *adjective*
vigilantly

vigorous *adjective*
vigorously

vigour

Viking *noun*
Vikings

vile *adjective*
viler
vilest
vilely

villa *noun*
villas

village *noun*
villages

villager *noun*
villagers

villain *noun*
villains

villainous *adjective*
villainously

villainy

vine *noun*
vines

vinegar

vineyard *noun*
vineyards

vintage *noun*
vintages

vinyl

viola *noun*
violas

violate *verb*
violates
violating
violated

violation noun
violations
violator noun
violators
violence
violent adjective
violently
violet noun
violets
violin noun
violins
violinist noun
violinists
viper noun
vipers
virgin noun
virgins
virginity
virtual adjective
virtually
virtue noun
virtues
virtuous adjective
virtuously
virus noun
viruses
visa noun
visas
visibility
visible adjective
visibly
vision noun
visions
visit verb
visits
visiting
visited
visit noun
visits

visitor noun
visitors
visor noun
visors
visual adjective
visually
visualize verb
visualizes
visualizing
visualized
vital adjective
vitally
vitality
vitamin noun
vitamins
vivid adjective
vividly
vividness
vivisection noun
vivisections
vixen noun
vixens
vocabulary noun
vocabularies
vocal adjective
vocally
vocalist noun
vocalists
vocation noun
vocations
vocational adjective
vocationally
vodka noun
vodkas
voice noun
voices
voice verb
voices
voicing
voiced
volcanic

volcano noun
volcanoes
vole noun
voles
volley noun
volleys
volleyball
volt noun
volts
voltage noun
voltages
volume noun
volumes
voluntary adjective
voluntarily
volunteer verb
volunteers
volunteering
volunteered
volunteer noun
volunteers
vomit verb
vomits
vomiting
vomited
vote verb
votes
voting
voted
vote noun
votes
voter noun
voters
vouch verb
vouches
vouching
vouched
voucher noun
vouchers
vow noun
vows

vow verb
vows
vowing
vowed

vowel noun
vowels

voyage noun
voyages

voyager noun
voyagers

vulgar adjective
vulgarly

vulnerable adjective
vulnerably

vulture noun
vultures

vulva noun
vulvas

wad noun
wads

waddle verb
waddles
waddling
waddled

waddle noun
waddles

wade verb
wades
wading
waded

wafer noun
wafers

wag verb
wags
wagging
wagged

wag noun
wags

wage noun
wages

wage verb
wages
waging
waged

wager noun
wagers

wager verb
wagers
wagering
wagered

waggle verb
waggles
waggling
waggled

wagon noun
wagons

wagtail noun
wagtails

wail verb
wails
wailing
wailed

★ **wail** noun
wails

☆ **waist** noun
waists

waistcoat noun
waistcoats

◉ **wait** verb
waits
waiting
waited

wait noun
waits

waiter noun
waiters

waitress noun
waitresses

✻ **waive** verb
waives
waiving
waived

wake verb
wakes
waking
woke
woken

wake noun
wakes

waken verb
wakens
wakening
wakened

walk verb
walks
walking
walked

walk noun
walks

walkabout noun
walkabouts

walker noun
walkers

walkie-talkie noun
walkie-talkies

Walkman noun
Walkmans

wall noun
walls

wall verb
walls
walling
walled

wallaby noun
wallabies

★ A **wail** is a loud sad cry. ! **whale**.
☆ A person's **waist** is the narrow part around their middle. ! **waste**.
◉ To **wait** is to delay, pause, or rest. ! **weight**.
✻ To **waive** a right is to say you do not need it. ! **wave**.

wallet noun
wallets
wallflower noun
wallflowers
wallop verb
wallops
walloping
walloped
wallow verb
wallows
wallowing
wallowed
wallpaper noun
wallpapers
walnut noun
walnuts
walrus noun
walruses
waltz noun
waltzes
waltz verb
waltzes
waltzing
waltzed
wand noun
wands
wander verb
wanders
wandering
wandered
wanderer noun
wanderers
wane verb
wanes
waning
waned
wangle verb
wangles
wangling
wangled

want verb
wants
wanting
wanted
want noun
wants
war noun
wars
warble verb
warbles
warbling
warbled
warble noun
warbles
warbler noun
warblers
ward noun
wards
ward verb
wards
warding
warded
warden noun
wardens
warder noun
warders
wardrobe noun
wardrobes
★ **ware** noun
wares
warehouse noun
warehouses
warfare
warhead noun
warheads
wariness
warlike
warm adjective
warmer
warmest
warmly

warm verb
warms
warming
warmed
warmth
warn verb
warns
warning
warned
warning noun
warnings
warp verb
warps
warping
warped
warp noun
warps
warrant noun
warrants
warrant verb
warrants
warranting
warranted
warren noun
warrens
warrior noun
warriors
warship noun
warships
wart noun
warts
wary adjective
warier
wariest
warily
was
wash verb
washes
washing
washed
wash noun
washes

* *

★ **Wares** are manufactured goods. **!** wear, where.

washable

washbasin noun
washbasins

washer noun
washers

washing

washing-up

wash-out noun
wash-outs

wasn't verb

wasp noun
wasps

wastage

★ **waste** verb
wastes
wasting
wasted

waste adjective and noun
wastes

wasteful adjective
wastefully

watch verb
watches
watching
watched

watch noun
watches

watchdog noun
watchdogs

watcher noun
watchers

watchful adjective
watchfully

watchfulness

watchman noun
watchmen

water noun
waters

water verb
waters
watering
watered

watercolour noun
watercolours

watercress

waterfall noun
waterfalls

waterlogged

watermark noun
watermarks

waterproof

water-skiing

watertight

waterway noun
waterways

waterworks noun
waterworks

watery

☆ **watt** noun
watts

○ **wave** verb
waves
waving
waved

wave noun
waves

waveband noun
wavebands

wavelength noun
wavelengths

waver verb
wavers
wavering
wavered

wavy adjective
wavier
waviest
wavily

wax noun
waxes

wax verb
waxes
waxing
waxed

waxwork noun
waxworks

waxy adjective
waxier
waxiest

✳ **way** noun
ways

✳ **weak** adjective
weaker
weakest
weakly

weakness

weaken verb
weakens
weakening
weakened

weakling noun
weaklings

wealth

wealthy adjective
wealthier
wealthiest
wealthily

weapon noun
weapons

✳ **wear** verb
wears
wearing
wore
worn

wear noun

wearer noun
wearers

weariness

. . . .

★ To **waste** something is to use more of it than is needed. ! **waist**.
☆ A **watt** is a unit of electricity. ! **what**.
○ To **wave** is to move your arm in greeting. ! **waive**.
✳ You use **way** in e.g. *can you tell me the way?* ! **weigh, whey**.
✳ **Weak** means 'not strong'. ! **week**.
✳ To **wear** clothes is to be dressed in them. ! **ware, where**.

weary adjective
  wearier
  weariest
  wearily

weasel noun
  weasels

weather noun

weather verb
  weathers
  weathering
  weathered

weathercock noun
  weathercocks

★ **weave** verb
  weaves
  weaving
  weaved or wove
  woven

weaver noun
  weavers

web noun
  webs

webbed

website noun
  websites

wed verb
  weds
  wedding
  wedded or wed

we'd verb

wedding noun
  weddings

wedge noun
  wedges

wedge verb
  wedges
  wedging
  wedged

Wednesday noun
  Wednesdays

weed noun
  weeds

weed verb
  weeds
  weeding
  weeded

weedy adjective
  weedier
  weediest
  weedily

☆ **week** noun
  weeks

weekday noun
  weekdays

weekend noun
  weekends

weekly adjective and
  adverb

weep verb
  weeps
  weeping
  wept

weft

◐ **weigh** verb
  weighs
  weighing
  weighed

✳ **weight** noun
  weights

weightless

weightlifting

weighty adjective
  weightier
  weightiest
  weightily

weir noun
  weirs

weird adjective
  weirder
  weirdest
  weirdly

weirdness

welcome noun
  welcomes

welcome verb
  welcomes
  welcoming
  welcomed

weld verb
  welds
  welding
  welded

welder noun
  welders

welfare

well noun
  wells

well adjective and
  adverb
  better
  best

we'll verb

well-being

wellington boots
  plural noun

well-known

went see go

wept see weep

were see are

we're verb

werewolf noun
  werewolves

west adjective and
  adverb

✳ **west** noun

westerly adjective
  and noun
  westerlies

western adjective

western noun
  westerns

- -

★ The past tense is **weaved** in e.g. *she weaved her way through the crowd* and
  wove in e.g. *she wove a shawl.*
☆ A **week** is a period of seven days. **! weak.**
◐ You use **weigh** in e.g. *how much do you weigh?* **! way, whey.**
✳ **Weight** is how heavy something is. **! wait.**
✳ You use a capital W in the **West**, when you mean a particular region.

westward adjective
and adverb

westwards adverb

wet adjective
wetter
wettest

wet verb
wets
wetting
wetted

wetness

we've abbreviation

whack verb
whacks
whacking
whacked

whack noun
whacks

★ **whale** noun
whales

whaler noun
whalers

whaling

wharf noun
wharves or wharfs

☆ **what**

whatever

wheat

wheel noun
wheels

wheel verb
wheels
wheeling
wheeled

wheelbarrow noun
wheelbarrows

wheelchair noun
wheelchairs

wheeze verb
wheezes
wheezing
wheezed

whelk noun
whelks

when

whenever conjunction

○ **where**

whereabouts

whereas

whereupon

wherever

whether conjunction

✳ **whey**

✳ **which**

whichever

whiff noun
whiffs

while adjective and
noun

while verb
whiles
whiling
whiled

whilst conjunction

whimper verb
whimpers
whimpering
whimpered

whimper noun
whimpers

whine verb
whines
whining
whined

✳ **whine** noun
whines

whinny verb
whinnies
whinnying
whinnied

whip noun
whips

whip verb
whips
whipping
whipped

whirl verb
whirls
whirling
whirled

whirl noun
whirls

whirlpool noun
whirlpools

whirlwind noun
whirlwinds

whirr verb
whirrs
whirring
whirred

whirr noun
whirrs

whisk verb
whisks
whisking
whisked

whisk noun
whisks

whisker noun
whiskers

whisky noun
whiskies

whisper verb
whispers
whispering
whispered

whisper noun
whispers

whist

- -

★ A **whale** is a large sea mammal. ! **wail.**

☆ You use **what** in e.g. *what are they doing?* or *I don't know what you mean.* ! **watt.**

○ You use **where** in e.g. *where are you?* ! **ware, wear.**

✳ **Whey** is a watery liquid from milk. ! **way, weigh.**

✳ You use **which** in e.g. *which one is that?* ! **witch.**

✳ A **whine** is a high piercing sound. ! **wine.**

whistle *verb*
whistles
whistling
whistled

whistle *noun*
whistles

whistler *noun*
whistlers

white *adjective*
whiter
whitest

whiteness

whitish

white *noun*
whites

whiten *verb*
whitens
whitening
whitened

whitewash *noun*

whitewash *verb*
whitewashes
whitewashing
whitewashed

Whitsun

Whit Sunday

whiz *verb*
whizzes
whizzing
whizzed

who

whoever

★ **whole** *adjective*
wholly

whole *noun*
wholes

wholefood *noun*
wholefoods

wholemeal

wholesale *adjective*

wholesome

wholly

whom

whoop *noun*
whoops

whoopee *interjection*

whooping cough

☆ **who's** *verb*

✪ **whose** *adjective*

why

wick *noun*
wicks

wicked *adjective*
wickeder
wickedest
wickedly

wickedness

wicker

wickerwork

wicket *noun*
wickets

wicketkeeper *noun*
wicketkeepers

wide *adjective* and *adverb*
wider
widest
widely

widen *verb*
widens
widening
widened

widespread

widow *noun*
widows

widower *noun*
widowers

width *noun*
widths

wield *verb*
wields
wielding
wielded

wife *noun*
wives

wig *noun*
wigs

wiggle *verb*
wiggles
wiggling
wiggled

wiggle *noun*
wiggles

wigwam *noun*
wigwams

wild *adjective*
wilder
wildest
wildly

wilderness *noun*
wildernesses

wildness

wildlife

wilful *adjective*
wilfully

wilfulness

wiliness

will *verb*
would

will *noun*
wills

willing *adjective*
willingly

willingness

willow *noun*
willows

wilt *verb*
wilts
wilting
wilted

. . . .

★ You use **whole** in e.g. *I saw the whole film.* **! hole.**

☆ You use **who's** in *who's* (= who is) *that?* and *I don't know who's* (= who has) *done it.* **! whose.**

✪ You use **whose** in *whose is this?* and *I don't know whose it is.* **! who's.**

wily *adjective*
 wilier
 wiliest

wimp *noun*
 wimps

win *verb*
 wins
 winning
 won

win *noun*
 wins

wince *verb*
 winces
 wincing
 winced

winch *noun*
 winches

winch *verb*
 winches
 winching
 winched

wind *noun*
 winds

wind *verb*
 winds
 winding
 wound

windfall *noun*
 windfalls

windmill *noun*
 windmills

window *noun*
 windows

windpipe *noun*
 windpipes

windscreen *noun*
 windscreens

windsurfer

windsurfing

windward

windy *adjective*
 windier
 windiest
 windily

★ **wine** *noun*
 wines

wing *noun*
 wings

wing *verb*
 wings
 winging
 winged

winged

wingless

wingspan *noun*
 wingspans

wink *verb*
 winks
 winking
 winked

wink *noun*
 winks

winkle *noun*
 winkles

winkle *verb*
 winkles
 winkling
 winkled

winner *noun*
 winners

winnings *plural noun*

winter *noun*
 winters

wintertime

wintry *adjective*
 wintrier
 wintriest

wipe *verb*
 wipes
 wiping
 wiped

wipe *noun*
 wipes

wiper *noun*
 wipers

wire *noun*
 wires

wire *verb*
 wires
 wiring
 wired

wireless *noun*
 wirelesses

wiring

wiry *adjective*
 wirier
 wiriest
 wirily

wisdom

wise *adjective*
 wiser
 wisest
 wisely

wish *verb*
 wishes
 wishing
 wished

wish *noun*
 wishes

wishbone *noun*
 wishbones

wisp *noun*
 wisps

wispy *adjective*
 wispier
 wispiest
 wispily

wistful *adjective*
 wistfully

wistfulness

wit *noun*
 wits

. . . .

★ Wine is a drink. ! whine.

★ **witch** noun
  witches

witchcraft

with

withdraw verb
  withdraws
  withdrawing
  withdrew
  withdrawn

withdrawal noun
  withdrawals

wither verb
  withers
  withering
  withered

withhold verb
  withholds
  withholding
  withheld

within

without

withstand verb
  withstands
  withstanding
  withstood

witness noun
  witnesses

wittiness

witty adjective
  wittier
  wittiest
  wittily

wizard noun
  wizards

wizardry

wobble verb
  wobbles
  wobbling
  wobbled

wobble noun
  wobbles

wobbly adjective
  wobblier
  wobbliest

woe noun
  woes

woeful
  adjective
  woefully

wok noun
  woks

woke see wake

woken see wake

wolf noun
  wolves

woman noun
  women

womb noun
  wombs

☆ **won** see win

wonder noun
  wonders

wonder verb
  wonders
  wondering
  wondered

wonderful adjective
  wonderfully

won't verb

❍ **wood** noun
  woods

wooded

wooden

woodland noun
  woodlands

woodlouse noun
  woodlice

woodpecker noun
  woodpeckers

woodwind

woodwork

woodworm noun
  woodworm or
  woodworms

woody adjective
  woodier
  woodiest

wool

woollen

woollens plural noun

woolliness

woolly adjective
  woollier
  woolliest

word noun
  words

word verb
  words
  wording
  worded

wording

wordy adjective
  wordier
  wordiest

wore see wear

work noun
  works

work verb
  works
  working
  worked

workable

worker noun
  workers

workforce noun
  workforces

workman noun
  workmen

workmanship

workout noun
  workouts

. . . .

★ A **witch** is someone who uses witchcraft. ! which.

☆ You use **won** in e.g. *I won a prize.* ! one.

❍ **Wood** is material from trees or a lot of trees growing together. ! would.

works plural noun
worksheet noun
worksheets
workshop noun
workshops
world noun
worlds
worldliness
worldly adjective
worldlier
worldliest
worldwide adjective
worm noun
worms
worm verb
worms
worming
wormed
worn see wear
worry verb
worries
worrying
worried
worrier noun
worriers
worry noun
worries
worse adjective and adverb
worsen verb
worsens
worsening
worsened
worship verb
worships
worshipping
worshipped
worship noun
worshipper noun
worshippers

worst adjective and adverb
worth
worthiness
worthless adjective
worthlessly
worthwhile
worthy adjective
worthier
worthiest
worthily
★ **would** see will
wouldn't verb
wound noun
wounds
wound verb
wounds
wounding
wounded
wound see wind
wove see weave
woven see weave
☆ **wrap** verb
wraps
wrapping
wrapped
wrap noun
wraps
wrapper noun
wrappers
wrapping noun
wrappings
wrath
wrathful adjective
wrathfully
wreath noun
wreaths
wreathe verb
wreathes
wreathing
wreathed

wreck verb
wrecks
wrecking
wrecked
wreck noun
wrecks
wreckage noun
wreckages
wrecker noun
wreckers
wren noun
wrens
wrench verb
wrenches
wrenching
wrenched
wrench noun
wrenches
wrestle verb
wrestles
wrestling
wrestled
wrestler noun
wrestlers
wretch noun
wretches
wretched adjective
wretchedly
wriggle verb
wriggles
wriggling
wriggled
wriggle noun
wriggles
wriggly adjective
wrigglier
wriggliest
◐ **wring** verb
wrings
wringing
wrung

★ You use would in e.g. *would you like to come to tea?* ! **wood**.
☆ To wrap something is to cover it in paper etc. ! **rap**.
◐ To wring something is to squeeze it hard. ! **ring**.

wrinkle noun
wrinkles

wrinkle verb
wrinkles
wrinkling
wrinkled

wrist noun
wrists

wristwatch noun
wristwatches

★ **write** verb
writes
writing
wrote
written

writer noun
writers

writhe verb
writhes
writhing
writhed

writing noun
writings

written see write

wrong adjective and
adverb
wrongly

wrong noun
wrongs

wrong verb
wrongs
wronging
wronged

wrote see write

wrung see wring

☆ **wry** adjective
wryer
wryest

Xx

xenophobia

Xmas noun
Xmases

X-ray noun
X-rays

X-ray verb
X-rays
X-raying
X-rayed

xylophone noun
xylophones

Yy

-y and -ey
Nouns ending in -y
following a
consonant, e.g. story,
make plurals ending
in -ies, e.g. stories,
and verbs, e.g. try,
make forms in -ies
and -ied, e.g. tries,
tried. Nouns ending
in -ey, e.g. journey,
make plurals ending
in -eys, e.g. journeys.

yacht noun
yachts

yachtsman noun
yachtsmen

yachtswoman noun
yachtswomen

yam noun
yams

yank verb
yanks
yanking
yanked

yap verb
yaps
yapping
yapped

yap noun
yaps

yard noun
yards

yard noun
yards

yarn noun
yarns

yawn verb
yawns
yawning
yawned

yawn noun
yawns

year noun
years

yearly adjective and
adverb

yearn verb
yearns
yearning
yearned

yeast

yell noun
yells

yell verb
yells
yelling
yelled

yellow adjective and
noun
yellower
yellowest

. . . .

★ You use **write** in e.g. *to write a letter*. **!** right, rite.
☆ You use **wry** in e.g. *a wry smile*. **!** rye.

yelp verb
yelps
yelping
yelped

yelp noun
yelps

★ **yen** noun
yens or yen

yeoman noun
yeomen

yesterday adjective
and noun
yesterdays

yet

yeti noun
yetis

☆ **yew** noun
yews

yield verb
yields
yielding
yielded

yield noun
yields

yippee

yodel verb
yodels
yodelling
yodelled

yodeller noun
yodellers

yoga

yoghurt noun
yoghurts

○ **yoke** noun
yokes

yoke verb
yokes
yoking
yoked

✻ **yolk** noun
yolks

Yom Kippur

yonder

✱ **you**

you'd verb

you'll verb

young adjective
younger
youngest

young plural noun

youngster noun
youngsters

your

you're abbreviation

yours

yourself pronoun
yourselves

youth noun
youths

youthful adjective
youthfully

you've abbreviation

yo-yo noun
yo-yos

yuppie noun
yuppies

Zz

zany adjective
zanier
zaniest
zanily

zap verb
zaps
zapping
zapped

zeal

zealous adjective
zealously

zebra noun
zebras

zenith noun
zeniths

zero noun
zeros

zest

zigzag noun
zigzags

zigzag verb
zigzags
zigzagging
zigzagged

zinc

zip noun
zips

zip verb
zips
zipping
zipped

zodiac

zombie noun
zombies

zone noun
zones

zoo noun
zoos

zoological adjective
zoologically

zoologist noun
zoologists

zoology

zoom verb
zooms
zooming
zoomed

★ The plural is **yens** when you mean 'a longing' and **yen** for Japanese money.
☆ A **yew** is a tree. ! ewe, you.
○ A **yoke** is a piece of wood put across animals pulling a cart. ! yolk.
✻ A **yolk** is the yellow part of an egg. ! yoke.
✱ You use **you** in e.g. I love you. ! ewe, yew.